COMPETITIVE ADVANTAGE
THROUGH DIVERSITY

COMPETITIVE ADVANTAGE THROUGH DIVERSITY

Organizational Learning from Difference

Peter Herriot and Carole Pemberton

SAGE Publications
London • Thousand Oaks • New Delhi

SAGE Publications Ltd
6 Bonhill Street
London EC2A 4PU

SAGE Publications Ltd
2455 Teller Road
Thousand Oaks, California 91320

SAGE Publications India Pvt Ltd
32, M-Block Market
Greater Kailash – I
New Delhi 110 048

British Library Cataloguing in Publication Data

A catalogue record for this book is available from the British Library.

ISBN 0 8039 8884 2
ISBN 0 8039 8885 0 (pbk)

Library of Congress catalog card number 94-068899

Typeset by Mayhew Typesetting, Rhayader, Powys
Printed in Great Britain by Redwood Books,
Trowbridge, Wiltshire

Contents

For Barbara and Bill

Introduction

Innovate or Perish

This is the stark choice facing organizations as the twentieth century draws to its tumultuous close. As competition grows ever more severe, it is no longer enough to be cost competitive. The recession's survivors are already as lean as it is possible to be without compromising quality; several have crossed that narrow line already. Today, competitive advantage can only come from being quicker to market with new and better products or services. Yet the habits of recession die hard. Cutting costs, avoiding risks, satisfying shareholders are still prime concerns. Agreed, any organization which is not cost competitive is dead already; but those priority concerns which secured survival in recession will not be sufficient now. The new priorities are over and above the continuing requirement for efficiency and productivity. They are the need to innovate and the need to learn.

How do we achieve these outcomes – without, of course, throwing out the productivity baby with the recessionary bathwater? This book isn't about a new method. We are not peddling the successor to performance-related pay or business process re-engineering. Nor is our book about a new movement. We are not preaching, with evangelical fervour, a new organizational culture such as total quality management. Methods and movements come and go; some of them are deservedly popular because for many they meet the needs of the moment. But methods and movements are here today and gone tomorrow. This is because they seldom take proper account of what we know about people at work, what they are each capable of, and how they work and learn together.

Ten Propositions

So how will people best innovate and learn in tomorrow's business environment? Here are 10 propositions which form the core of our argument:

1 Knowing beyond – going beyond the evidence to imagine what might be done – is already more important than knowing how (the capacity to solve problems in the light of past experience).

2 Everyone, at all levels in an organization, is capable both of knowing how and of knowing beyond.
3 The diversity of individuals' frameworks of understanding is the key potential source of innovation.
4 However, their capacities for innovation won't be fully used unless they work well together.
5 Successful teamworking requires people to play a variety of skilled roles to make sure a few key things get done.
6 Neither individuals nor teams will innovate unless they also learn continuously.
7 Learning is both about how to do something better and also about how better to learn.
8 Learning does not occur unless there is a favourable context for it to happen.
9 That context is the process of organizational learning. The most useful definition for the future organization is, as the process whereby people learn together.
10 In such an organization information is not held by a few in order to control others. It is shared, so that people use it to exercise control for themselves and more important, to learn and innovate.

None of these propositions is new. Many of them are articles of faith to human resource professionals. Yet many of the management methods and movements popular in recent years are clearly incompatible with one or more of them. For example:

◆ Culture change programmes seek to make employees' values and behaviour more homogeneous, not more diverse.
◆ Performance-related pay systems reward individuals, whereas innovation and learning are social processes.
◆ Selecting out high-flyers for fast-track careers inhibits others from developing their potential.
◆ Using biographical data which predict current career success in order to select new recruits clones those in power.
◆ Quality procedures which require employees to 'get it right first time every time' inhibit innovation and the taking of calculated risks.

So although our propositions are nothing new, their implications for practice certainly are.

People, Practice, and Process

Taken together, our 10 propositions imply the 3P model shown in Figure 1. Our book is structured in three parts, to fit the 3P model.

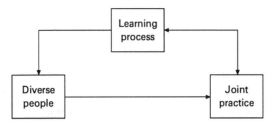

Figure 1 *The 3P model*

We start with the people. Books about organizations seldom start with people. They talk about structures or environment or strategies or markets. If the future survival of organizations depends upon their capacity to create and use knowledge, it will only happen through people. For it is only people who can know beyond and create their future. An organization doesn't manage its human resources. An organization *is* its human resources. Or, to be more precise, it is people who organize themselves to learn.

The first part of our book, then, 'Diverse People', looks at the different knowledge that different sorts of employees bring to work. We demonstrate that they each bring distinctive capacities for knowing how and for knowing beyond.

Diverse knowledge can only contribute to innovation if very different people can work together. We propose in Part Two, 'Joint Practice', that teamworking itself has to be put into its own context. Who are the team's clients and what tasks do they expect the team to achieve? How can clients be managed? How do we elicit ideas freely but also evaluate them critically? How can we respect and recognize individual differences as sources of strength? And finally, how do we know whether we've achieved our task(s)? If one task is always to learn from what we've done, how do we check that we've learned something? Our new model of teamworking proposes some solutions to these issues.

Such learning cannot occur unless people organize themselves to learn. We argue in Part Three, 'Learning Process', that it is knowing beyond which is at the heart of organizational learning. Imagining what might be done (knowing beyond) determines the know-how we need, the projects we take on, and the sense we make of their outcomes.

Our argument, then, is that innovation can only bring us competitive advantage if we address the issues at three levels of analysis – individual, team, and organization. Only if diverse individuals work together in teams in a context where they can learn from the outcomes of their actions will successful innovation occur. To support our case, we call as witnesses organizations as diverse as *She* magazine and British Rail; authorities ranging from Charles Handy to Shoshana Zuboff; and individual workers at the organizational coalface.

Knowing How, Knowing That, and Knowing Beyond

Before we start exploring people at work in all their diversity, though, we want to distinguish three different sorts of knowing in a bit more detail. Knowledge as the key organizational asset is nearly as much of a cliché as people construed as assets. What's usually meant by knowledge is what we call 'knowing how' – expertise in how to solve particular sorts of problem on the basis of past experience. A second sort of knowledge we have called 'knowing that'. By this phrase we mean possessing information about what's actually happening at the moment. Finally, we've coined the phrase 'knowing beyond'. By this we mean imagining from the viewpoint of the present what we might do in the future.

Current thinking and practice is certainly coming to recognize the importance of knowing how. Skill shortages in a wide range of areas are predicted for the European and the American economies. Competitive advantage is believed to derive from the possession of certain core competences: key areas of expertise which competitors find it hard to imitate (Prahalad and Hamel, 1990). The importance of up-to-date information, of knowing that, is also being recognized, as information technology permits us to receive and act upon vast amounts of immediate information. Electronic funds transfer at point of sale (EFTPOS) allows both supermarket chains and finance houses to respond instantly to changing customer behaviour. But knowing beyond is at present seldom treated as a general form of organizational knowledge. It usually masquerades as 'the vision', handed down from on high by chief executives as part of an attempt to win over hearts and minds. Yet knowing beyond, rather than knowing how, is the real key to innovation.

Telescoping Time

The three sorts of knowing are all about time. Knowing how involves solving present problems in the light of past experience. Knowing that involves getting a fix on the here and now, while recognizing that such information is continuously becoming out of date. Knowing beyond means developing a theory about how the present might be transformed into a set of radically different future activities. So knowing how is using the past to help in the present: knowing beyond is imagining the future as a transformation of the present.

This is why knowing beyond is most central to our argument. For the speed of change has telescoped time. In previous periods of our economic history we could use a large sample of past experience to help us with the present. Change was relatively slow, and so our approaches to present problems were based on the outcomes of our attempts to solve the same sort of problem in the past. Our main form of knowledge was knowing how.

With the pace of change in the environment increasing exponentially, solutions to the problems of the past become less relevant. Many of our problems are new ones; we have never faced them before. All we can do is try to make sense of what is going on – of the changes that crowd in upon us. Knowing that is now crucial, for if we do not continuously scan our environment, we may fail to interpret appropriately. Key features of the present situation will never have been experienced before. We have to work with the information we've got at the moment, making sense of it in terms of the futures it could potentially lead to. In other words, we have to know beyond on the basis of knowing that.

We cannot generate our ideas of the future on the basis of concrete past events; the situations in which those events occurred have gone for ever. Instead, we have to theorize the present in an abstract way and construct the future from our theories. Very often, these theories will be analogies. A good example is our attempts to understand the current state of our organizations and create their future (Morgan, 1986). We've moved from machines (1950s) through organisms (1960s) to networks (1990s) as pictures of the current nature of organizations. Each of these analogies generated visions of how organizations would be in the future. The machine metaphor suggested more of the same, but more efficient. The organism analogy suggested gradual evolutionary adaptation to the environment. Our present images of organizations as networks or amoebas predict continuous self-transformations.

Back to Earth

Our speculations about the future have to be continuously reanchored in reality; knowing beyond has to go hand in hand with knowing that. For the speed of continuous change often renders our earlier constructions of the future unattainable. This is why chief executives' statements of vision often acquire a dated look rather rapidly. Instead, it's more a case of Alice continuously stepping back and forth through the looking-glass.

To anchor all these theoretical flights of fancy in reality, recall your reaction to the recent recession. In the latter part of 1989, as the downturn came, did you analyse it in terms of the 1981 recession? Did you perceive it as likely to last about a year? Did you initially attempt to deal with it by means of cost reductions? Did you expect to get back to the status quo ante? Did you fight World War II using World War I strategies?

These responses were based on previous experience of recession. An alternative would have been to analyse the situation more in terms of what you might like to be doing some time ahead. Perhaps you see yourself concentrating more upon a single niche market internationally and succeeding abroad by forming alliances with business partners there. This future perspective might have made you look at the recession in different terms. You might have construed it as an opportunity to divest your non-core businesses, thereby retaining liquidity. Rather than looking for internal cost reduction opportunities, you would have been searching out information on possible purchasers and partners. At the same time, however, you would have been focusing hard upon your core competence as an organization, which gives you competitive advantage in your niche market. You would have been knowing that – gaining information about your environment and yourselves in terms of where you wanted to go.

We could have regarded the recent recession, then, through the rear-view mirror; we could have interpreted it in the light of the previous recession. However, we could also have viewed it in terms of the opportunities it offered for moving towards a vision of our future. These two perspectives lead us to search out different sorts of information. Looking through the rear-view mirror, we would have monitored our costs with great care. We might well have reanalysed our business in order to discover hitherto hidden costs, so that we could reduce them. Looking ahead, on the other hand, we might have spent some time analysing the knowledge assets of our organization and those of potential business partners. We might also have been acquiring information about potential market niches abroad.

In the next chapters, we will look at five different sorts of employee in organizations. Their know-how we almost take for granted; they are all, of course, the people who know most about their own jobs. We will emphasize their access to unique information – their opportunities to know that. But above all, we will demonstrate that all of them are capable of knowing beyond.

Knowing beyond is not just the preserve of the chief executive or the boffins in corporate planning. It is in everyone's repertoire, waiting to be tapped to create innovative new products, services, and processes. We need to recognize two things: that everyone has that capacity; and that the differences in knowledge and approach when all do contribute, are themselves the source and spring of innovation.

References

Morgan, G. (1986) *Images of Organizations*. Beverly Hills, CA: Sage.

Prahalad, C.K. and Hamel, G. (1990) 'The core competence of the corporation', *Harvard Business Review*, 90(3): 79–91.

PART ONE   DIVERSE PEOPLE

1
Diversity as Strength

Dealing with Diversity

Our second and third propositions stated:

+ Everyone, at all levels in an organization, is capable both of knowing how and of knowing beyond.
+ The diversity of individuals' frameworks of understanding is the key potential source of innovation.

These are controversial statements; we will spend the first part of this book attempting to justify them.

Most organizations have had the utmost difficulty in responding to differences between people. The recession has given them an excuse for their continued refusal to respond. For the recession has stressed the need for efficiency and productivity. The outcomes have been achieved by even tighter control: control of money and control of people. People of the same sort are much easier to control; they start out with similar assumptions, values, and work patterns. When we add fear of unemployment to this homogeneity of outlook, the opportunity for control is there to be seized, and often has been.

Yet homogeneity and control are inherently hostile to innovation. One of the reasons why many organizations are unable to keep up with the pace of change is that they have either assimilated diversity and homogenized it, or else rejected diverse people and sent them packing. The diversity which is the potential source of new ideas is at the same time the stumbling block which prevents the benefits of those ideas being realized.

There are three sorts of response to diversity which organizations use:

+ Assimilate it: otherwise known as the vindaloo model, whereby everything that's put into the dish ends up tasting the same, however different it was to start with.
+ Protect it: the *nouvelle cuisine* approach, in which we put a very delicate decoration to the side of the plate so as not to

damage it, not being quite sure whether we should be eating it or not.

♦ Value it: the traditional English Sunday lunch, wherein roast beef, Yorkshire pudding, roast potatoes, gravy, and mustard are all indispensable to the success of the meal.

Assimilation: the Vindaloo Model

All the evidence suggests that the vindaloo is the most popular dish. In a powerful theoretical paper entitled 'The people make the place', Ben Schneider (1987) argues that we restrict the range of diversity within our organizations. This we do by seeking to attract and select others like ourselves. Any dissimilar people who pass through the net are subsequently more subject to attrition, either voluntary (they can't stand it) or involuntary (they are rejected). This restriction in range is both of value priorities and also of personality characteristics. For example:

♦ In eight accounting firms in San Francisco, new auditors were selected according to eight narrow but different sets of values (e.g. aggressive, people oriented) (Chatman, 1991). Moreover, those auditors already in post differed across firms in terms of their value priorities. These differences cannot be attributed to the profession which these recruits were entering: it was the same for all of them.

♦ In four UK organizations from different sectors, differences in the personality characteristics of managers were found. These held true even after differences due to functional specialization, age, education, and aptitude were allowed for (Jordan et al., 1991).

♦ In 28 UK and US organizations, career progress in terms of salary was related to degrees of fit (Ansari et al., 1982). Those middle managers who placed a similar value on achievement as others in the organization were more highly paid. Interestingly, this pattern wasn't repeated right at the top, where it paid to be a little less overtly ambitious and conventional.

The overall picture supports Schneider's suggestion. Organizations attract, select, retain, and reward those who are like those already in place in the organization. Where they select those unlike themselves, they either socialize them into at least behaving like themselves; or, if they fail to homogenize them, they spit them out.

What is true of organizations as wholes is also true of their boards. Where you would expect diversity to be most valuable, it is

Table 1.1   *Comparison of diversity on boards by sector*

Dimension of diversity	Retail (%)	Finance (%)	Engineering (%)	Food and drink (%)
Board members over 50	64	80	76	80
Women board members	8	4	3	0
Non-UK board members	7	5	10	18
Attended public school	42	37	53	40
Attended Oxbridge	16	26	17	20
Board members with public sector experience	15	16	23	10
Career primarily with one organization	28	16	26	57
Board member for more than five years	52	33	38	44
Board members with international work experience	17	24	25	38
Board members holding other directorships	55	75	68	47

Figures based on analysis of board membership of 30 major UK companies in spring 1992.

least apparent. Boards have to make sense of an inherently ambiguous business and organizational context. Yet they perversely seem set on perpetuating themselves in their own image. Table 1.1 presents the membership of 30 UK boards by sector. These boards seem ill-fitted to take the perspective of their company's customers, or of international markets. In the food and drink sector, for example, fewer than half of board members are equipped by their experience to take a perspective from outside their own organization!

The research evidence indicates that boards with diverse members have a higher turnover rate, and those likely to leave are those least like their colleagues (Jackson et al., 1991). If boards do succeed in maintaining their diversity, though, they are likely to do better. In particular, if they are made up of people who have worked in a variety of functions (especially those like marketing and sales which deal with customers) (Norburn and Birley, 1988) and for a variety of organizations (Wiersema and Bautel, 1992), they are likely to perform better (fewer bankruptcies) and to be more adaptable to change. So it pays boards to be different; but if the organization is a vindaloo, and if the board members are home grown, then they are likely to be the most homogenized of all the employees.

Why assimilate?
So at organizational and at board levels of analysis, most organizations seek to assimilate their members into the club. Why do they do so? Two levels of explanation suggest themselves. The first makes some generalizations about human nature; the second outlines some of the difficulties that arise when we try to work with people different from ourselves.

Generalizations about human nature normally tell us more about the generalizer than about human nature. However, perhaps the following observation will ring some bells. We feel very comfortable in a club. A *Punch* cartoon about clubland had the club officer lifting the newspaper from the deeply upholstered armchair to find a skeleton underneath. The comfort comes from being able to identify with each other. We're all like-minded and congenial people. We feel we can't argue too much; we take too much on trust because it's not gentlemanly to question; we want to be unanimous since there must be a right solution for a problem we all perceive in the same way; we come to rapid conclusions based on little evidence because we feel we all share the same expertise. Above all, we treat anyone from outside our club as an inferior. For the more powerful the common identity we share, the more different to us we perceive them to be; and since we have a pretty high opinion of ourselves . . .! Perhaps this is the most dangerous consequence of all; we often look down on those with perspectives or values different from our own. We therefore devalue their contribution and refuse to take on board knowledge based upon different perspectives. We also happily attribute failure to their shortcomings, and successes to our own wisdom. And we stereotype them into gross categories – out-of-touch senior managers, hysterical women, snooty and uncommitted professionals, deadwood stick-in-the-mud experienced managers, feckless and reckless youth, automated operatives, and mad IT people – each with *their* own set of worthless prejudices!

In case you think we are exaggerating the exclusiveness of clubbery, consider a famous social psychology experiment (Billig and Tajfel, 1973). People arriving for the experiment were randomly divided into two arbitrary groups. Each person was told which group he or she belonged to, but was not told which of the two groups other individuals belonged to. The subjects were then given an opportunity to earn some money. They could make more for themselves if they agreed that an anonymous member of the other group would actually get more than they would. They could, alternatively, earn less for themselves, but get the pleasure of knowing that the member of the other group got even less than they did. There was a clear tendency for experimental subjects to prefer the latter option! An analogy is with wages, where employees often want differentials to be maintained at the cost of personal benefit. That happened when the only thing that united the group was the arbitrary label they were given. How much greater the exclusivity when there are real similarities of background and value!

Difficulties of Diversity
We seem predisposed to prefer people like ourselves, and reject those who persist in remaining different. But apart from this general aspect of human nature, there are specific difficulties which are likely to arise in working with diverse people. Here are a few of them:

+ The others don't agree with our longer-term vision.
+ These differences in vision are likely to be based on differences in values, and probably in identity. Where identities are involved, we easily feel threatened, and defensive behaviour ensues.
+ Differences in vision lead to major disagreements on what are the basic issues to be addressed, and therefore what are worthwhile projects to tackle.
+ Analyses of the situation will be different, since they will be derived from different perspectives.
+ Difference in expertise will create disagreement about how things ought to be done.

Being in a minority of one is a difficulty of diversity: it's difficult for the outsider! Consider the board of a major financial organization. All of the board come from a banking or accounting background except one: the human resources (HR) director. He wishes to enlist the board's support for a management development programme. This is because he sees the situation in terms of the know-how needed to carry through the board's currently favoured strategy. This is to develop financial services particularly suited to new markets in Central and Eastern Europe, and to claim a large share of that market before it becomes colonized. The rest of the board, however, construe the situation in a different way. They see it in terms of the investment of funds in the project and the length of time before appreciable returns can be expected. They place these considerations into the context of the annual accounts due shortly, and the size of the dividend expected by shareholders and the marketplace. The issues are thus perceived to be different, and the priority of projects follows suit. The board wishes to minimize costs, the HR director to improve skills. The HR director's project, which will increase costs, is therefore incompatible with the board's priorities. The board members come from somewhere different, and therefore are likely to be trying to go somewhere different too. Many of them may know beyond to a scenario where the organization's financial position is not so dependent on national political events. Now the HR director also knows beyond. He envisages a scenario where employees are so flexible in their skills and knowledge that they are capable of adapting to a variety of strategic directions.

The HR director and the others differ in their backgrounds and values, in their visions of the future, and consequently in how they view the real issues and the appropriate action projects. This does not mean that he cannot persuade them to support his project, though it's fairly unlikely that he will do so. One way he might try is to argue that investment in management development is only a cost in the very short term. In the longer term, it is likely to result in a financial benefit. He might support this argument with estimates of the costs of buying in the new staff with the skills necessary to exploit the Eastern Europe opportunity. He has now approached his board colleagues in terms of *their* intellectual framework, a financial one, even though he has personally retained his own 'human capital' assumptions. It will help him greatly however if he has had experience in other functions, especially finance. Of course, he still has to address the short-term versus long-term benefits issue. Nevertheless, he has made the effort to persuade them in terms of their view of the situation and of what the key issues are. It's worth noting that it is the difference in intellectual frameworks which has resulted in his putting up his project in the first place; it wouldn't have been considered or championed if this difference was not present in at least one person on the board. It's also worth noting that while the HR director and the others may have different visions of longer-term activities, these different visions are not necessarily incompatible. Indeed, the development of a flexible workforce may actually assist the organization to be less dependent financially on national political events.

On his own, the HR director is unlikely to win the day, however. This is because there is insufficient diversity among the board. Because he was there, at least the issue got raised. The rest of the board were probably irritated by this seemingly irrelevant intervention. If one person irritated them, imagine what several could do! The HR director on his own stood little chance. However, if he had had one or two allies, they might have got their way, even though they were initially in the minority.

A famous social psychology experiment demonstrates how they might have done so (Nemeth et al., 1974). Groups of six people were tested for colour blindness. Provided they passed, they were then shown 36 slides, all of them obviously blue in colour and differing only in their brightness. When asked to name the colour on each of the slides, the first group of six were over 99 per cent correct. In other groups, however, the experimenters planted two confederates. These two, as instructed, consistently said that the slides were either green (the brighter ones) or green-blue (the duller ones). On average, the four naïve subjects said that 21 per cent of the slides were green!

The two confederates were completely consistent in their responses, in that they always said that the blue slides were something other than blue. They also showed a clear pattern in their replies, using green for brighter and green-blue for duller slides. The implication is that a minority can influence a majority, providing they are consistent; but not so consistent as to seem rigid and extreme, and therefore as not worth taking seriously. Rather, they are seen as certain and confident, and so their behaviour needs explaining. Perhaps they've got something, think the other four. While the four may start privately wavering in their conviction that the slides are blue, they won't show it aloud because they won't wish to appear the odd one out. However, once one of the four breaks ranks, the others may follow. They have no more need to comply. But it's clearly important for at least one of the majority to break ranks, otherwise the minority may not affect the actual decision, even though they have sown private doubts.

The experiment, together with such current trends as the successes of special interest groups, demonstrates that it may take an active minority to make us reassess our view of reality. When there are no consistent minority groups present, however, other research shows that discussion only reinforces the existing majority point of view (Lamm and Myers, 1978).

Catastrophes of Clubbery

So dealing with diversity is difficult, and so is being in a minority of one. But while diversity may be difficult, clubbery can be catastrophic. What happens when the diverse sources of knowledge are ignored and we become a cosy little club instead?

Real crises give us the ultimate consequences. The Bay of Pigs fiasco saw 'groupthink' at its most extreme (Janis, 1972). The advisers of President Kennedy were characterized by:

- a shared illusion of invulnerability
- collective efforts to find ways of discounting warning signs
- a shared belief in the inherent morality of the group
- stereotyped views of outsiders as evil, weak, or stupid
- disapproval of those who questioned the way the group was thinking and working
- self-censorship of any doubts
- the illusion of unanimity
- the censoring out of any evidence casting doubt on their plans.

Business crises can have the same effect if a club is in charge of the business. All the traditional shipping companies, for example, shared an illusion of their blue-chip invulnerability. They ignored the Wickenden brothers as they emerged from the remains of Townsend Thorenson to grow the biggest cargo route – the UK to the Continent. The management literature is replete with many more examples.

Protection: the Nouvelle Cuisine Model

A second way of dealing with diversity is to protect it like a delicate culinary decoration. This approach involves taking categories of people who tend to suffer unfair treatment in society at large (for example, ethnic minorities, women, gay people, the disabled) and trying to make sure they are treated fairly at work. These efforts have taken a variety of forms, most of them concentrated upon equal opportunities of employment; some have been enforced by legislation, especially in the USA where affirmative action has been widespread.

However, as Thomas (1990) puts it: 'Minorities don't need a boarding pass, they need an upgrade.' In other words while, in the United States at least, selection into organizations may no longer be discriminatory to any great extent, subsequent progress certainly is. Interesting evidence (Fine et al., 1990) indicated that white men in organizations believe that state legislation and/or organizational systems remove discrimination. Many, indeed, believe that the discrimination is now reversed, and that women and the ethnic minorities receive preferential treatment. Women, on the other hand, believe that their struggle has only just begun. They see attitudes and culture barriers impeding their progress. The jury is out on whether the cohorts of women recently admitted into organizations and indeed into their management structures will progress through. Current evidence isn't hopeful.

From the viewpoint of our argument, however, those in power in organizations should not be regarding people who are visibly different and who are likely to differ from others in identity and values as endangered species. They should not concentrate merely upon doing their duty and being fair. Rather, they should be recognizing that the diversity of outlook which often derives from biographical differences is their major asset.

Anyway, protection of embattled minorities begins to look a little *passé* when those to be protected outnumber their protectors. Already in the United States, white males form less than half of the workforce (Thomas, 1990). In Europe and the UK, the proportion of the workforce that is female is increasing annually and approaches 50 per cent. In the UK, much of this employment is part-time, with the diminution of rights and power that this presently entails. This points to the continued inequalities suffered by those who used to be numerical minorities. We are not arguing that employees' rights should be ignored; rather, we hold that it is their potential rather than their rights which should be the greater focus of our attention in the future.

Value: the Sunday Lunch Model

The final approach to diversity, and the one which innovative organizational survivors of the twenty-first century will have embraced, is the Sunday lunch model. While roast beef and Yorkshire pudding will probably have been banished by then in the interests of health and the environment, the principle will remain: the whole is enhanced by each of its parts. Each will therefore be valued for what it adds to the whole experience (Rosenor and Loden, 1991).

The examples of differences we have given so far relate to gender and ethnicity. This is because these are the differences which have been recognized as among the most powerful origins of unfair treatment. They are also powerful differences from the point of view of the individual's psychology. For many women and ethnic minority members, their gender and/or ethnicity is a major aspect of their identity, their idea of who they are. Since we derive our identity largely from the way we are dealt with by others, this is hardly surprising. For the differences which have clear visual or behavioural signals are the ones which others use to categorize us. Gender and ethnicity are clearly signalled and those on one side of these categories suffer inequalities of power relative to those on the other.

However, they are only some of the differences between people. There are many others: our national or socio-economic culture or subculture, with its differences in assumptions, values, and behaviour; our personality; our aptitudes and abilities; our attitudes, opinions, and interests; the varied roles we play; our habits and personal style; our social status, wealth, and power; our appearance; our health and strength; and so on.

Which of these are we interested in? Which should we value in organizations? Arguments have been put forward for many of these differences as crucial. For example, it has been argued that women are likely to bring additional qualities to the task of management, since in general they are stronger on interpersonal skills than men. Ironically, much of the effort in equal opportunities has gone into ensuring that gender and ethnicity do not enter as criteria into selection or promotion decisions. Other favourite dimensions of difference are abilities and personality. The whole of the psychometric industry is based on the premise that differences along these dimensions predict subsequent job performance. The actual practice of selection relies more on an estimate of cultural fit. Do this individual's assumptions, values, and behaviour style fit in with our own? In this latter case, the dimension of difference under consideration is the degree to which the individual resembles our culture or can be persuaded to do so.

What dimensions of diversity should organizational members be most interested in? Every dimension of difference carries the danger of stereotyping – the danger of assuming that because an individual is high or low, or falls into this category or that, he or she exhibits the characteristics which we attribute to that category. We may or may not be correct in attributing more developed interpersonal skills to women, but we are certainly incorrect in inferring that because Mary is a woman, she has more developed interpersonal skills than the person sitting next to her who happens to be a man. On the other hand we desperately need to make generalizations about people, simply in order to understand and describe them as individuals. I cannot describe Mary as interpersonally skilled unless I have some notion of people behaving in skilled or unskilled ways.

The differences we have chosen to work with are those of roles at work. There are several reasons for this choice:

- ◆ We are interested in the different frameworks of understanding and knowledge which people bring to work.
- ◆ We believe that those frameworks can have their origins in all sorts of more fundamental differences.
- ◆ For example, the framework of understanding brought by a production engineer may derive from his perception that he is a professional engineer, that he is a man, that he has strong

Table 1.2   *Elements of diversity and how to achieve them*

Elements	Tools
Pluralism: getting different perspectives	Training programmes using varied inputs to solving problems
Structural integration into the organization in all job roles	Education, affirmative action, career development, new reward systems and packages (e.g. childcare)
Integration of informal networks	Mentoring, social events, support groups
Absence of prejudice and discrimination	Focus groups, awareness training, internal research, monitoring practice of policies
Identification with the organization	Consequences of all the other interventions described
Low levels of inter-group conflict	Evidence on promotion rates, conflict resolution training

Source: Cox (1991)

spatial and mechanical aptitude, high general intelligence, and an interest in making things work.

♦ However, the most available source of evidence for the knowledge that people bring to work is what they do at work.
♦ Unfortunately, many are in roles which prevent them from demonstrating the depth of their understanding in their action.
♦ Therefore our evidence from different roles will sample exceptional as well as typical activity and performance.

Preparing Sunday Lunch

What characterizes organizations which actively value diversity? How do they set about it? There have been two recent lists of prescriptions for policy. The first (Cox, 1991) lists the tools for achieving six key elements of a truly multi-cultural and diverse organization (Table 1.2).

A second recipe (Copeland, 1988) for Sunday lunch suggests the following 10 ingredients:

1 Recruitment: recruit diversity.
2 Career development: ensure the same development jobs are open to all.
3 Provide diversity training for managers.
4 Provide diversity training for other employees.
5 Make efforts to break glass ceilings.

6 Seek views from diverse groups rather than just from their managers.
7 Ensure networks and support groups for minorities.
8 Hold managers accountable for development of all their subordinates.
9 Accommodate organizational systems to individual needs (holidays, religious observance, family, etc.).
10 Install visible outreach programmes into the community.

Proposing recipes is one thing; cooking the meal is another. Different chefs will do it their way, but here is how Grand Metropolitan sought to value diversity.

Case Study: Grand Metropolitan

In 1988–9 Grand Metropolitan took over the American food company Pillsbury (Greenslade, 1991). In so doing, they acquired some famous brands – Burger King, Jolly Green Giant, and Häagen Dazs among them. What they also acquired was considerable anxiety from the Pillsbury workforce, centred on Minnesota. Employees were particularly concerned that the affirmative action department had been sacrificed by Pillsbury in their effort to become more cost competitive to fight the takeover.

Not only did Grand Metropolitan reinstate the department; they renamed it the 'culture diversity' function. This new name reflected Grand Metropolitan's conviction that there were business benefits to be derived from multi-culturalism. They realized that if their customers were represented in the workforce, they would have a better understanding of their expectations of the products and services. They also perceived that organizational assumptions and values needed challenging if they were to match the changing business environment.

The initial emphasis was still on women and blacks as the sources of diversity. However, working style, age, education, and sexual preference were soon added to the list. An organization-wide education and training programme was implemented in the foods business, attended by all top management from the chief executive down. The programme sought to demonstrate the added value that was derived from diversity. It challenged stereotyped thinking about what people were capable of at work. In addition to the training programmes, senior managers were made accountable for encouraging diversity, and for mentoring individuals, and their bonuses were contingent partly upon their success in so doing.

The chief executive of the food business in the USA, Ian Martin, summed up the rationale by writing to all employees: 'By securing the best talent from all parts of our corporate culture, we will improve our own business performance as well as ensuring a fair and just working environment.' Martin had gone beyond *nouvelle cuisine*. His food company was into English Sunday lunch.

Seeing this true piece of our national heritage being appropriated by the Americans, Grand Metropolitan HQ in the UK took a major conceptual leap. They agreed that the business case was universal. It would have been only too easy to identify the USA, with its history of equal opportunities legislation and larger ethnic minority groups, as a special case. Resisting this temptation, Grand Metropolitan determined to manage diversity from a corporate multinational perspective. In view of the relative autonomy given to subsidiaries by Grand Metropolitan corporately, this was indeed a major commitment.

Progress has yet to be reported, but if the diversity of Grand Metropolitan's board is anything to go by, the omens are good. The board contains people with a variety of educational, organizational, functional, and national backgrounds. The non-executive directors are powerful and outspoken individuals in their own right, not in the least beholden to the chairman. The board are reported to have been faced with a black female store manager recently, who told them just what it was like at the sharp end.

Summary

- Most organizations restrict diversity by attracting, selecting, and retaining people like those already working in them.
- One reason is that we like people who are similar to ourselves, and treat those outside the club as inferior.
- Another reason is that it is easier to work with those who are similar to ourselves.
- However, while diversity may be difficult, clubbery is often catastrophic.
- Another way of dealing with diversity is to treat minorities as needing protection.
- A final way is to treat it as the potential source of creativity and innovation; in particular, in terms of the different mental frameworks of those in different organizational roles.

References

Ansari, M., Baumgartel, H. and Sullivan, G. (1982) 'The personal orientation – organizational climate fit and managerial success', *Human Relations*, 35: 1159–78.

Billig, M. and Tajfel, H. (1973) 'Social categorization and similarity in intergroup behaviour', *European Journal of Social Psychology*, 3: 37–52.

Chatman, J.A. (1991) 'Matching people and organizations: selection and socialization in public accounting firms', *Administrative Science Quarterly*, 36: 459–84.

Copeland, L. (1988) 'Valuing diversity. Part 2: Pioneers and champions of change', *Personnel*, July: 44–9.

Cox, T. (1991) 'The multi-cultural organization', *Academy of Management Executive*, 5(2): 34–48.

Fine, M., Johnson, F. and Ryan, S. (1990) 'Cultural diversity in the workplace', *Public Personnel Management*, 19(3): 305–19.

Greenslade, M. (1991) 'Managing diversity: lessons from the United States', *Personnel Management*, 23(12): 28–32.

Jackson, S.E., Brett, J.F., Sessa, V.I., Cooper, D.M., Julin, J.A. and Peyronnin, K. (1991) 'Some differences make a difference: individual dissimilarity and group heterogeneity as correlates of recruitment, promotions, and turnover', *Journal of Applied Psychology*, 76(5): 675–89.

Janis, I.L. (1972) *Victims of Groupthink: a Psychological Study of Foreign Policy Decisions and Fiascos*. Boston: Houghton-Mifflin.

Jordan, M., Herriot, P. and Chalmers, C. (1991) 'Testing Schneider's ASA theory', *Applied Psychology: an International Review*, 40(1): 47–53.

Lamm, H. and Myers, D.G. (1978) 'Group-induced polarization of attitudes and behaviour', in L. Berkowitz (ed.), *Advances in Experimental Social Psychology*, Vol. II. New York: Academic Press.

Nemeth, C., Swedland, M. and Kanki, G. (1974) 'Patterning of the minority's responses and their influence on the majority', *European Journal of Social Psychology*, 4: 53–64.

Norburn, D. and Birley, S. (1988) 'The top management team and corporate performance', *Strategic Management Journal*, 9: 225–37.

Rosenor, J.B. and Loden, M. (1991) *Workforce America: Managing Employee Diversity as a Vital Resource*. Homewood, IL: Business One Irwin.

Schneider, B. (1987) 'The people make the place', *Personnel Psychology*, 40: 437–53.

Thomas, R.R. (1990) 'From affirmative action to affirming diversity', *Harvard Business Review*, March–April: 107–17.

Wiersema, M.F. and Bautel, K.A. (1992) 'Top management team demography and corporate strategic change', *Academy of Management Journal*, 35(1): 91–121.

2

The General Managers: Flexible Frameworks

The Pressures

It is obvious that general managers need to know something. But what is the nature of their knowing? Is it more knowing how, knowing that, or knowing beyond? What unique perspectives do they bring?

Four companies in the microcomputer industry were facing strategic problems (Bourgeois and Eisenhardt, 1988). This was hardly surprising. There is a constant state of flux in demand, competition, technology, and regulatory legislation in that industry. It is very hard indeed to get reliable information about these crucial factors, so actions have to be taken largely in the absence of data. The strategic decisions with which they were faced were fundamental:

♦ Should we be IBM compatible?
♦ What should be our new business strategy?
♦ Do we need a new name?
♦ Should we go public?

The solutions had to be innovative ones: the hostile competitive environment meant that imitation of competitors was not a viable option since all market niches were occupied. Furthermore, given the capital and knowledge investment, mistakes would be costly and result in being left behind in the race. Solutions not only had to be innovative; they also had to be good, rational ones with a low probability of failure. What's more, they had to be taken fast, and be rapidly implemented.

Two of the four companies succeeded in taking decisions which resulted in competitive advantage; two failed. What made the difference? The successful ones succeeded in balancing three paradoxes:

♦ They made their decisions carefully but quickly.
♦ Their solutions were innovative and high risk, but their implementation was safe and gradual.
♦ The CEO was powerful and took the final decision, but the rest of the top team were powerful too, and ensured implementation.

How do top management teams work together to achieve such successes as these? Research (Thomas and McDaniel, 1990) shows that the more participative, informal, rule free, open, and equal the team members are, and the more they feel free to form *ad hoc* groups to tackle particular issues, then the greater the benefit to the CEO. In particular, he or she is likely to feel more positive about the strategic issues and consider them more controllable than before. What's more, the CEO will be prepared to gather more information before arriving at a decision.

What about the failures? As soon as they construe the situation as one of threat, top management teams start making maladaptive responses (Staw et al., 1981). They restrict the information they gather (Janis, 1972), they exercise as much centralized control as they can, and they stick to well-learned and trusted solutions. Any member who deviates from the group line is pressured to conform. While such responses might be appropriate where the problem is powerful, immediate, and familiar, they are hardly going to work when it's a radically new situation. Instead of adopting new frames of reference, managers understand the situation in terms of existing ones. Past experiences and past ways of understanding then become the touchstone; a new understanding of the present and a new vision for the future are out of the question. Chrysler and Swiss Watches are historical examples, but today as we come out of recession we can see organizations still striving for increased control and efficiency in the face of competition when only new and innovatory frames of reference will save them.

So there are expert general managers and there are journeymen. What is the nature of the expertise which distinguishes them? We will argue that expert general managers *know beyond* much more frequently than they *know how*. We will also show that they express this knowledge in action. Those actions which embody knowing beyond are usually more important than those which reflect know-how. The expert general manager knows beyond. For example, Clive Thompson, CEO of Rentokil, spends most of his time trying to ask new questions or have new ideas. He actively resists involvement in the routine of the business.

General managers are in an exciting but exposed position. A wide range of stakeholders in the organization expect them to keep the show on the road. Putting it more formally: 'The distinctive nature of managerial activities lies in their contribution to the establishment and development of firms as significant economic resource controlling entities' (Whitley, 1989). Executives are expected to ensure their organization's survival both by managing resources internally and by adapting to the external environment, a difficult enough balancing act in itself. Yet their basic responsibility is augmented by many other expectations from a variety of stakeholders:

◆ Individual shareholders may have ethical agendas.
◆ Pension fund shareholders want short-term profits.
◆ Employees expect continued employment.
◆ The local community requires environmental concern.
◆ Clients and customers want individualized and excellent service at their convenience.
◆ Suppliers request predictable and regular orders.
◆ Corporate HQ wants budget targets exceeded.
◆ Non-executive directors insist on the formulation of a business strategy.
◆ Departmental heads want disputes over resources settled.

Immediate and medium-term issues assault the executive from all directions, hurled in his or her direction by a variety of stakeholders. Truly, the label 'general' manager' is apt. For general managers are expected to cope with a general and broad range of problems in a particular situation; professional specialists, in contrast, cope with a narrow range of issues in a wide variety of situations.

However, it is the survival and growth of the organization which is the chief responsibility of executives. And there's the rub. For survival is within the competitive environment, which is changing ever more rapidly. Unless they understand these changes and their implications, executives are unlikely to secure their firm's survival or seize new opportunities as they arise. Here are the general manager's requirements for knowing that:

◆ In the competitive environment, executives need to appreciate trends such as increasing cost competitiveness and productivity and decreasing time to market.
◆ They need to know what competitors are doing both domestically and in an increasingly global marketplace (Bartlett and Ghoshal, 1989).
◆ They have to be aware of possible takeovers and mergers and be on the look-out for potential allies and partners.
◆ They should understand the nature of technological change and its likely impact on their business and markets.
◆ Their political antennae should pick up new policy directions and legislative changes which affect their business.
◆ They should be sufficiently socially aware to pick up those sea-changes in social trends which will affect both their workforce

and their business: current emphases on individuals' rights and quality of life, for example.

What a demanding but stimulating mixture! Short-term fire fighting, medium-term target reaching, long-term scanning, all at the behest of an army of stakeholders. Effectiveness can be defined as keeping a reasonable proportion of them reasonably happy for a reasonable period of time (Stewart, 1991) – hardly the stuff of which folk-heroes are made.

The Activities

So how do they cope? The first thing they do is talk to each other. Some 78 per cent of the time of the five CEOs whom Henry Mintzberg (1973) studied was spent talking to others. A large proportion of this time was devoted to others at their own level, many of them in other organizations. Of course, apart from telling us that general management is a highly social art, this finding is hardly very informative. We don't know what they are talking about or what are their purposes and intentions (Hales, 1986). They may be persuading, threatening, tapping, informing, negotiating, promising, gossiping, flattering, selling, discovering the score in the test match, or 101 other social acts. On the other hand, we do know that the more they socialize and politicize, the faster their career progress has been this far (Luthans et al., 1985). When they aren't talking to people, general managers are doing other things in brief episodes (Kotter, 1982). Those who have followed them around with stop-watches tell us that they average just over 20 discrete activities in any one day; this is considerably less, however, than junior and middle managers who average between 100 and 200 (Carroll and Gillen, 1987).

Stop-watches are all very well but we need to get inside the heads of our general managers and see how they are thinking. One ridiculous conclusion has been that because executives seem to be talking and doing things all the time, they can't do much thinking. Thinking isn't behaviour like talking and walking; thinking is more an adverb than a verb. We do things more or less thoughtfully, rather than spending our time in either one or the other activity, thinking or acting (Weick, 1983). In order properly to understand general managers' expertise, then, we have to look at how thoughtfully they are acting. We won't swallow the prescriptive sequence of popular mythology that people sit down to think and plan and then get up to act. Rather, we will seek to tease out on what basis they are acting.

General managers' activities have been categorized in an extra-ordinary variety of ways, ranging from descriptions of their physical behaviour (making a phone call) through types of activity (holding a planning meeting) to different roles and functions (strategic planner, team leader) (Hales, 1986). However, these lists represent only a surface analysis of the art of senior management. Descriptions at the level of behaviour or activity are mere catalogues; they offer no explanatory power at all. Descriptions in terms of roles and functions at least put the behaviour into the context of the organization. However they don't get at the psychology underlying the role activities; they don't explore the nature of the expertise. It is certainly no explanation to put these roles and functions inside general managers' heads as though this accounted for their performance. It doesn't help us understand how general managers work if we generate a list of functions that they perform and call them competences. Strategic planning, for example, is a role activity expected of general managers; it isn't a mental faculty or ability located inside their psyche. Rather, what we need to discover is how they get their information and how they act upon it.

So how do expert general managers get information from their environment? Many information systems are at their disposal in modern organizations. In process industry, for example, data from automated systems can reveal deviations from the programme and the situations in which they occur. In retail, changes in buying behaviour across the country can be monitored and acted upon. In most businesses, financial control systems provide a whole raft of bottom-line indices. At first blush, then, general managers have a wide range of information instantly available; why do they need to search out more?

Some analysis of *the idea of information* will help towards an answer. We talk and think about information as though it is an objective given: something that we receive ready-made and act upon according to what it tells us. However, we need to ask the questions: who decided what information we should be given, and on what grounds? Consider the information systems we quoted above. The automated control system in the process industry was probably designed by an engineer. He or she set the system up in the first place in order to control the process. The data which the system provides will be based on the control parameters within which the process operates efficiently. The recipients of such data can interpret them with benefit; for example, they can formulate hypotheses as to why the process periodically breaks down on the basis of their observations. The engineer's purpose of automation can be extended to inform others (Zuboff, 1988). But the fact remains that the system was set up for a particular purpose – automated control. Therefore only certain parameters were measured: those that were relevant for this purpose. The information, therefore, is not neutral. Its parameters were selected from within an engineering frame of reference to achieve an engineering objective. Moreover, any use to which it is further put depends on the meaning with which it is invested. Thus both the selection of what information to obtain and its interpretation depend on the meaning and purpose with which it is invested.

Exactly the same is true of the other examples. Financial control systems, for example, are usually designed by accountants. It is from an accountancy frame of reference that the parameters are derived. For general managers to interpret these as the sole indices of organizational performance is to accept the accountants' assumptions about what really matters. Information, then, is never value free. It is sought out and interpreted from within the mental framework of the individuals who are acquiring it and making sense of it.

If general managers were to acquire their information solely from the system we have described, they would be limiting themselves to narrow professional-based frameworks with which to make sense of their world. This they cannot afford to do. Their environment is so rapidly changing and so ambiguous that it is very hard to invest it with meaning. Anything like a coherent picture will certainly fail to emerge for an expert executive from a few sets of figures. Indeed, only non-experts will seek to impose meaning on ambiguity by limiting their data in this way.

So how do the experts do it? Here are some of the ways in which successful executives get their information and act upon it:

- They carry a set of action agendas around with them in their heads (Kotter, 1982).
- They rapidly seize opportunities to further these agendas as they arise.
- They notice and learn from the consequences of their agenda actions.
- They think about different agendas at the same time, and relate them to each other.
- They change constantly the agendas in their list and the priority they put on them.
- They talk about their agendas with other people and clearly articulate a joint interpretation of the outcomes.
- The people they talk to are different from each other and different from them.

♦ They talk not only about the meaning of the present but also about possible futures.

This list suggests that expert executives are very active people, who are always concerned to get things done. They are flexible people, who can switch easily from one agenda to another; and they are social people, who constantly give to and receive from others. Above all, they *act thoughtfully*; their actions are aimed at creating meaning out of ambiguity.

However, even this list doesn't really explain their thinking. What are the mental frameworks within which they are operating, where do they come from, and how do they change? After all, most executives probably fill the above bill moderately well. How do the real experts think?

Frameworks for Action

There is a wide range of possible assumptions and values that could form executives' mental framework. We could ask them, for example:

♦ To what extent can we understand business in terms of cause and effect, or is a lot of business activity essentially random?

♦ Consequently, can we predict the outcomes of present events or is the future unpredictable?

♦ How much of what happens in and to my organization is the consequence of my actions, and how much is outside my control?

♦ Do people behave rationally and in their own interests, or irrationally and for no discernible reason?

♦ Are organizations unified wholes, or are they a conglomeration of conflicting interests?

♦ Do people live to work or do they work to live?

♦ Is the sole major purpose of organizations to create profits for shareholders, or is there a range of legitimate stakeholders?

♦ Do employees have to be controlled, or can they control themselves?

♦ Do markets exist or can they be created?

♦ What is the organization's major asset: capital or people?

♦ Are disagreements a good thing or a bad thing?

♦ Do the same few things motivate everyone, or do different things motivate different people?

♦ Is the organization a fortress, a bearpit, or a ball game?

♦ Is business life primarily a competition or a collaboration?

- Is my own or my organization's future more important to me?
- Is the business environment becoming more difficult, or is it offering increased opportunities?
- Are management skills general across organizations, sectors, and countries, or are they more specific?
- Which is preferable – objective numerical information or subjective impressions from people you trust?
- Is performance best assessed individually or by unit?
- Will we ever return to a period of stability, or will it be continuous change from now on in?
- Can a common corporate culture be engineered, or will there always be different subcultures?
- Is major risk-taking inevitable, or can we minimize risks by foresight?

Some of these values and assumptions may strike us as being more appropriate in an area of ever increasing rate of change than others. However, the more important questions are where they came from and how they change.

The origins of senior managers' mental frameworks are many and varied. They may have absorbed assumptions and values from their organization's culture, or the subculture of a part of it; once an IBM person, always one. They may have acquired them from their professional or functional membership (Hambrick and Mason, 1984); try going through the questions about values and assumptions listed above and asking how you think an accountant and a marketer would respond to each of them. Compare the relative importance which an engineer, an accountant, and a marketer would give to information about product flow, cash flow, and the competition respectively.

Previous job roles may well predict how they perceive their present position. Middle managers often see their work in terms of defined activities, areas of responsibility, and objectives (Shrivasta and Schneider, 1984). To continue viewing one's job in the same way when a general manager would be inappropriate. Most expert executives seem to view their job holistically and don't worry too much about control or setting boundaries. Delving more deeply, mental frameworks may derive from individuals' identity. To the extent that our identity derives from our gender, we might expect two people with a strong male and a strong female identity respectively to demonstrate different assumptions and value priorities. Similarly with the degree of centrality of our work in our view of ourselves; a CEO whose self-concept has always been bound up in achieving such power is likely to operate with a different framework from one who has had greatness thrust upon him or her (Marshall and Stewart, 1981).

Given all these powerful determinants of their frameworks, how do general managers succeed in continuously adapting to that state of flux and chaos that masquerades as their business world? Their frameworks are vital to them: they enable them to give enough meaning to the flux to generate an action agenda. An interesting recent piece of research (Isenberg, 1986) contrasted the way in which 12 general managers solved a business case study with the methods adopted by business students. The managers arrived at an action plan much sooner, and asked for less information before they did so. They engaged in a lot more reasoning, especially reasoning by analogy, and paid less attention to specific detail. Clearly, general managers apply their frameworks to situations much more quickly. They are used to minimizing the time and effort costs of information search, and maximizing the use of what little information they have. A major danger, therefore, is that they arrive at premature conclusions by seeking out information which confirms their frameworks.

There are so many easy ways to do this (Kiester and Sproull, 1982). Inexpert executives can create their agendas for action solely on the basis of their own view of the situation. This view can be buttressed by the provision of filtered management information which is devised to serve the organization's administrative systems. They can create their agendas on the basis of existing agendas and projects to which they are committed.

Expert executives, on the other hand, create their agendas on the basis of others' frameworks as well as their own. Sir Allen Sheppard, CEO of Grand Metropolitan, actively recruits powerful and opinionated non-executive directors such as Sir John Harvey-Jones and encourages them to challenge his own strategic agenda. As Table 1.1 shows, different sectors have different degrees of diversity on their boards; some even have women, foreigners, and people under 50! The more agendas are based on different frameworks, the less likely one is to be tempted to seek to confirm one's own. Like Karl Popper's good scientist, expert executives act in ways which permit the refutation of their hypotheses.

However, it is in making sense of the outcomes of their agenda actions that the greatest difficulties face executives. All sorts of temptations lie in wait to retain their existing frameworks. After all, they have three alternatives (Norman, 1982). First, they can interpret the outcomes of their actions in terms of their existing frameworks: our sales promotion failed because we didn't give it a big enough budget. This interpretation buttresses an existing frame of reference which assumes that sales volume is a linear function of amount spent on advertising. Executives could have ignored evidence that the product line is out of fashion. Second, they can adapt their frame of reference to accord with the outcome; sales volume can only be increased by costly promotions if there is already a strong market for the product. Alternatively, they can adopt an entirely new frame of reference; let's stop thinking about selling a product and construe our task as marketing a service instead.

Keeping one's framework intact and unchanged is very comfortable. After all, agendas and their justifications have a lot invested in them. The framework that supports and justifies an agenda is often a risky personal judgement that a course of action will result in a desired outcome. What happens if it doesn't? Usually the situation is ambiguous enough to pretend that it has to some extent, or that it will soon, or that it hasn't for some unforeseeable and uncontrollable reason. There are 1001 ways of rationalizing failure, and they are usually designed to preserve the self-esteem and the interpretative framework of the actor. Expert executives are prepared to admit failures and to adapt their frameworks accordingly.

Moreover, experts are extremely sophisticated in avoiding two opposite interpretative errors. One error arises from a framework which stresses the ability of executives to make anything happen. Consequently, such can-do executives run the risk of believing that whatever happens after they've taken action is a consequence of that action: illusory causation (Schweik, 1986). They consequently credit (or occasionally blame) themselves for events for which they had no responsibility, and are unlikely to surrender the illusion of power. An entirely different error is for executives to interpret a situation in a particular way without realizing that they have brought it about in the first place: the ultimate in self-fulfilling prophecy (Weick, 1983). So eager are we to impose a causal explanation upon events that we imagine causation exists when it doesn't, or we make things happen so that it does.

Expert executives don't just avoid these pitfalls. They adjust their old frameworks or they create new ones. They operate in a continuous loop, with their agendas resulting in outcomes which require changed or new frameworks which create new agendas which result in outcomes – and so on (Figure 2.1). They interpret the present in new ways, which allows them to generate new agendas for the future. That is why they are so busy: they need to do a lot in order to generate new frameworks which enable them to do a lot more!

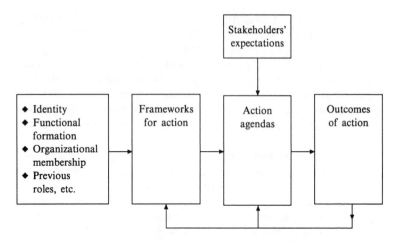

Figure 2.1 *Executive behaviour*

New frameworks generate new agendas. They can also generate new desired outcomes. Warren Bennis (1983) describes the art form of leadership as being to create and communicate clearly a compelling vision of a desired state of affairs. So many of the frameworks and agendas of individuals are tacit and intuitive. That is why executive teams are more likely to generate a communicable vision: they have to express themselves to each other to do so.

Our analysis of the work of expert executives suggests that there is very little specific know-how about it. No sooner have they established a frame of reference that meets their needs than they change it for a different one. They aren't faced with recurring problems for which they gradually develop better solutions. Rather, they are continuously doing new things and putting new interpretations on the consequences. They are imagining what could be; they are knowing beyond.

Summary

- Expert executives are expected to meet the short-, medium-, and long-term expectations of a wide variety of stakeholders.
- They have to be aware of many aspects of their changing environment.
- They operate on the basis of flexible action agendas, about which they communicate with a variety of others.

♦ Their mental frameworks for action are likely to consist of a wide range of assumptions and values about people, organizations, and the business environment.
♦ These frameworks are likely to be based on their identity, their professional formation, or their organizational membership.
♦ They may find it difficult to change their frameworks on the basis of the outcomes of their actions unless they invite others' interpretations.
♦ To the extent that their frameworks for action envisage a different future, they know beyond.

References

Bartlett, C.A. and Ghoshal, S. (1989) *Managing Across Borders*. London: Hutchinson.

Bennis, W. (1983) 'The artform of leadership', in S. Srivastva (ed.), *The Executive Mind*. San Francisco: Jossey-Bass.

Bourgeois, L.J. and Eisenhardt, K.M. (1988) 'Strategic decision processes in high velocity environments: four cases in the microcomputer industry', *Management Science*, 34(7): 816–35.

Carroll, S.J. and Gillen, D.J. (1987) 'Are the classical management functions useful in describing managerial work?', *Academy of Management Review*, 12(1): 38–51.

Hales, C.P. (1986) 'What do managers do? A critical review of the evidence', *Journal of Management Studies*, 23: 88–115.

Hambrick, D.C. and Mason, P.A. (1984) 'Upper echelons: the organization as a reflection of its top managers', *Academy of Management Review*, 9(2): 193–296.

Isenberg, D.J. (1986) 'Thinking and managing: a verbal protocol analysis of managerial problem solving', *Academy of Management Journal*, 29(4): 775–88.

Janis, I.L. (1972) *Victims of Groupthink*. Boston: Houghton-Mifflin.

Kiester, S. and Sproull, L. (1982) 'Managerial response to changing environments: perspectives on problem sensing from social cognition', *Administrative Science Quarterly*, 27: 548–70.

Kotter, J.P. (1982) *The General Managers*. New York: Free Press.

Luthans, F., Rosenkrantz, S.A. and Hennessey, H.W. (1985) 'What do successful managers really do?', *Journal of Applied Behavioural Science*, 21(3): 255–70.

Marshall, J. and Stewart, R. (1981) 'Managers' job perceptions. Part 1: Their overall frameworks and working strategies', *Journal of Management Studies*, 18(2): 177–90.

Mintzberg, H. (1973) *The Nature of Managerial Work*. New York: Harper and Row.

Norman, D. (1982) *Learning and Memory*. San Francisco: W.H. Freeman.

Schweik, C.R. (1986) 'Information, cognitive bias, and commitment to a course of action', *Academy of Management Review*, 11(2): 298–310.

Shrivasta, P. and Schneider, S. (1984) 'Organizational frames of reference', *Human Relations*, 37(10): 795–809.

Staw, B.M., Sandelands, L.E. and Dutton, J.E. (1981) 'Threat-rigidity effects in organizational behaviour: a multi-level analysis', *Administrative Science Quarterly*, 26: 501–24.

Stewart, R. (1991) *Managing Today and Tomorrow*. London: Macmillan.
Thomas, J.B. and McDaniel, R.R. (1990) 'Interpreting strategic issues: effects of strategy and the information processing structure of top management teams', *Academy of Management Journal*, 33(2): 286–306.
Weick, K.E. (1983) 'Managerial thought in the context of action', in S. Srivastva (ed.), *The Executive Mind*. San Francisco: Jossey-Bass.
Whitley, R. (1989) 'On the nature of managerial tasks and skills: their distinguishing characteristics and organization', *Journal of Management Studies*, 26(3): 209–24.
Zuboff, S. (1988) *In the Age of the Smart Machine*. Oxford: Heinemann.

3

The Professionals: Opening Up the Club

Professional Empires and Their Enemies

General managers face a wide variety of problems in a particular context – their organization. That's why they need a lot of knowledge specific to their own organization and sector. Professionals claim the opposite: that they can only solve certain sorts of problems but they can do so just about anywhere (Whitley, 1989). What's more, they claim to be the only ones who can.

The professions have in the past done a good marketing job for themselves. They have persuaded us that they are primarily concerned for our benefit rather than their own; that they possess expert knowledge which only those who have undergone their lengthy initiation rites can share; that they can and should police themselves, since they pay allegiance to a demanding set of professional ethics; and that they rather than their clients know what to do for the best. Their success in persuading us of their wisdom and virtue has tended to obscure what they really are: occupational groups which have gained more power than their rivals in the occupational marketplace (Child and Fulk, 1982). Professions arose to make individuals' occupational careers invulnerable to the instabilities of capitalist employment. They are nothing more than 'somewhat exclusive groups of individuals applying somewhat abstract knowledge to particular cases' (Abbott, 1988). They have no divine right to retain their elevated status: 'When a profession's performance no longer meets the values and needs of the society that suffers it, the demise of that profession is but a matter of time' (Van Maanen and Barley, 1984).

Instead of occupations slowly progressing towards a condition of professional grace and joining the elect in a permanent state of bliss, the reality is much more tarnished. Occupations compete with each other in their effort to annex more and more areas of work into their empire, or to acquire as clients more and more prestigious elements of society. In the 1980s, for example, a variety of occupations scrambled to annex the territory politely termed 'financial advice', and to offer it to the richest clients.

In their territorial ambitions, professions use a variety of weapons:

- They claim exclusive competence to carry out certain sorts of work; they are the sole operators.
- They control entry into the profession by qualification and certification.
- They regulate themselves, and so have greater freedom to compete.
- They legitimize their activities by claiming that they are founded on an abstract body of knowledge.
- They maintain a sufficiently generalized range of activity for their professional judgement to remain necessary.
- They use a private language which serves to mystify others, but to unify their members.
- They aim for a variety of markets for their services so that their clients are diverse and unorganized.

Some professions have succeeded remarkably well in achieving and maintaining a dominant position. British lawyers and doctors, for example, keep a relatively firm grip on their territory, despite repeated assaults by central government over the last decade. Government is not the real enemy of most other professions, however. Their toughest foes are their organizational clients.

To claim that clients are enemies is a paradox indeed; after all it is they who enable a professional occupation to survive. What is dangerous, however, is to be dependent on powerful clients who can call the tune. What is even more dangerous is the absence of reciprocity. You as a professional forecaster, for example, might be dependent on your organization for employment: you couldn't get work as a freelance. Your organization might treat its planners, however, as peripheral to its main purpose, and dispensable in recession.

Professionals may depend on organizations, then, for

- employment itself, the means to make a living
- the resources to do the work, the means of professional production
- a degree of security, the means of professional independence.

It's all very well for lawyers, doctors, and accountants. They can set up on their own, independent of organizations. Scientists, engineers, and computer people, though, are more dependent. As a consequence, their organization can define their work objectives and determine how their performance is to be evaluated. It can even claim a considerable say in how those objectives are to be achieved, a major intrusion on traditional professional autonomy. Even when professionals band together to create an organization of their own – a large firm of solicitors or accountants, for example – their individual autonomy is limited. For the major concern of that organization is to survive and prosper in the commercial market-place, and some professional values may be sacrificed to that imperative.

There are other, more pressing current reasons why organizations have the whip hand over their professionals. Increased competition implies that advantage is to be gained by decreased time to market. Scientists and engineers are consequently expected to:

◆ work in multi-disciplinary project teams
◆ telescope the product or service cycle
◆ be satisfied with meeting specifications rather than doing the best job possible
◆ discover and act upon what the customer wants
◆ share their knowledge with non-professional colleagues
◆ be business managers as well as technical professionals.

Organizations are losing patience with warring professions in their midst: the battle for resources is often ferocious when it is between functional departments each consisting of one sort of professional. And professional values and practices are quite often explicitly contradictory to senior management's messages.

Now, organizations are requiring business relevance even from those professions most central to the organization's mission. R&D staff, for example, in 12 high-tech firms are now expected to acquire a customer-facing business perspective relatively early in their career (Pemberton and Herriot, 1993). Unilever send their PhD recruits, eager to thrust back the frontiers of knowledge in the laboratory, out on secondment for months on end to production, marketing and sales.

It is not by acquiring more diverse knowledge that professionals are threatened, however. It is rather by giving away their professional knowledge. Organization by project rather than by department requires such surrender. So does the power of information technology to model their regular skills. The IT revolution has created the tools for turning much professional knowledge into a commodity available to all. Commercial credit risk assessment and medical diagnosis of common ailments are two examples. Architects have yielded up certain design skills to computer-aided design (CAD) systems. Basic auditing of accounts can now be carried out by accountancy technicians using software systems, leaving professionals to do more judgement-based work.

Indeed, it pays to be fairly general and vague in one's area of expertise; then one's knowledge can't be modelled. The knowledge of the general manager would be very hard to model systematically; and psychoanalysts are unlikely to invent a program which can match the tortuous complexity of their explanations of mental illness. So IT presents both a threat and a challenge: a threat because it gives away some of the knowledge and practice previously exclusive to the profession; and a challenge to discover new knowledge which cannot be immediately modelled.

To make these abstract arguments concrete, we will consider the case of *accountancy* as a profession, since it exemplifies many of the features of professions that we have outlined so far in this chapter. Of course, it is dangerous to generalize across professions. Some (e.g. engineering) are central to some organizations and non-existent in others. Others (e.g. law) tend to be peripheral in all except for professional law firms. Those professions which are central to manufacturing industry in particular (science, engineering) tend to be the ones which need an organizational setting in which to practise. Those which are peripheral tend to be able to find work for themselves.

Accountants started off as people who were called in to stave off bankruptcy. They then acquired their core function, audit, as a preventive annual event for all large business organizations rather than as an occasional remedy for some. They succeeded in promoting regulations which enforced an annual audit and made them its sole practitioners. Realizing that their market increasingly consisted of larger and larger organizations, they organized themselves into large professional bureaucracies to serve them. Accountancy firms now employ a wide variety of support professionals as well as accountants. Moving out from their core function of audit, they annexed tax, insolvency, and aspects of management consultancy. Realizing the importance of controlling costs for competitive advantage, cost accountants served organizations' needs by telling them how much they were spending on overheads, labour, and materials, for example, and how much they ought to be spending. With the advent of IT, they seized the territory of management information systems, fighting off information scientists in the process.

And all this while, they were controlling access to the profession by professional qualification. So attractive have these qualifications become as a general business preparation as well as an entrée to the profession, that many graduates seek initial employment with accountancy firms in order to obtain them. Indeed, some 250 of the UK's engineering graduates are lost annually to the accountancy profession, and we produce many times more accountants than our continental competitors.

In accountancy, then, we see many of the key features of professions exemplified:

- They continuously lay claim to new areas of work as they become available.
- Some of their work is a statutory requirement laid upon organizations (audit).
- There is a professional hierarchy, with those providing the statutory requirements and more general services (chartered accountants) at the top.
- There is a degree of exclusivity, with the chartered accountancy profession now predominantly graduate.
- They are largely immune to economic swings, since they are required all the time for audit, in bad times for insolvency, and in good times for consultancy.

Theory and Practice

What accountants haven't got is a strong abstract academic body of knowledge to give their profession greater legitimacy. This may be one of the reasons why accountancy still does not rank so high in status as medicine, scientific research, or law. It is also the main clue we have got to help us understand professionals in organizations and the way they think and work.

There is a major distinction to be made between expert *knowledge in practice* and *knowledge in theory*. Knowledge in practice is about dealing with the particular; it is about knowing how. What should we do in this particular situation, or to cope with this particular problem? Knowledge in theory is about generalizing in a formal, rational and abstract way about classes of situation. Knowledge in practice involves experts in using their personal theories in action to diagnose, infer, and deal with particular problems. Knowledge in theory requires them to produce evidence which confirms (but could have denied) their theoretical propositions. The problems dealt with by the practitioners originate from their client (although they may redefine them). The problems dealt with by the theorists are generated by their theory. Practitioners have theories of action in their heads which are seldom coherently expressed; theorists have formal theories which are not accepted by their peers unless they *are* coherently expressed.

What has abstract theory got to do, if anything, with professional practice? To the lay person, there is little if any distinction. A prestigious scientific knowledge base must result in sound and effective practice, we assume. A new discovery in medical science will surely lead almost automatically to a more successful treatment of a disease. A professional who knows more science must of course be a better practitioner as a result.

Yet almost the opposite assumptions are held in organizations about professionals. They are valued if they are practical and down to earth, and address pressing business problems. In Anglo-Saxon culture, the word 'academic' is used as a term of abuse in organizations. 'Of academic interest only', we say, as we dismiss a theoretical attempt to understand a situation. Unless the theory is a theory in action, we aren't interested.

How has this state of affairs come about? To a considerable extent, professions are to blame. They realized early that in order to gain esteem they had to stop being a mere craft, and acquire a respectable rational basis. After all, many of them gained their power in the nineteenth century, the age of reason itself. They then made the acquisition of this formalized knowledge base a condition for entry into the profession; the ability to practise was assumed to follow on later. It could be acquired during a probationary period and certificated by professional membership. So engineers, for example, usually have to have advanced level school qualifications in mathematics and physics, a degree in engineering, and professional membership achieved after a probationary period in which they have been supervised by a senior professional.

This abstract knowledge base gave professions a great deal of prestige and legitimacy. In some cases, it was very clear that knowledge of the abstract base really was necessary to the practitioner. Actuaries have to know the mathematical and statistical theory of actuarial science; physicists have to know their physics. Their knowledge base is clearly marked out and highly formalized. In other activities, no such knowledge base is available. This is why general management has never become a profession; despite the efforts of business schools with their MBA degrees, there is no coherent body of theory underlying managerial work. We have to rely on metaphors and analogies rather than testable theories to help us understand it.

In general, however, formal theory legitimates professions in the eyes of the public, and often the client. More dangerously, it has also bestowed status within the profession. The professionals have, as it were, swallowed their own propaganda. Instead of valuing those who meet the needs of the clients at the coalface, they esteem most highly those who are furthest removed from the client: those to whom other professionals refer the most difficult or interesting problems, or those who train professionals and research the knowledge base in academia. Clients value knowledge in practice; many professionals themselves value knowledge in theory.

This is highly dangerous for the profession. It directs professionals' attention away from the clients upon whose custom they depend and internally towards their own individual status. It also passes on a sense of what is valued and what bestows status to those who are receiving their professional formation. If the undergraduate student or the probationer professional has eyes to see and ears to hear, they will notice that the most eminent professionals see only the most unusual or prestigious clients. They will have as their role models professionals who live an alluring life of consultancy, passing on their wisdom through conferences, professional policy discussion, and writing.

This is trebly tragic. It is tragic because clients' needs tend to take second place, although we may be sure that hungrier professions will move in to provide a better service in time. It is tragic because entrants to professions pick up during their formation values and assumptions which do not endear them to their individual or their organizational clients. And it is most tragic of all because, as we will argue, theoretical knowledge is the most potent source we possess for generating innovations. Its potential is ignored in many organizations because of its abuse by the professions which own it.

Professional Frameworks

So what sort of professional emerges, wet behind the ears and blinking, into the harsh competitive world of the organization? We may ask the same questions about professionals as we asked about general managers: what are their frameworks of values and assumptions, and how do these affect their perceptions of the present and the future? Hopefully our lengthy analysis of professions as social institutions will have paved the way for some insights into the professional mind.

Try the following questionnaire, devised by Gerpott and colleagues (1988). How important is it to you to:

- Make a contribution to a body of scientific and technical knowledge?
- Establish a reputation as an outstanding professional?
- Publish results of significant research findings?
- Be evaluated on the basis of scientific and technical skills?
- Be evaluated on the basis of management skills?

- Advance to the upper levels of management?
- Develop and utilize management skills?
- Help the company enhance its economic success?

Respond to each question with a rating of:

0   of no importance
1   of little importance
2   of moderate importance
3   of considerable importance
4   of extreme importance.

Add the scores for the first four items and those for the latter four. The first four are an index of professional orientation, and the second four of managerial orientation. You may have scored high on both; low on both; high on professional only; high on managerial only. All four patterns have been observed in research and development scientists and engineers (Aryee and Leong, 1991) and software developers (Garden, 1990). How do you score? And are you a professional?

We cannot assume, then, that professionals all hold exclusively professional/technical values and assumptions. Nor may we infer that a professional and a managerial orientation are mutually exclusive: some score high on both. Taking engineers as an example, we can say that those with a technical orientation are likely to be from lower socio-economic class origins than those with a managerial orientation (Taylor, 1979; Keenan and Newton, 1986). Further, this difference in values was evidenced during university, and affected choice of engineering specialization. Those with a technical orientation were more likely to want jobs in research and development or design, those with a managerial one jobs in operations or outside engineering altogether (Taylor, 1979; Rynes, 1987). When they actually left university, engineering students were often disappointed. They expected more autonomy, influence, and development of their abilities than they got; and they found less opportunity than they had hoped for to apply the knowledge they gained at university (Keenan and Newton, 1986). In one large UK organization in the petroleum field, engineers and computer scientists decreased in their personal growth, tangible rewards, and psychological adjustment over two to five years, relative to marketers, traders, planners, and personnel specialists (Nicholson and Arnold, 1991). However, they did do more analytic work, honing the skills they acquired at university.

So while there is evidence of students being socialized into a technical, abstract, and academic set of values at university, individuals differ in their response to these influences. Some allow the social, enterprising, and conventional sides of their personality to take them into managerial jobs, even within R&D, while the technical specialists have more artistic interests (Hill and Roselle, 1985) and want to be autonomous and creative (Garden, 1990).

To discover the framework held by professional and technical employees, then, we might ask them the following questions:

◆ Whose approval do you value more: your boss's or your fellow professionals'?
◆ What's more important: to meet the specification on time or to make a really good job of it?
◆ How many work problems can one deal with properly at any one time: one, several, or many?
◆ Who should be your line manager: a professional colleague or a project manager?
◆ Who should decide which projects you work on: you or your boss?
◆ Can only someone with your qualifications do the work you do?
◆ Should professional ethics always override business 'opportunism'?
◆ Is furthering knowledge through publications and conferences more important than keeping commercial advantage?
◆ Should managing people or money be part of your job?
◆ Can you continue to specialize, or do you have to become more general?
◆ Are organizational politics a nuisance or a necessity?
◆ What's more important: pragmatic solutions for now, or principled ones for the longer term?
◆ What gives individuals authority: what they know or what position they hold?
◆ What do you prefer: to do the work you want to, or promotion?
◆ How do you describe your work: 'I'm an X' (profession) or 'I work for Y' (organization)?
◆ Do younger people now know more than you do, and does it matter?
◆ Which is more important for you: your organizational network or your professional one?
◆ Is nearly all your knowledge transferable across organizations? across sectors? across national cultures?
◆ Are there one or more academic disciplines which underpin your knowledge?

The mental frameworks of professionals and general managers are markedly different (see Table 3.1); so much so that it is amazing

Table 3.1   *Mental frameworks of professionals and general managers*

Professionals	General managers
Defined problem area	Unlimited problem area
Action knowledge and theory knowledge	Action knowledge only
Esteem from other professionals	Esteem from satisfied stakeholders
Career is more knowledge and expertise	Career is more power and responsibility
Optimum solution sought	Workable solution sought
Prefer rationality	Justify intuition

that so many professionals succeed in making the transition successfully. Professionals have a defined area of problems which they think they alone are qualified to solve; the world is their stage for general managers, who have to tackle any and every major problem. Professionals operate with both action knowledge as to how to perform their task, and also theory knowledge which they may seldom use in practice; general managers usually use action knowledge alone. Professionals look to other professionals for esteem and recognition as well as to their employing organization; general managers have to keep a wide variety of stakeholders happy. Professionals perceive their career as a growth in knowledge and expertise, general managers as a growth in responsibility and power. Professionals want to solve problems according to the optimum solution their knowledge can provide; general managers tend to be satisfied with what works. Professionals need to have rational accounts for what they do; general managers are prepared to act intuitively, and say so.

Chalk and cheese, it seems. Indeed, the potential for conflict is always there. But out of diversity comes strength. The outstanding strength of professionals is not so much their know-how, which can often be more successfully applied by means of models and systems; it is their possession of theory-based knowledge. The reason is this: abstract ideas organized into theoretical systems are the most productive source of new ideas. Because they are symbolic, they can be transformed into different combinations without having to try them out in action. And because they are abstract, they can often be applied to a wide range of concrete situations. The vast technological advances of the present century have mostly occurred as a consequence of new theories aimed at understanding phenomena; consider, for example, biotechnology and DNA.

Problems with Professionals

So potentially, professionals are a major source of the new ideas for products and services which will give competitive edge from now on. Unfortunately, many of them operate from within one single frame of reference *alone* – their professional one. This means that their ideas are the products of closed systems, of sets of symbols which can only be transformed into variants of themselves. As Thomas Kuhn (1970) observed, theoretical frameworks exist for long periods during which they are fruitfully mined and explored. Then there is a scientific revolution, and new paradigms, new theoretical frameworks take their place. The whole of professionals' formation has been geared to developing a single theoretical framework (at university) applied to a particular area of expertise (during accreditation and professional membership). No wonder so much effort is currently being put into broadening their frameworks when they start their organizational careers. For it is only when they start thinking in terms of customers, products, and services as well as of their professional knowledge that they will come up with fruitful and applicable ideas.

There is currently a misplaced and counter-productive denigration of many technical professionals in the UK. This is partly a consequence of the recent devaluing of the public sector, in which many of them work. It also has to do with the perceived importance of effective general management in enabling organizations to survive in recession. General managers have cut costs, courted unpopularity, and worked all the hours God sends; on the other hand, professionals have been thought to show little allegiance to their organizations. Yet the evidence does not support this view. On the contrary, for 159 US computer specialists Bartol (1979) found that the greater their desire for professional autonomy, the greater their commitment to their profession and to its ethics, the greater was their organizational commitment. It also helped if they were rewarded for their:

◆ ability to work without much guidance
◆ concern for client interest
◆ high-quality work in their field
◆ participation in professional organizations
◆ keeping up with the latest developments in their field.

Dalton and Thompson (1986) found that, of 550 professionals (155 scientists, 268 engineers, 52 accountants, and 75 academics), many:

◆ developed other colleagues
◆ led ideas teams

- managed relationships with clients
- highlighted strategic opportunities and threats
- represented the organization to the outside world.

No, professionals don't lack organizational commitment. They are as loyal as the next person, provided that organizations honour their side of the bargains they have struck with them (Herriot, 1992). Nor should they be blamed for being theoretical; as someone once said, there is nothing so practical as a good theory. Indeed, a theoretical understanding is far more likely to generate good new ideas than an entirely action-based intuitive know-how. The fault, if fault there is, lies with educational and professional institutions. The academic gateways to professional work lead to limited discipline-based frames of reference; and the territorial preoccupations of professions limit those areas of practice in which professionals feel competent to work. It is the professional institutions which are concerned with territory; many individual professionals are genuinely motivated by the desire to provide excellent service to their clients.

We may contrast Germany, where the position of professionals is very different. Many fewer professions are represented within German organizations than in the UK and the USA (Child et al., 1983). In the UK we typically have many professionals exclusively engaged in one function: finance, human resources, research and development, quality control, maintenance, etc. Their purpose is to help line management in its task of actually producing or delivering products or services, and their active involvement in that core process itself is usually minimal. In Germany, line managers are the most prestigious professionals in the organization. They have been formed by a higher-education system which treats applied knowledge seriously. Degrees take much longer than in the UK, and usually consist of a mix of theoretical and organization-based training. University staff transfer between university and industry throughout their career. The consequence is that, even when differences between organizations are allowed for, German research and development professionals are less professionally oriented than their UK and USA counterparts (Gerpott et al., 1988).

So in terms of our basic distinction between knowing how and knowing beyond, professionals have a very ambivalent stance. Their whole professional identity rests upon a claim to be sole owners of an area of know-how. Yet organizations are forcing them to share that know-how with others, and information technology is making it available to all in the form of models and knowledge-based systems. On the other hand, professionals have the basic

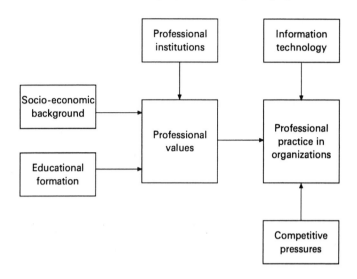

Figure 3.1 *Professional practice*

tools and capacities for knowing beyond, since they have abstract yet explicit frames of reference. In principle, they could generate lots of different transformations of the present into imagined futures. Yet for many of them the delimited nature of their frames of reference makes this very difficult. If one's framework is discipline or profession based only, and if one's action agenda is limited to that profession's area of practice, then knowing beyond is hard. Organizations can do their best to both cherish professional theoretical expertise and broaden it; but we need a cultural and institutional revolution as well. If Figure 3.1 accurately represents the factors affecting professionals in organizations, then the need to relate professional formation to the realities of organizational life becomes apparent.

Summary

- Professionals are members of more or less powerful occupations which have annexed areas of work activity for themselves.
- Some professionals are dependent on their organizational employers for the means to practise. They are also losing power because their know-how is being programmed.
- Professionals have both theories of action and abstract theories.

Knowledge in theory carries prestige within the profession, knowledge in action with their clients.

♦ Professionals are formed within the abstract theoretical framework and in the context of a ring-fenced area of professional activity.

♦ Their theoretical framework is a potential aid to knowing beyond, but they will not exploit it fully until they broaden it with other frameworks.

References

Abbott, A. (1988) *The System of Professions*. Chicago: University of Chicago Press.

Aryee, S. and Leong, C.C. (1991) 'Career orientations and work outcomes among industrial R&D professionals', *Group and Organization Studies*, 16(2): 193–205.

Bartol, K.M. (1979) 'Professionalism as a predictor of organizational commitment, role stress, and turnover: a multi-dimensional approach', *Academy of Management Journal*, 22: 815–21.

Child, J., Fores, M., Glover, I. and Lawrence, P. (1983) 'A price to pay? Professionalism and work organization in Britain and West Germany', *Sociology*, 17(1): 63–78.

Child, J. and Fulk, J. (1982) 'Maintenance of occupational control: the case of professions', *Work and Occupations*, 9: 155–92.

Dalton, G.W. and Thompson, P.H. (1986) *Novations: Strategies for Career Management*. Glenview, IL: Scott-Foresman.

Garden, A.M. (1990) 'Career orientations of software developers in a sample of high tech companies', *R&D Management*, 20(4): 337–52.

Gerpott, T.J., Domsch, M. and Keller, R.T. (1988) 'Career orientations in different countries and companies: an empirical investigation of West German, British, and US industrial R&D professionals', *Journal of Management Studies*, 25(5): 439–62.

Herriot, P. (1992) *The Career Management Challenge*. London: Sage.

Hill, R.E. and Roselle, P.F. (1985) 'Differences in the vocational interests of research and development managers versus technical specialists', *Journal of Vocational Behaviour*, 26: 92–105.

Keenan, A. and Newton, T.J. (1986) 'Work aspirations and experiences of young graduate engineers', *Journal of Management Studies*, 23: 224–37.

Kuhn, T. (1970) *The Structure of Scientific Revolutions*. Chicago: University of Chicago Press.

Nicholson, N. and Arnold, J. (1991) 'From expectation to experience: graduates entering a large corporation', *Journal of Organizational Behaviour*, 12: 413–29.

Pemberton, C. and Herriot, P. (1993) 'Can purity damage your health? The fate of technical professionals in the 1990s', *Recruitment, Selection and Retention*, 2(2): 17–27.

Rynes, S. (1987) 'Career transitions from engineering to management: are they predictable among students?', *Journal of Vocational Behaviour*, 30: 138–54.

Taylor, R. (1979) 'Career orientations and intra-occupational choice: a survey of engineering students', *Journal of Occupational Psychology*, 52: 41–52.

Van Maanen, J. and Barley, S.R. (1984) 'Occupational communities: culture and control in organizations', in B. Staw and L. Cummings (eds), *Research in Organizational Behaviour*, Vol. 6. Greenwich, CT: JAI Press.

Whitley, R. (1989) 'On the nature of managerial tasks and skills: their distinguishing characteristics and organization', *Journal of Management Studies*, 26(3): 209–24.

4

The Experienced Manager

The Changing Contract

Time was when having spent 25 years with an organization gave an individual status, endorsed by a public ceremony in which that commitment was thanked and recognized. Nowadays such ceremonies are increasingly rare, and a question as to how long a manager has spent with the company draws embarrassed smiles from those with service in double figures. That times have changed is highlighted in this bitter comment from one American senior executive: 'I have 28 years of experience. I've made millions for the company and have knowledge that will cost them millions more to duplicate in someone else. Yet they were willing to spend $500,000 to get rid of me' (Veit, 1992). His comments were made from the perspective of an employee who had been 'offered' early retirement. A similar comment could be made by thousands of experienced managers who are still employed by their organizations, but who see little future in their continued presence: 'I have 28 years' experience. My skills have helped this company be profitable. Now all they want is for me to share what I know with younger colleagues in order that they can take over my job. They seem resigned to my staying here costing them a lot of money, rather than looking to let me further grow my experience.'

Somewhere in the business changes that have marked the last 10 years, the idea of experience has become devalued. If professionals are learning that holding a body of knowledge gained through extended periods of study is an insufficient defence for survival within organizations, then experienced managers are learning that the link between age and knowledge acquisition has also been broken.

The positive relationship between age and experience is one which is deeply embedded in us. The confidence we feel when the doctor is greying at the temples; the use of actors of uncertain years when advertising financial services; the presence of a father figure in detective series acting as a counterbalance to the sometimes misdirected energies of younger colleagues. We have learned to seek comfort in the presence of an older person, someone who has seen it before and can bring wider perspectives to our consideration of an issue.

Until recently these same beliefs have held true in many of our largest organizations. As organizations grew in size, and as they moved from the start-up to the maintenance stage of the business cycle, they inevitably acquired increasing numbers of long-serving employees. The growth of business, and increasing confidence that the organization would be able to sustain itself, led to the creation of more functions, to new departments, to additional layers of bureaucracy. People stayed in organizations because there were continually developing opportunities for them. Alongside their formal contractual relationship with the organization a psychological contract developed between the two. At first it was largely transactional (Rousseau, 1990): I'll stay here for as long as you continue to reward and promote me. Over time, however, the nature of the contract changed. The employee became as much committed to the organization as to the job itself. The contract became one of a long-term relationship, with all the strengths and weaknesses such relationships embody:

- tolerance of weaknesses and imperfections
- a valuing of the whole person rather than individual qualities
- a taking for granted on both sides
- a willingness to go the extra mile when there is a problem for the other party
- an acceptance that the balance of power constantly shifts between the two
- a tendency not to notice when things are changing for the other side
- a combined history of pleasure and pain that binds them together.

This willingness of individuals to commit themselves to one organization over time was seen as a good thing. It was a sign of career maturity on the individuals' part – evidence that they had settled down, and were establishing their career identity (Super, 1968). For the organization it was beneficial to have a pool of people who had a body of organizational knowledge that went outside the strict confines of their job, and who identified with the organization as much as with their job. Think of the identification British Rail employees have with rail travel, regardless of whether they are a booking clerk or a train driver; or the equal commitment to the National Health Service of the hospital porter and the consultant. It is through such identification that organizational cultures are defined and strengthened (Schein, 1985).

Somewhere along the way, however, the organizational rules about long-standing relationships seemed to have changed.

The Organizational Change

Whereas military models have shaped the design of large organizations for much of the twentieth century, with their emphasis on hierarchy, roles, and time served as a prerequisite for promotion, the late twentieth century has seen a radical challenge to those models. Where once multiple levels were a mark of organizational success, writers such as Tom Peters (Peters and Waterman, 1982) have recommended that organizations follow the model of the Catholic Church with its four layers from Pope to priest. This delayering, it is argued, is vital if organizations are to succeed against global competition. Delayering has come to be presented not simply as an economic necessity but as a necessary condition for freeing up innovation and busting bureaucracy (Peters, 1992). Where once age was equated with the acquisition of organizationally useful experience, now it is presented as likely to block the innovation process. The talk now is of inverting pyramids (Handy, 1989), of rewarding performance over longevity, and of extracting the knowledge of all workers, rather than forcing managerial knowledge into the heads of subordinates.

In order for organizations to be able to make difficult business decisions about who is to be rewarded in the new order it has been necessary to create a new paradigm. That new paradigm is one in which experience is viewed negatively because, it is argued, it holds back the speed of change. Organizations have stopped talking about the importance of having an organizational memory available to them. They no longer speak of the value of long-serving managers who have seen it all before, or of the cultural importance of the older manager who can talk of the 'old days' and remind the organization of its roots (Deal and Kennedy, 1988). Now the talk is of the inability of long-service managers to adapt to the new business realities, of their resistance to becoming computer literate, of their blocking up the shrinking career paths for younger colleagues. Where once Handy (1985) had spoken admiringly of the shift from 'energy to wisdom', organizations now act as though energy is all and wisdom is obsolete.

The Creation of the Plateaued Manager Problem

It is now commonplace to recognize the need for faster, more frequent change than ever before. The cult of chaos has been

created (Peters, 1987). This imperative for change leaves organizations with a difficulty. Even after voluntary and involuntary
redundancies and retirements, they still employ significant numbers
of experienced managers. One recently privatized organization
claimed to have 60,000 of such people – managers who may no
longer be receiving the regular promotions by which they previously
marked their value to the organization, but who are nonetheless
likely to remain with the organization for some while. We know
from our work with such managers that a strong organizational
focus ill equips managers for keeping in touch with the labour
market and their own external marketability (Herriot et al., 1993).
A mark of their diminishing status within organizations is that
these managers are now redesignated as plateaued. The phrase is
unlikely to be openly used within the organization; it has become a
closet term used by those who see themselves outside the dangerous
circle. For those within it is a taboo word. So what do we mean by
plateaued?

The term is in itself neutral. It was defined by one group of
researchers (Ference et al., 1977) as 'the point in a career where the
likelihood of additional hierarchical promotion is very low'. Based
on the idea of careers as rounds of a tournament in which we
compete until knocked out of the competition (Rosenbaum, 1979),
it is, given the structure of most organizations, an inevitability for
all except the chief executive. The term itself is simply an objective
statement of reality. The point at which that reality looms is defined
by the norms of the organization. For a bank which has
traditionally promoted good performers every two years, and has
sufficient layers to sustain this over considerable periods of time,
plateauing has until recently remained a late career stage. In a
design company which has few layers, a long-serving management
team and long time gaps between promotions, a young entrant can
plateau very early in his or her career. Given the restructuring
which has hallmarked the 1980s, plateauing is for most of us an
inevitability and one which is occurring earlier and earlier in our
careers.

That an inevitability should create a problem in the organizational mind is the product of a connection that has been made
with the individual life cycle. As Ference and his colleagues (1977)
have identified, we have a picture of organizational careers as
shown in Figure 4.1. This model links with life cycle theorists who
view life as the succession of growth, stability, and decline. No
room here for regeneration.

Individuals enter organizations and are exposed to learning
(either formally or informally). As a result of displaying the

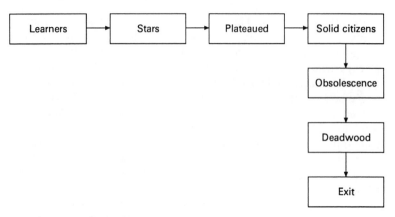

Figure 4.1   *Plateauing as viewed by some organizations*

application of that learning they are rewarded with promotions, until such point as their learning is deemed insufficient for the demands of the next job (the Peter principle). At this point they plateau. From this point further opportunities for planned learning are deemed inappropriate, and they will be expected to sustain performance for a while, until there is an inevitable decline into obsolescence – at which point they will be encouraged to leave.

In considering the likely consequences of plateauing, then, organizations are hidebound by confusing structural change with supposed life cycle patterns and individual performance. The thinking goes: it is not possible to promote this person further, we must concern ourselves with the survival of the fittest. At best we can leave this person and trust he or she will not undermine our business goals. Or at worst, this person is out of touch with the new realities, and is a problem to us. In the organizational mind, plateaued managers are divided into two groups (Ference et al., 1977): 'solid citizens', good performers who carry the bulk of organizational work and will be left to get on with it; and 'deadwood', low performers with little potential who demand a disproportionate amount of attention. Of course this distinction is seldom made explicit, and so the two groups become coalesced into one identity: the plateaued manager.

So far, plateauing has been seen as an outcome of structural change, but there are other ways of defining the phenomenon. Judith Bardwick (1986) highlighted that managers can be plateaued by the demands of a job which stops developing. Alternatively, they can be plateaued by their own internal processes, when they become bored with the demands being made on them. These views of plateauing confirm an alternative definition, which sees it as the point at which 'his or her likelihood of receiving further assignments of increased responsibility is low' (Feldman and Weitz, 1988). The importance of these alternative perspectives is that they focus on continuing to develop the knowledge of experienced managers, distinct from any position they may occupy in the hierarchy.

There could be scope here for experienced managers continuing to build on their experience, and yet if we look at the evidence of the treatment of long-serving employees the chances of this happening are not high (KPMG Peat Marwick, 1990; Webb and Townley, 1990):

◆ Development is focused on the new entrant to the organization or to a job.
◆ Development is focused on the extremes of the employee continuum, the high-flyers and the low performers. Do your job to the standard expected over time, and you are unlikely to receive regular development.
◆ The longer you are with an organization, the less performance feedback you will receive.
◆ The longer you are with an organization, the less the organization feels the need to praise your efforts.
◆ It will be assumed that you are willing to pass your knowledge down the line to younger subordinates rather than further developing your own expertise.

The Experienced Manager: How Is It for Them?

So far we've focused on the organizational perspective of the reducing opportunities for experienced managers, and hinted that there is an organizational cost in the neglect of an important knowledge base. Now it's time to consider what it's like to be an experienced manager in a large organization in the 1990s. If you are an experienced manager, it is likely you will have observed some of the following:

◆ the disappearance of colleagues with whom you built your career, as a result of expediency linking redundancies to age rather than performance
◆ the disappearance of services and products on which the organization's reputation rested, as a result of competition or legislation
◆ the disappearance of the internal labour market, as people from outside the organization are brought into senior jobs

- the disappearance of old career paths, without the apparent building of new ones
- the appearance of new jobs which seem to bear little relationship to any skills you have acquired
- the rapid advancement of younger colleagues who don't seem to need to serve time getting to know the organization, its customers and its services/products before they are rewarded.

From your perspective it seems that there is no place for the sort of experience you have built up over the years and that having an organizational history is a distinct disadvantage, as it marks you with the taint of past organizational behaviours. It appears that creating a new organizational culture involves removing any sign of the previous one, rather than building on its strengths.

And yet, you also see signs that the organization is still somewhat ambivalent in its regard for you:

- When presenting to a prospective client it wants to be able to include you in the team as reassurance to the client, although you may not be heading up the project.
- It wants you to mentor younger colleagues, to teach them the political skills of how to get things done.
- It wants you to coach younger colleagues in order that they can learn from your know-how (and assumes you will be happy to share this selflessly).
- Younger colleagues seek you out for advice on how to manage their careers, even though their careers will inevitably be different from your own.
- It wants you to be involved in cross-departmental projects, where knowing the individuals and how to get them to do things is important to success. It wants to use you as an organizational lubricant.
- It wants you to be available for special projects which require multiple perspectives, but without assuming this will lead to promotion.

In other words, there is a level at which the organization does value experience, without acknowledging the potential for building on it.

There is an irony in the organization seeking to utilize the know-how of long-serving employees for the benefit of those with less experience, without helping the long-serving employees to put that experience within the framework of new realities and new learning. There is also an implicit assumption in the ways in which organizations are using experience that managers of experience are similar in their needs and motives and in what they have to offer.

The Need to Differentiate Experienced Managers

In looking at the burgeoning of plateaued managers, and the ways in which organizations are looking to utilize experience, we have so far assumed that this group are homogeneous in their needs and aspirations. This is as dangerous as assuming that all chief executives are the same, all women managers are the same, or all old people are the same. If organizations are to get the best value out of experience then they need to know more about this large group than they do at present. One American study of HR practices (Rosen and Jerdee, 1990) in 600 of the largest organizations in the US concluded that plateaued employees constituted one-third of the workforce, and that nearly half the organizations saw them as constituting a moderate to very great HR problem. They were seen as sending negative messages to younger workers about their own future career development, and as too likely to rest on past accomplishments. Further ammunition for the discard experience school of thought? Yet before discounting the over 40s, organizations need to remind themselves of the reality that older workers will comprise an increasingly large part of the work population, as the impact of declining numbers of 16–25-year-olds hits the workplace over the next 10 years. In order to start making sense of these contradictions, and to maximize the potential of experience, organizations need to start looking at the issue in a more differentiated way.

Separating Out Motivations

While we have recognized that plateauing is more than an outcome of structural changes, and can occur whenever a job stagnates in its content or an individual becomes unstimulated by the demands being made on him or her, we have so far talked of experienced managers globally. If, however, organizations are to increase the value they can obtain from experience they need to know more about the sources and consequences of plateauing in order that they can respond. Feldman and Weitz (1988) have helped our understanding by putting together a taxonomy of the causes, consequences and possible interventions to maximize outcomes. They defined them as follows:

◆ The individual lacks the skills and abilities to cope with new demands.
  Consequence: poor performance and job attitude.
  Solution: improve training and appraisal feedback.
◆ The individual lacks motivation because the job lacks variety, significance or challenge.

Consequence: minimally acceptable job performance; declining job attitude.

Solution: increase the scope of the job; put into a project group; increase the client relationship aspect of the job; open up feedback between the individual and his/her manager.

- The individual has low growth needs, his/her security needs are more important than the need for challenge, and therefore he/she self-imposes constraints on further career progression.

  Consequence: solid job performance and good job attitude.

  Solution: provided performance remains strong, continue to reward; provide careers information on lateral moves within the organization.

- The individual is demotivated by the lack of extrinsic rewards; given the diminished opportunities for promotion, there is little likelihood of substantially increasing his/her salary.

  Consequence: poor performance and job attitude.

  Solution: redesign compensation system; encourage highly dissatisfied to leave.

- The individual is burnt out by the demands of the organizational climate; he/she experiences role conflict as expectations change.

  Consequence: poor performance and job attitude.

  Solution: job rotation, off-site training, sabbaticals.

- The individual is plateaued by a slowing down of organizational growth, and by restructuring in response to external business conditions.

  Consequence: performance holds up in the short term, but over time job attitudes will decline.

  Solutions: individuals who would otherwise be organizational 'stars' should receive adequate resources; poorer performers should be encouraged to leave.

These solutions may appear pat: easy to say, but hard to apply. However, the overall message that they offer organizations is of value. Give attention to the individual, and organizations may be able to obtain more from long-serving employees for future organization benefit than they currently recognize. Such an approach would better equip them to separate the wheat from the chaff, in making decisions as to who should leave or stay.

The Nature of Their Expertise

In arguing the case for nurturing rather than neglecting the experienced manager, we have so far taken for granted the expertise which they have to offer. The following are examples of ways in which we have seen experience used in organizations, but the list is by no means exhaustive. After reading it, think of ways in which your organization specifically uses long-serving managers.

♦ New recruits are sent to them as part of induction, in order to learn some of the unofficial rules and norms of the organization.
♦ High-flyers are attached to them in order that they can learn the behaviours that help people get on.
♦ People call them up when they want to find out information that is never officially recorded.
♦ People refer to them to recall incidents that have been important to the organization's/department's success or failure.
♦ People use them to short-circuit learning – to find out how to do something without the pain of trial and error.
♦ People build relationships with them in the hope of being able to access networks and informal groups that would otherwise be closed to them.
♦ People build relationships with them because they believe they have influence beyond their formal title on issues such as promotion.
♦ Colleagues use them as sounding boards on how to handle a difficult boss, colleague or client.

In other words, both younger colleagues and more senior colleagues recognize that organizational experience gives access to a wealth of know-how that is invaluable in helping the organization to move more smoothly, and in helping individuals to move smoothly within organizations. What is implicit in this is that past experiences form a strong basis for understanding and dealing with the present. In some areas this will still be true. As much as organizations talk of change, they fail to talk of those things which do not and need not change. There is, however, a danger in relying on know-how as the prime asset of the experienced manager. When Sundridge Park surveyed managers as to their perceptions of older managers in their organizations (Horack and Adler Associates, 1991), they found a clear split between a valuing of those skills which were seen as current know-how – e.g. understanding how the political system works within the organization, helping with performance coaching – and a lack of regard for the future orientation of experienced managers. They did not believe that older managers could be creative or innovative; they were uncertain as to the value of their receiving further training and development. They saw them as looking towards the past rather than the future, and as likely to avoid rather than embrace risk. In the terms of our model, they were happy to recognize their know-how, but had clear reservations as to their ability to know beyond.

At the beginning of the chapter we identified a link in the organizational mind between the individual life and the organizational career, and showed how this limited the value which a long-serving employee could be to an organization. We have subsequently argued that by giving attention to developing their knowing beyond, rather than watching the atrophying of their know-how, experienced employees could be harnessed and would prove a valuable competitive weapon. As one academic commented on the poor performance of a major high street bank: 'By sacking long-serving managers every time they made a business mistake, they wiped out the organizational memory, and increased the chances of making further mistakes.' The aim for the future should be to redesign the model so that the plateau becomes a platform from which to know beyond rather than a diving board to obsolescence.

Summary

+ While we value evidence of experience in our role as customers, organizations have come to devalue it in recent years.
+ That devaluing has been a consequence of organizational restructuring which has reduced the opportunities for promotion, and inevitably has led to larger numbers of managers than ever before plateauing at earlier career stages.
+ A structural necessity has become confused in the organizational mind with personal disability.
+ Organizations fail to distinguish the different needs and motives of experienced managers, and so miss out on opportunities to maximize the contribution they can make.
+ While organizations see plateaued managers as problematic, conversely they continue to want to use them in roles which make use of their know-how.
+ While organizations recognize their know-how they fail to build on it in order that experienced managers can be developed to know beyond.

References

Bardwick, J. (1986) *The Plateauing Trap*. New York: Amacom.
Deal, T. and Kennedy, A. (1988) *Corporate Cultures: the Rites and Rituals of Corporate Life*. London: Penguin.

Feldman, D.C. and Weitz, B.A. (1988) 'Career plateaus reconsidered', *Journal of Management*, 14(1): 69–80.

Ference, T.P., Stoner, J.A. and Kirby Warren, N.E. (1977) 'Managing the career plateau', *Academy of Management Review*, October: 602–12.

Handy, C. (1985) *The Future of Work*. Oxford: Blackwell.

Handy, C. (1989) *The Age of Unreason*. London: Century Business Books.

Herriot, P., Pemberton, C. and Pinder, R. (1993) 'Misperceptions by managers and their bosses of each other's preferences regarding the managers' careers: a case of the blind leading the blind?', *Human Resource Management Journal*, 4(2): 39–51.

Horack and Adler Associates (1991) *Older Managers: Assets or Liabilities?* London: Sundridge Park Management Centre.

KPMG Peat Marwick (1990) *Age . . . Has its Compensations*. London: IPM.

Peters, T.J. (1987) *Thriving on Chaos: Handbook for the Managerial Revolution*. London: Macmillan.

Peters, T.J. (1992) *Liberation Management: Necessary Disorganisation for the Nanosecond Nineties*. London: Macmillan.

Peters, T.J. and Waterman, R. (1982) *In Search of Excellence*. New York: Harper and Row.

Rosen, B. and Jerdee, T. (1990) 'Middle and late career problems: causes, consequences, and research needs', *Human Resource Planning*, 13(1): 59–70.

Rosenbaum, J.E. (1979) 'Tournament mobility: career patterns in a corporation', *Administrative Science Quarterly*, 24: 220–41.

Rousseau, D. (1990) 'New hire perceptions of their own and their employer's obligations: a study of psychological contracts', *Journal of Organizational Behavior*, 11(5): 389–400.

Schein, E.H. (1985) *Organizational Culture and Leadership*. San Francisco: Jossey Bass.

Super, D.E. (1968) 'A theory of vocational development', in B. Hopson and J. Hayes (eds), *The Theory and Practice of Vocational Guidance*. Oxford: Pergamon Press.

Veit, K. (1992) 'The reluctant entrepreneur', *Harvard Business Review*, November–December: 40.

Webb, S. and Townley, A. (1990) *Valuing Maturity*. London: Industrial Society.

5

Information Workers: the Organizational Hub

This chapter is about secretaries and the ways in which they are presently used within organizations. So why have we headed the chapter as being concerned with information? The title is deliberate because while managers and professionals are readily recognized as workers who work with information, it is less often that secretarial staff are recognized as 'distinguished from other workers because the primary value added by their labour results from creating, manipulating or providing data/information/knowledge' (Kraemer and Danziger, 1990). Of course we recognize that they work with information, the information of others, but they are not seen as being in control of that information or, even more radically, of creating it.

Office Wife and Mother

Consider a secretary in your organization and enumerate the things she (*sic*) does. The list you are likely to come up with may look something like this:

- answers letters and enquiries
- drafts letters and enquiries (for boss's signature)
- manages her boss's time through his (*sic*) diary
- arranges conferences and meetings
- follows through on projects
- places telephone calls
- takes minutes at meetings
- develops own filing system and maintains files
- distributes and sends out mail
- inputs and edits data
- orders stationery.

The striking thing about this list is how much of the secretary's time is given to receiving information from others, and taking decisions which are invisible to others.

If your list looks like this, it's likely you are not a secretary. If you were, or if you are a perceptive colleague, then you may additionally find on the list:

- keeps people away from her boss when he does not wish to see them
- makes reservations for boss's social arrangements
- acts as a sounding board for boss
- picks up jobs which could be seen as managerial, but which her boss does not want to do
- listens to (but does not pass on) organizationally sensitive information about other members of staff, other departments, policy matters
- corrects boss's work
- builds up rapport with boss's contacts and customers
- makes coffee and orders food
- cleans up
- collects organizational gossip and information from other secretaries (and passes it on where she feels it appropriate)
- performs private errands – gift buying, laundry collection, etc.

You could probably add to the list, and we all have stories of the secretary who protects her boss like a lioness protecting her cub; the secretary who everyone knows manages the office and provides a cover for her less than able boss; the secretary who remembers his family's birthdays; and the secretary who swapped being his office wife in order to be his housewife. That it is possible to interpret the role so widely is the result of the fact that we remain unsure of what a secretary is, and where the role boundaries lie. The term 'secretary' has 'no generally accepted meaning, but rather is a catch-all word for a person performing a variety of clerical, administrative and personal tasks' (Watstein, 1985). What is missing from this definition is one critical element: she is performing these tasks for a superior.

When she looked at a number of US corporations in the late 1970s, Rosabeth Moss Kanter (1978) made the observation that secretaries fulfilled the requirements of being in a lord–vassal relationship along three dimensions:

- They are subject to the arbitrary power of their boss, who defines their job description, and sets the limits of fair practice.
- There is a strong emphasis on loyalty, with symbolic and emotional rewards to replace economic ones.
- Their status is defined by the rank and power of their boss.

Where a working relationship is so defined by the nature of the personal relationship between two individuals, it can be no surprise that the criteria against which performance is judged are often personal. Moss Kanter found in her study that secretarial ratings were defined by two main traits: the enthusiasm and initiative of the secretaries, and their anticipation of, and response to, personal needs. Within this model of the ways in which secretaries work, the focus on the personal service aspects of the role have masked much of the more highly skilled 'invisible work' which they perform (Murphree, 1987). In a study of legal secretaries, it was found that in order to do their jobs well these women made expert social and cognitive judgements and used sophisticated negotiating techniques. They knew who was who in their managers' worlds, they knew how to get things done through working across departments and levels, they knew how to interpret poorly given instructions (Murphree, 1984). In other words they displayed a good deal of know-how, but know-how which is largely invisible to the organization because of its focus on the servicing aspect of the secretarial function. Yet consider the power and influence of Jeeves *vis-à-vis* Wooster. Yes, Jeeves is a vassal to the lordly Wooster, but his power and influence is based on the universal recognition that he can see issues more widely than his boss, he can negotiate his way around difficulties, and he can think more creatively than his master. Most important of all, Wooster knows this too, and looks to make use of those skills (if only for his own protection), rather than to deny their existence.

The Impact of Information Technology

But as we write this, we can hear you thinking: 'Well, things used to be bad for secretaries, but it's not like that anymore. Not now that secretaries no longer take dictation; only the most senior bosses have their own secretaries, and we are all doing our own keyboarding. It's all changed.' Or has it? Information technology was seen as the great hope of the secretarial profession, the opportunity to redefine how the skills of often highly able women could be better used; a chance to offload routine work, in order to free them up for managerial roles; a chance to get away from the keyboard and into the work team; an opportunity to put know-how to more creative uses. The jury is still out, as we will see, on whether that is happening, but what is clear is that organizations are still failing to get the full value of the knowledge that secretaries could bring to their jobs, if the climate allowed them to.

The difficulty of weighing up the impact of information technology on the work of secretarial staff is summed up in Amin Rajan's (1990a) assessment of jobs which will increase/decrease in number, and those that will reskill/deskill in the 1990s. Simultaneously he forecasts an increasing number of deskilled secretaries (often part-time), together with an upskilling of a decreasing number of others. This response highlights the tension in assessing what IT means for the secretarial employee. An early male writer on the impact of IT saw it as a means of job enrichment, allowing women to leave the dictation pad and keyboard behind, to discover instead the excitement of data manipulation, financial analysis and project management (Hirschhorn, 1984). At the same time, a survey of 5447 women in 10 EEC countries was finding that working women felt far less optimistic than men that technology was going to increase the interest and skill level of their work, although they perceived that customers and top management would benefit from the introduction of IT (Riffault and Tchernia, 1984). The women's own feelings were supported in another study, which found that women were performing few of the higher-level, autonomous, information processing tasks (Gutek and Bikson, 1985). This was partly because the improved efficiencies of IT were encouraging organizations to cut costs by having secretaries work for several managers, where once they worked for one. It was also because the dazzling possibilities offered by IT encouraged bosses to make more revisions to work than they ever did when the only tools to hand were correction fluid and carbon paper (Zimmerman, 1983). Under the cost competitive pressures of recession, it is easy to see how IT has provided organizations with the means of increasing the work of its secretarial staff, without necessarily enriching it.

When Amin Rajan (1990b) was looking to discover the skills which would be essential for survival in the 1990s, he defined five skills groups:

- ◆ procedural skills: awareness of procedure for routine and non-routine tasks
- ◆ technological skills: ability to design, develop and operate information systems to the specified level of efficiency and budget
- ◆ interpersonal skills: effective written and oral skills with peers, customers and teams
- ◆ knowledge-based skills: both knowledge directly related to job needs, and intellectual skills that show the ability to conceptualize
- ◆ intrapreneurial skills: proactivity in initiating ideas that can be beneficial to the organization.

Looking at these skill areas from the perspective of organizational use of secretarial staff, the daily use of the first three is clear. The freedom to conceptualize beyond know-how is less clear, and the opportunities to act intrapreneurially are rare indeed. There is even evidence that opportunities to develop higher-level contributions are diminishing, as managers take to the keyboard. The newly computer-literate manager reserves for himself the more creative and rewarding tasks: the writing of original material, the manipulation of financial programmes and the creation of project management systems (Bikson and Gutek, 1983).

The news is not all bad. No one would claim that secretaries were more fulfilled or gave more value to the organization when their days were spent typing and retyping paper documentation, and manually manipulating files. There are many information workers who can appreciate how their service to their customers is enhanced by the speed with which they can provide information, or the higher-quality documentation they can now produce. Listen to this account of job enrichment by one secretary:

> When I first came here, I was strictly a secretary. Then my boss noticed how I enjoyed figures, and gave me the job of looking after the revenue from his work. This meant issuing manual invoices, which led me into using spreadsheets. Now I work with a variety of software packages, and I have been attending evening courses in computer studies, finance for non-financial managers and project management. Now I not only monitor revenue, I forecast it for the year ahead, and report to the chief executive on progress to date and on comparisons with previous years. I spend one-third of my time inputting data, another third generating invoices for work done, and the last third networking by telephone or direct contact to get the rest of the information I need. Just relying on information that is easily available for input would not give me the full picture, I need to be constantly talking with other secretaries in order to learn what work is on-line. Having information easily accessible on my PC means that I can often see patterns in business. I can spot where one type of customer is more buoyant than others, and where customers are returning year after year.

This employee is still defined as a secretary, and yet the whole basis of her work is now the provision and analysis of information. Her chief executive trusts her judgement as to whether targets will be met based on her analysis of revenue patterns. Her information is used to help set targets for the next year, and what is interesting is that she is not a passive recipient of information. She spends much of her time actively seeking out information in order that as full a picture as possible is available to her senior managers. In Zuboff's (1988) terms, while much of her work is automated, she sees her task as 'informating'.

At a more general level, the introduction of E-mail has led to another means of informating. Research has shown (Sproull and Keisler, 1986) that 60 per cent of messages sent by electronic mail would not have been sent via paper communication, and that its accessibility helps to reduce status differences as to who communicates with whom. Look at your own E-mail messages, and you will probably find a large number of them are generated by secretarial staff; individuals who would have thought twice about putting it on paper will happily buzz a message around the network. Look at the contents of the messages, however, and you will probably find that they are more likely to be concerned with procedural or social arrangements than with knowledge skills or intrapreneurial thinking.

Secretary as Team worker?

So far we have defined secretaries in terms of their relationships with bosses, seeing them in a one-to-one relationship, or a series of concurrent one-to-one relationships as increasingly they work for more than one individual. This definition of how they work separates them from the model of teamworking which increasingly is talked of as the norm for effective and creative working in the future. They have been seen as 'task-oriented helpers . . . management frequently does not recognize a secretary as someone capable of offering worthwhile opinions or of generating valuable ideas for the organization' (Demongeot, 1986). The very nature of the master–servant relationship dictates that the servant can be a valued helpmate, but she is unlikely to be seen as a fellow team player.

When Honeywell (1983) surveyed its staff, it found that secretaries were twice as likely as their bosses to believe that a stronger team relationship would improve office productivity. So despite the many years in which managers have attended team building workshops, and happily accepted that teams need individuals with different characteristics and role preferences in order to produce effective and creative solutions, they implicitly mean teams of people of similar standing in the organization. A challenge to this was made at NASA's Lewis Research Center in Cleveland, Ohio, where there was a top-down commitment to moving from an authoritarian management culture to one based on employee participation. A training programme was implemented which helped staff look at collective working and generating solutions, influencing styles in good and less good conditions, and motivation. The programme unearthed the reality that participative working demanded far more of staff. They had become used to taking the line of 'tell me what to do and I'll do it – but it's your fault if it's wrong.' Follow-up on the programme found that secretaries had been able to work with engineers in producing a creative and satisfactory solution to a difficult office problem. That this example merited a journal article tells us that such a story is still unusual enough to deserve special attention.

In recounting such a story, it is easy to put the blame on management, to engage in the outsider's paranoia that *they* deliberately exclude us, that all *they* need to do is to allow us into their team and we will show them. A few may, but more likely letting the outsiders in on the team without a recognition of the difficulties of speaking out will simply reinforce distances, and a preference for dealing with the boss on a one-to-one basis.

Consider this recent scenario. An organization which actively wants to encourage more ideas and innovation announces a seminar at which the issue of encouraging ideas will be launched. The seminar attracts a lot of interest amongst all staff, because at a time of economic difficulty everyone is concerned that they should help the organization survive and flourish. The meeting is noticeable because such seminars are usually only attended by the 'professional' staff, but on this occasion the majority of those who attend are secretarial and support staff. In the meeting the reasons why lots of good ideas either fail to be put forward, or fail to survive early scrutiny, are aired, and well-known research findings on the importance of support and teamworking for the nurturing of ideas are shared. What is noticeable is that throughout the meeting the only people who speak are the professional staff, although secretarial staff can be heard mumbling dissensions under their breath. The one point at which they become involved is when the Japanese idea of anonymous suggestion boxes is put forward by a male colleague. The meeting ends, and within an hour three women members of staff have sought out the seminar leader to explain why they did not contribute, although it was an issue on which they felt strongly. The professional group members can be criticized for not recognizing the difficulties for non-practised group speakers in airing their views. However, the secretaries need to be helped to give themselves permission to be creative, rather than waiting for it to be given. They need to be helped to see the right to contribute on grounds other than size of salary cheque and paper qualifications.

A recent writer on creativity argued: 'Many people also believe that creativity is the result of the amount of intelligence that one possesses. Verifiable geniuses (as measured by IQ tests and similar instruments) tend to do very well for themselves vocationally (but) . . . they haven't made much of a dent in terms of making creative contributions to the world' (Anderson, 1992: 43). He goes on to expose the myth of the sole creative genius, working in isolation from the ideas of others, and exhorts organizations: 'First – realize that no structure, process, incentive system or management reorganization is going to make your firm creative unless you first help the individuals within those structures and systems unlock their willingness to try. And that isn't done at arm's length . . . Hold up a mirror for your people and help them see their own creative potential by identifying it for them' (1992: 46). While Japanese management has highlighted the importance of this message in terms of production workers, the need for a similar message for secretarial and clerical workers has yet to be recognized. We love them as helpers, we need them as sources of knowledge that cannot be tapped elsewhere, we rely on them to work the system, and yet neither they nor we yet recognize their potential to contribute creatively to the organization's future.

In the three previous chapters we have argued the ability of, and the need for, key groups of workers to know beyond. It will hardly come as a surprise, therefore, that we make this claim for secretarial staff also. But what is our evidence for this claim? Let's return to where we started this chapter with the duties that a secretary carries out. We recognize that some of her time is taken with acting as gatekeeper, with filtering out those people who she judges should not be taking up her boss's time. In an average week, these could include salespeople trying to sell a new service or product, market researchers wanting some informed response on one issue or another, students wanting help with projects, competitors wanting to get inside information on the state of the business, or disgruntled customers.

Without even trying, a secretary is constantly scanning the environment, picking up on her radar a range of current concerns which could have implications for the future of the business. She will unconsciously note patterns in the sort of people who are making contact, the types of products they are trying to sell, the kind of questions they are asking. Much of the information she acquires will remain unconscious because no one will see a use for it. How likely is it that her boss will ask, 'Who did you stop me having to speak with this week?'; yet if he did, he might find there was a wealth of information to work with. If salesman A is contacting your organization, then it's a fair bet he is also contacting your competitors. The conversation could have been used to discover the response the salesman received from your competitors, and how they intend to use the product or service. Instead of the secretary being seen as a gatekeeper to keep out the unwelcome, she could be encouraged to become a reconnaissance agent. She could be actively gathering and analysing data on what is happening outside, in order to help the organization make better-informed and faster leaps forward.

Summary

♦ The role of secretary is usually construed as a one-to-one personal service role. It typically consists of a wide range of tasks.

♦ The impact of technology is to upskill some secretaries, but to deskill more.

♦ The potential contribution of secretaries as teamworkers has seldom been utilized. When it has, their ability to know beyond has been evident.

♦ Part of what secretaries have to offer derives from the amount of information, both internal and external to the organization, with which they deal.

References

Anderson, J. (1992) 'Weirder than fiction: the reality and myths of creativity', *Academy of Management Executive*, 6(4): 40–7.

Bikson, T.K. and Gutek, B.A. (1983) *Advanced Office Systems: an Empirical Look at Utilization and Satisfaction*. Santa Monica, CA: Rand Corporation Publication Services.

Demongeot, C.A. (1986) 'Secretaries: the unrecognized members of the management team', *Training and Development Journal*, November: 28–9.

Gutek, B. and Bikson, T.K. (1985) 'Differential experiences of men and women in computerized offices', *Sex Roles*, 13 (3,4): 123–36.

Hirschhorn, L. (1984) *Office Automation and the Entry Level Job: a Concept Paper*. Management and Behavioural Science Center, Wharton School, University of Pennsylvania.

Honeywell (1983) *National Survey on Office Automation and the Workplace: a National Survey of Managers and Secretaries*. Minneapolis, MN: Honeywell Inc.

Kanter, R.M. (1978) *Men and Women of the Corporation*. New York: Basic Books.

Kraemer, K.L. and Danziger, J.N. (1990) 'The impact of computer technology on the worklife of information workers', *Social Science Computer Review*, 8(4) Winter: 593.

Murphree, M.C. (1984) 'Brave new office: the changing role of the legal secretary', in K. Sachs and D. Remy (eds), *My Troubles are Going to Have Trouble with Me: Everyday Trials and Triumphs of Women Workers*. New Brunswick, NJ: Rutgers University Press.

Murphree, M.C. (1987) 'New technology and the office tradition: the not so changing world of the secretary', in I. Hartmann (ed.), *Computer Chips and Paper Clips*, Vol. II. Washington: National Academy Press.

Rajan, A. (1990a) *A Zero Sum Game – Business Know How and Challenges in an Integrated Europe*. London: Industrial Society.

Rajan, A. (1990b) *Capital People – Skills, Strategies for Survival in the Nineties*. London: Industrial Society.

Riffault, H. and Tchernia, J. (1984) *European Women in Paid Employment*. Brussels: Commission of the European Communities.

Sproull, L. and Keisler, S. (1986) 'Reducing social context cues: electronic mail in organizational communication', *Management Science*, 32(11): 1492–512.

Watstein, E. (1985) 'Administrative assistant: just another title?' *Biz*, 16(1): 4.

Zimmerman, J. (ed.) (1983) *The Technological Woman*. New York: Praeger.

Zuboff, S. (1988) *In the Age of the Smart Machine*. London: Heinemann.

6

So What About the Operatives?

Operatives' Know-how

In considering the way in which people's knowledge is used within organizations, we have ignored a group whose numbers far outweigh the other groups combined, but whose know-how is largely ignored by organizations. So whom do we mean? We are referring to a group which can be defined as operatives, although to use that term immediately raises a problem. Just what do we mean by an operative?

An examination of Roget's *Thesaurus* identifies why the term 'operative' is problematic. The thesaurus offers us as alternative words: agent, artist, craftsman, labourer, navvy, drudge, and hack. Even to a casual observer these words conjure up very different images. Are we to see an operative as a creative thinker, a person who holds detailed know-how in his head which is made visible in his physical actions? As we shall argue in this chapter, the history of the workforce over the last 100 years has driven us to see the operative as an increasingly deskilled labourer, whether in the factory or the office. This deskilling process limits both what operatives can bring to the workplace, and how they work with information technology. If other groups have been rewarded for their know-how, operatives have often been rewarded for 'knowing nothing'. The limitations this places on organizational learning are increasingly visible.

In order to simplify, we are defining operatives as people who are paid in order to produce an effect, but whose freedom of action is strictly defined. Both a customer service clerk and a process worker are operatives by this definition. So are a fast food order assistant and a clerk processing insurance claims. These are people who have a profound effect on our feelings of satisfaction with a product or service, but who in organizational hierarchy terms receive little recognition.

One reason why the knowledge of operatives receives little attention in Western culture (Zuboff, 1989) is because of our distaste for physical labour. Our social mobility has been based on escaping from physical work. That's why several years ago tabloid newspapers ran stories on the millionaire hodcarrier, who used his physical strength to carry vast numbers of bricks. Through doing so he was able to earn himself the trappings of a life style normally associated with chief executives. He merited attention because a hodcarrier living on an executive estate is as much an oxymoron as a bricklaying prime minister.

In our concern to distance ourselves from physical labour, we have forgotten that knowledge is held as much in the body as in the head, and that craftsmen hold knowledge in their legs, arms, hands, wrists, fingertips, eyes, nose, and ears as well as in their brain. Their knowledge has been traditionally gained from an apprenticeship of observation, of sitting alongside and talking with more experienced craftsmen. Through the imitation of others, and feedback on their performance from their senses, they have been able to refine their skills. This results in a form of knowledge which is hidden from those who do not physically labour. The knowledge is not visible because it is not verbalized. Ask a craftsman how he knows that the engineering piece still needs final adjustment, and he may not be able to explain in words because the information he is using is sensory. In a similar way, trying to explain how we are able to ride a bike is beyond words, because the learning we assimilated in order to master the task has been absorbed by our physical senses. Extend this to other operatives and the model still holds. Ask an experienced cabin crew member how she can tell which passenger needs reassurance, or a successful sales assistant how he can tell when to approach a potential customer, and they may not be able to give a clear model. However, it's clear from their actions that they have one, and the model is likely to include sensory data. The know-how such people hold is 'knowledge that is derived from action and displayed in action' (Zuboff, 1989: 41).

The Deskilling Process

Traditionally operatives have embodied two forms of physical labour: physical strength and stamina which allow them to sustain effort; and physical know-how which defines their skill. It was Frederick Winston Taylor in his establishment of scientific management who was first able to identify and divide these two forms of labour (Hounshell, 1988). He sought to make the skills explicit, in order to keep what was efficient and to discard the rest. The very fact that craftsmen often could not verbalize how they did things led him to believe that their learning could be captured by having someone observe and record what they were doing. Time study not only assumed all knowledge was visible in action, but also captured it and then handed it over to management.

In this way cognitive aspects of the craftsmen's jobs which until then had given them autonomy – planning, monitoring, controlling, and analysing – were taken from them. The embodiment of Taylor's philosophy is captured in the story of the 'sluggish' German immigrant Schmidt. Schmidt was promised, by Taylor, a daily rate of $1.85 for loading 48 tons of pig iron a day (a fourfold increase on his previous daily target), on the condition that when his manager 'tells you to walk, you walk; when he tells you to sit down, you sit down' (Taylor, 1947).

If Taylor systematized the separation of skill and effort in the operatives' work, the process gained momentum when Ford added technology to the division of labour (Hayes et al., 1988). The use of conveyor belts and overhead rails at Ford's first auto assembly plant caused one industrial journalist to write enthusiastically: 'First all needless motions were eliminated from the worker's actions; second the task was organized to require the least expenditure of will power and brain fatigue' (Zuboff, 1989: 147).

Ford's model became the basis of mass production techniques, and the cause of what has been called the 'degradation of work' (Braverman, 1974). From our perspective the extension of the ideas of Taylor and the increasing application of technology to work has resulted in an operative workforce where 'know nothing' has been rewarded over know-how, and where the resistance of workers to deskilling has led them to be seen as problematic.

The supremacy of technology-controlled mass assembly, in which the skills of the workforce are increasingly irrelevant, held sway until the obvious success of Japanese manufacturing led outside observers to deify what they saw as the flexible, holistic skills of the Japanese employee. Hayes et al. (1988), in criticizing the decline of American manufacturing, saw the cause in the contrasting approaches to learning adopted by both cultures. They wrote: 'World class manufacturing organizations do not divide people into those who think and those who act. Learning and applying knowledge must be high on everyone's agenda at every level in the organization.' The key, however, is not just to have knowledge, but to be able to hold and direct that knowledge, rather than it being extracted into the hands of management.

They wrote as outside researchers looking in; for employees the analysis may be somewhat different. Consider, with Zuboff (1989), the life of process workers in a pulp mill: men who understood pulp wood and its characteristics in the same way as winemakers know their vines. Their experience had been gained in the same way as the winemaker, through spending every day with their product, smelling it, feeling it, knowing when more heat was needed and when less. They felt ownership and responsibility for the quality of the pulp in much the same way as the winemaker is concerned to exert control over this year's vintage. Imagine then their feelings when computerization means that there is no need to come into physical contact with the pulp. Indeed operatives are actively discouraged from venturing on to the mill floor. Instead they spend their day in front of a computer screen in a sealed environment interpreting electronically presented data. Now they take action on the basis of symbols, rather than the senses that experience has developed in them. The result is a feeling of lack of control, of fear that skills are being lost to the computer, and a lack of connection between actions taken at the screen and their physical consequences.

Where the shop floor operative would have seen and averted the risk of spillage as temperatures rose, the hermetically sealed operative may without concern press buttons which guarantee that spillage occurs. The difference is not because of conscious disengagement from responsibility by the operatives, but because the nature of the skills required is different. Where once they used the action skills on which traditional operative work has been based, now they are being asked to abstract, infer, and visualize the consequences from electronically presented data. Where these skills remain undeveloped the risks to the organization are high, but where the operator is able to acquire what Zuboff (1989) defines as intellective skills, the potential gains are enormous. Where previously pulp operators would have been concerned with the machines in their physical proximity, now they can receive data from the whole factory floor, and have the potential for making much wider connections. As one operator reported: 'Things occur to me now that never would have occurred to me before. With all of this information in front of me, I begin to think about how to do the job better. And, being freed from all that manual activity, you really have time to look at things, to think about them, and to anticipate' (1989: 75).

The Reskilling Process

So far we have highlighted the threat that technology has presented to operatives in challenging their know-how. We also believe, however, that technology has the potential to change the nature of the contribution that operatives can make, and in particular to develop their intellective skills so that they are able to broaden the focus of their expertise.

Our argument has been that the skills of groups of people defined as manufacturing operatives have been systematically reduced through the techniques of Taylor, and the increasing application of technology to work processes. Technology has been presented as in opposition to the interests of craft workers, but is this necessarily so? When looking at the performance of a robotics line, a group of British researchers (Wall et al., 1992) found that where the operator assumed responsibility for fault management, the amount of downtime decreased. Where the operator was allowed to acquire new skills, and was able to act locally and autonomously, applying his or her own judgement, the outcome was to the benefit of the organization. Rather than the robotics line being seen as a sophisticated piece of technology, and the operator as an unsophisticated piece of machinery, the organization discovered that with training the operatives could outperform technological specialists not only in rectifying immediate problems but also in diagnosing and preventing problems. The reason they could do this was because of their closeness to the technology. This finding clearly supports the views of quality experts such as Deming (1986) and Juran (Juran and Gryna, 1988), who have long argued that the major impediment to workers performing effectively is the barrier to their discretion imposed by management.

While the recent attention paid to total quality management (TQM) makes the logic of recognizing the potential contribution of manufacturing operatives more easily acceptable, we believe that the same logic applies to other areas of operative input. Consider this description of Taylorism in action described by Gareth Morgan: 'A hundred and seventy to 189 sandwiches per gallon. That's how many servings of Big Mac sauce the manual says you should get from a jar of the stuff . . . 24–28 sandwiches per pound of lettuce . . . 111–135 slices per pound of pickles . . . there's a whole book of regulations for McDonald's you know . . . Why, the manual even gives you a special chore for every day of the year. July 25th, clean the potato peelers' (1989: 272). The McDonald's way is a proven method of ensuring a global standardization of quality in a high-turnover employment sector, but it's a model which is unlikely to produce innovative thinking amongst those who are closest to the customer. It's the perfect embodiment of the belief that things work best if the operative doesn't need to know anything.

Deskilling Office Operatives

The office, too, can deskill its employees. If manufacturing was the early target for deskilling, the target for the 1980s and 1990s has been the office operative: people involved in routine, clerical tasks, many of which have been automated in an attempt both to cut costs and increase efficiency. From the organization's and the individual's perspectives, there are some losses and some potential gains from this development.

In introducing technology, the first loss is often human memory. Think of your first calculator. How long was it before you stopped even trying to do mental arithmetic, and trusted instead to the infallibility of the 'chip'? The same is true in office systems. Once the office memory was held by individuals, who often felt pride in their ability to remember file references, or the telephone numbers of key customers. Within a short period of time it's accepted that the computer knows more, and individual amnesia is legitimized.

Yet as memory declines as an asset, the importance of physical labour increases. The operatives become defined by their physical mastery of the keyboard, and use of software applications, rather than their know-how. Equally important, the social interaction by which information was gathered diminishes, and is even blocked by the appearance of physical barriers between colleagues. It is perhaps not surprising that as the focus of the office operatives' work has shifted to their physical skills, attention to the physical risks has increased. Nowadays we are constantly hearing about back pain, repetitive strain injury, headaches and eyestrain.

The similarities between the use made of production line work and that of office operatives are highlighted in the complaints of this airline reservations clerk quoted by Studs Terkel (1974):

> My job as a reservationist was very routine, computerized. I hated it with a passion. Getting sick in the morning, going to work feeling 'Oh my God! I've got to go to work . . . I was dealing with the same people everyday. This is so and so from such and such a company and I want a reservation to New York and return, first class. That was the end of the conversation. They brought in a computer called Sabre . . . With Sabre being so valuable, you were allowed no more than three minutes on the telephone. You had twenty seconds, busy out time, it was called, to put the information into Sabre. Then you had to be available for another phone call. It was almost like a production line. We adjusted to the machine.

It is not difficult to empathize with the frustration of the reservations clerk in her desire for more meaningful interactions, and a greater sense of control.

As a result of technology, the office operative has become more isolated, with a loss of potential for collaboration and knowledge exchange. From the individual's point of view this loss makes work less satisfying, while at an organizational level it needs to be redressed if opportunities for service enhancement are to be seized. Organizations have been so concerned to automate procedures that the potential for wider outcomes led by operative analysis is often lost. This potential was identified by a Brazilian bank manager when he said: 'If people aren't aware of the opportunities in the data-base environment to use the integrated information it can make available, then they will only be terminal operators. They will be filling in the blanks on the screen rather than thinking' (Zuboff, 1989: 167). Sometimes, however, these connections are made. A telephone sales operative in a service organization identified that the client information she collected could be of benefit for the field sales consultants, and could be enhanced by input from the consultants on their work with clients. Individual consultants kept client knowledge in their heads, which was never made available to others unless they made a direct request. It needed an operative to act as a catalyst, by drawing a colleague's attention to the business potential of enhancing the data base. To take such a stand single-handed requires a degree of courage and self-confidence that many operatives will lack. It is far more likely to emerge when, as in this instance, operatives are able to collaborate and gain the support of others before the idea is opened up to organizational evaluation.

The office operatives' experience tells us that information technology redefines many as labourers whose physical and attentional stamina are the source of their reward. It also offers the possibility of integrating operator with management, where the operative is able to identify the additional value that working creatively with data can bring. Paradoxically, removing operatives' know-how by automation has increased the possibility of their knowing beyond – if they are encouraged by their organization to do so.

In this first part of the book, we have described a wide range of roles. What has emerged is that all of the players have knowledge that is of potential use to the organization. We have recognized again what has been frequently recognized already: all of these characters possess know-how; they are all in possession of knowledge and skills based on their past experience; and some of them are true experts. Moreover, all of them have access to information about what's going on – often information which is available only to them. What we have also argued, and what is not often recognized, is that they are all capable of knowing beyond.

They can all imagine different activities and different ways of doing things in the future.

In the rest of the book, we will address two further issues. How can they work together so that their knowledge is utilized to innovate and gain competitive advantage? And how can they organize so as to continuously learn from working together?

Summary

- Operatives are people whose actions directly impact on the quality of the products and services we receive, but whose field of discretion is narrow.
- Traditionally operatives have been defined as working within manufacturing, but the definition needs to be extended to include those involved in clerical and service occupations.
- The history of manufacturing operatives in this century has been the systematized diminution of their know-how through the application of scientific management and mass production techniques.
- There is evidence that working with technology can also upskill the operatives' contribution, where they are able to apply intellective skills to the electronic data they receive.
- The application of technology to routine clerical tasks has led to the loss of knowledge that was once held in individuals' heads, and a reduction in the informal interactions by which many decisions were made. Office operatives have seen the focus on their physical skills increase.
- By working in collaboration with others, there are means by which the office operative, through using technology, can add to the organization's knowledge base.

References

Braverman, C.F. (1974) 'Labor and monopoly capital', *New York Monthly Review*.

Deming, W.E. (1986) *Out of the Crisis*. Cambridge, MA: MIT Center for Advanced Engineering Study.

Hayes, R.H., Wheelwright, S. and Clark, K. (1988) *Dynamic Manufacturing: Creating the Learning Organization*. New York: Free Press.

Hounshell, D. (1988) 'The same old principles in the new manufacturing', *Harvard Business Review*, 6: 54–61.

Juran, J.M. and Gryna, F.M. (1988) *Juran's Quality Control Handbook*. New York: McGraw-Hill.

Morgan, G. (1989) *Creative Organization Theory*. London: Sage.

Taylor, F.W. (1947) *Scientific Management*. New York: Harper and Row.

Terkel, S. (1974) *Working*. New York: Pantheon Books.
Wall, D.T., Jackson, P.R. and Davids, K. (1992) 'Operator work design and robotics system performance: a serendipitous field study', *Journal of Applied Psychology*, 77(3): 353-62.
Zuboff, S. (1989) *In the Age of the Smart Machine*. London: Heinemann.

PART TWO   JOINT PRACTICE

7

Teams: Old Myths and a New Model

Using Knowledge through Teams

Knowledge is to be found everywhere in the organization. Everyone from the cleaner to the chief executive has know-how; everyone knows that various things are currently happening, inside and outside the organization; and everyone knows beyond the present, at least in personal if not yet in organizational terms. We already have the *diverse people*, and their different frameworks of knowing provide the varied perspectives we need for input to the knowledge process.

How are these potentially valuable perspectives to be used to get things done? Can we simply place all the ingredients of Sunday lunch into the melting pot and hope it will come out all right? We haven't papered over the difficulties that valuing diversity involves. Such difficulties, we argue, usually happen for two sorts of reason. First, people can't manage the job of working together on particular tasks or projects. Second, the overall organizational context doesn't encourage recognizing the value of diversity and learning from it. The second part of the book, 'Joint Practice', looks at better ways of working together. We'll label them teamworking, since 'team' is a word which implies that all the members are valued because of the different things they have to offer.

Table 7.1 demonstrates the increase in teamworking in UK organizations. In response to the enquiry as to what they were doing to respond to new challenges and opportunities within their business environment, 79 per cent cited increased teamworking (Coulson-Thomas and Coe, 1991). Organizations have been busily introducing project teams, focus groups, autonomous work groups, quality circles, multi-function work teams, and top teams in the boardroom for the last decade. Back in 1982, Peters and Waterman's excellent companies, alas not all so excellent today, were distinguished by their use of small groups. So much so that the authors called teams 'the basic organizational building blocks'.

Table 7.1   *UK organizations' responses to business challenges*
          and opportunities

Response	%
Creating slimmer and flatter organizations	88
More teamworking	79
More responsive networks	78
More interdependence of functions	71
Procedures resulting in greater flexibility	67
More interdependent organizations	55

Source: Coulson-Thomas and Coe (1991)

How is it, then, that teamworking has seldom transformed organizations into examples of the knowledge process? After all, teamworking is specifically designed to make the most of everyone's knowledge and skills. 'A team opportunity', we are told, 'exists anywhere where hierarchy or organizational boundaries inhibit the skills and perspectives needed for optimal results' (Katzenbach and Smith, 1993). Looking at our own organizations, we might all be tempted to reduce this sentence to 'A team opportunity exists anywhere.'

So if practice and opportunity are widespread, why the apparent lack of impact? Definitions of teams and their critical success factors suggest some answers. It's not the mechanics but the practice that matters; not the structure itself, but whether it changes the way we work. A true team, according to the textbook, 'is a small number of people with complementary skills who are committed to a common purpose, set of performance goals, and approach for which they hold themselves mutually accountable' (1993: 112). Real teams, as opposed to other sorts of organizational group, have (1993: 113)

◆ shared leadership roles
◆ individual and mutual accountability
◆ specific team purpose that the team itself delivers
◆ collective work products
◆ open-ended discussions and active problem-solving meetings
◆ measures of collective work products as performance indicators
◆ discussions, decisions, and real work.

These aren't just academic definitions – textbook recommendations on how to do things which the author hasn't tested or observed in practice. These are the features of real teams in organizations as diverse as Hewlett-Packard and the Girl Scouts. Just to emphasize the generality, here are the eight critical success factors for an even more diverse set of teams, ranging from the team that investigated the Challenger space shuttle accident, through a football team and a cardiac surgery team, to the people who developed the IBM personal computer (Larson and Lafasto, 1989):

- a clear elevating goal
- a results-driven structure
- competent team members
- unified commitment
- a collaborative climate
- standards of excellence
- external support and recognition
- principled leadership.

These findings demonstrate that merely bringing a diverse set of people together is certainly no guarantee of success. A lot more has to happen as well. But what if we combined the two lists of features and brought teams together according to those criteria? Surely we'd be on the way to success then, wouldn't we?

Two Pervasive Myths

We believe not. We believe that the features that are listed above do indeed distinguish successful from unsuccessful teams. But the successful teams were not necessarily successful *because* of these features alone. Researchers chose to compare teams on the basis of those particular features because they had certain beliefs about what it was important to look at. These views were probably influenced by two long-held myths about how teams work and why they are successful.

The first myth is that you have to get the interpersonal relationships among the group right before you can get down to your real task: the 'all friends together' myth. The second is related. It is that you have to go through a sequence of stages of group development in a particular order to be successful: the 'seven stages of team' myth. Both of these myths focus upon internal interpersonal processes to the exclusion of the relationship of the team to its environment. Perhaps influenced by the mythology, the researchers we have quoted above included only one external team feature in a combined list of 15 factors: external support and recognition.

The 'all friends together' myth is derived from a long-past period in the history of organizational theory and practice: the so-called human relations era, with its spin-off, the T group. Once we more fully understand and accept ourselves and others, it was optimistically argued, we could work together more effectively. The assumption was that we could be trained to relate better in general, and that this learning would transfer to the workplace. Further, it was implied that we would work better together because we related to each other better.

The glad new dawn of the post-war era generated this hopelessly naïve optimism. The evidence, alas, fails to support the myth. There is no evidence that interventions aimed at improving relations between members of the team improve the team's effectiveness at its task (Sundstrom et al., 1990). Those interventions into group process which *do* sometimes boost outcomes are about helping people with how best to work together on their task: defining objectives, for example, or allocating tasks to the right people (Guzzo and Shea, 1991).

The 'seven ages of team' myth derives from the same historical period and the same assumptions. Why does a sequence of developmental stages have to be passed through before the team can tackle its task? Because learning about how to operate together has to happen before real work can start. Or rather, more preciously, because we have to 'work hard at our relationships' before we can start the task. This myth was supported by a widely quoted rhyming mnemonic – forming, storming, norming, and performing (Tuckman, 1965) – which is still the staple fare provided by many trainers and consultants.

Yet here again, the evidence fails to support the myth. In organizational settings, teams don't spend a lot of time on process. On the contrary, they usually leap rapidly (perhaps too rapidly) into the task they think they have been given. Then they have alternate periods of getting on with their work and changing the way they do it (Gersick, 1988). It's hardly surprising that there is no fixed sequence or pattern. After all, there is a tremendous variety in the nature of the tasks they undertake: resolving problems, devising strategy, achieving a tactical objective, reporting on feasibility, planning a restructuring, running a campaign. Tasks differ in ambiguity and familiarity: imagining a new service or product that people might be persuaded to buy is a much more ambiguous task than designing an improved model of an automobile. Different tasks require different ways of working (Larson and Lafasto, 1989).

A New Model

What we need is a much broader model of teams and teamwork. We are not saying that the process of how team members work together is irrelevant. On the contrary, it is the core of the team concept; our next four chapters are all about processes. What we do argue is that to concentrate on team processes in isolation from the tasks and their context is meaningless.

The traditional model has been as follows:

Get the processes right and success at the tasks will follow. We want first of all to reverse the sequence to:

In other words, the nature of the task will determine the ways we tackle it. Then we need to add in the context:

It is the organizational context which sets the tasks that the team has to tackle. However, we also need to add another relationship, as follows:

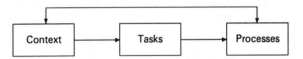

The organizational context has an impact on what sort of work processes are used (for example, it may determine the number and the identity of team members). Also, the processes have an impact on the context, in the sense that the team will seek to influence and persuade its organizational and external clients. Next, we need to add a fourth component, roles:

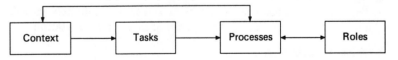

Roles are the different parts people play in helping along each of the processes (which are in their turn, what get the tasks done). Finally, we have to remember what it's all for (Figure 7.1). Team members can enjoy their activity no end. Indeed, they can gain great satisfaction in their work and believe, incorrectly, that they are being successful (Gladstein, 1984) Ultimately they are evaluated

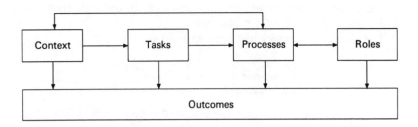

Figure 7.1   *The teamworking model*

not only by themselves but more importantly by their clients and customers; outcomes matter.

We need now to explore the model in Figure 7.1 in greater depth. We need to understand more fully its components and their relationships. Only then can we decide how to teamwork more effectively.

Context and Tasks

First, then, we examine the context in which the team works, and how it determines the tasks:

The organization is the most immediate context, and other organizational members have usually tasked the team to achieve some sort of outcome. Of course, this does not mean that the team may not redefine the task or consider issues that were not in its original remit. What it does mean is that the team has to produce something, normally to a deadline (Gersick, 1988).

The range of tasks a team can be tasked with is infinitely varied. Think of three teams currently operating in your organization:

- What is their name?
- What are their tasks?
- Along which dimensions do the tasks differ?

The last question is the tough one. It's very hard to think of ways tasks differ apart from difficult, very difficult, and next to impossible. One way is to think of tasks in terms of the knowledge process. Some tasks have a high level of knowing beyond, others

Table 7.2 *Some tasks and their knowledge requirements*

Task	Know beyond	Know how	Know that
Feasibility study	Low	Medium	High
Problem solution	Medium	High	Medium
Devising strategy	High	Medium	High
Tactical objective	Medium	Medium	High
Restructuring	Medium	Medium	Low
Running a campaign	Medium	High	Medium

imply a large dose of know-how, others again require a great deal of information: see, for example, Table 7.2.

Clearly, organizations exist within a business environment, the condition of which will affect the nature of the task. During recession the dominant tasks are likely to be those requiring less knowing beyond, since most organizations are concerned with short-term survival.

Not only does the state of the business environment affect what tasks organizations give to their teams. It also means that organizations themselves are changing. The consequence is that the organizational context in which teams operate is often in a state of flux. The task that the team started off with may be changed as a consequence, part way through. Think back to the three teams you enumerated from your own organization:

◆ Which of them now has a different task from the one it was tasked with at the beginning?
◆ When and why did this change occur?
◆ Were there new organizational circumstances which triggered this change?

The variety of primary tasks, then, is immense. But in the knowledge-based organization, every team has an identical secondary task. It is to increase that knowledge base – to learn. As we work through the team model, then, we have to ask continuously how *both* tasks are being achieved. In terms of the components we are currently considering, we have to ask:

◆ Have others in the organization explicitly tasked the team with learning?
◆ Do they require from the team an output which demonstrably adds to the knowledge base?
◆ Have they established systems which capture the team's outputs and make them available for others?

Tasks and Processes

The second relationship in our team model (Figure 7.1) is between tasks and processes:

We believe there are four processes necessary if teams are to achieve their tasks – both their primary task, and their task of learning. They are:

♦ achieving motivation and momentum
♦ defining issues and getting ideas
♦ managing the boundaries
♦ evaluating progress and outcomes.

All of these processes are necessary if tasks are to be completed successfully. However, they may well differ in their importance for different kinds of task. Some examples are shown in Table 7.3. Take the example of reaching a tactical objective. The need to maintain motivation is high since the task is not inherently of great interest. However, there is little need for ideas, since the objective may be a routine one. Boundaries need to be managed but, more important, progress has to be evaluated. This evaluation is vital since tactical objectives are usually specific and progress can be estimated.

Some processes may be very important at particular points in the time span of tasks. For example:

♦ Issues and ideas are going to be crucial near the beginning of the strategy-making task.
♦ Managing boundaries will be important at the end of a problem-solving task when the solution has to be sold to the problem's owners.
♦ Keeping motivation and momentum going will prevent a campaign from sagging in the middle.
♦ Constant evaluation of progress will ensure that the tactical objective is adhered to.
♦ Evaluation of progress and outcomes is essential for the universal task of learning, which cannot occur unless activity is reflected upon.

So, as we have shown, the nature of the task affects which processes are important and when.

Table 7.3 *Some tasks and their process requirements*

	Motivation and momentum	Issues and ideas	Managing boundaries	Evaluating progress and outcomes
Feasibility study	High	Low	Medium	Medium
Problem solution	Medium	High	High	Medium
Devising strategy	Low	High	Low	Medium
Tactical objective	High	Low	Medium	High
Restructuring	Low	Medium	High	High
Running a campaign	High	Medium	Medium	High

Context and Processes

The third relationship in our model (Figure 7.1) is that between context and processes:

Components include:

- the cooperation others in the organization give or fail to give the team
- the time pressure they put the team under, for they usually set the deadlines
- the resources they allocate for the team's use
- the degree of autonomy they allow the team.

All of these are contextual features which affect how well the four basic processes work.

As we all know from bitter experience:

- It's hard to keep up momentum if you haven't been given the resources; and motivation is difficult to summon up if you believe that lack of resources indicates no one's really interested in what you're doing.
- You don't have time for issues and ideas or for evaluating progress if they're on your back all the time for an answer. In other words, you don't have time for innovation or learning.
- There's no room to define issues and there's little motivation to succeed if they take away your autonomy by telling you precisely what the problem is and precisely how to tackle it.

Now think of a team of which you are currently a member:

♦ In what ways do others in the organization support and help you?
♦ In what ways do others hinder you from achieving your task?
♦ What efforts do you make to maximize support and minimize hindrances?
♦ How successful are these efforts?

The last two questions direct our attention to the two-way nature of the relationship in our model between context and processes. Teams actively seek to manage their context (Ancona and Caldwell, 1992): they

♦ protect their boundaries
♦ buffer themselves against pressure and threats
♦ promote their cause to important people
♦ keep their ears to the political ground ˙
♦ make alliances with other teams.

They coordinate what they're doing with suppliers and colleagues, and negotiate specifications and deadlines with customers. They scan their business sector and competitors for ideas, both marketing and technical. And they keep or gradually release as appropriate the team's secrets. So teams aren't necessarily at the mercy of their environment; they influence it too.

Processes and Roles

The next relationship in our model (Figure 7.1) is that between processes and roles:

We believe not only that different processes require different roles, but also that the role-playing skills available affect how well each of our four basic processes actually operates in practice: the relationship is two way.

There is already a large number of different theoretical frameworks relating to team roles. The best-known set of team role definitions is that of Belbin (1981). However, it's important to note that despite its widespread use, there is little published evidence to demonstrate that these roles are used and work in the organizational setting when real tasks are to be tackled by real teams. On the contrary, Belbin's team roles were derived from observations of senior managers engaged in simulation exercises. Where the task isn't real, attention focuses inevitably on roles which become objects of attention in their own right, divorced from the task. Furthermore, recent research indicates that Belbin's measure of the roles lacks reliability and validity (Furnham et al., 1993).

We propose instead to differentiate four basic ways of approaching and understanding task situations. We will call these 'roles', even though they are more general and broad ranging than the term usually implies. Each individual prefers one of these four roles, and each of the four team processes is dependent on particular roles being played.

What are they, then? They are derived from one of the two best-researched measures of personality in existence, the Myers-Briggs Type Indicator (Myers, 1988). The MBTI identifies consistent patterns of behaviour which stem from differences in the ways we use our perceptions and judgement. In terms of perception, the MBTI identifies two basic ways of perceiving reality. These are called sensing (S) and intuition (N). People who prefer sensing use their five senses as a way of becoming directly aware of things. They look for hard facts and tangible information. In contrast, people who prefer intuition tend to look for inferences, insights, and relationships. It is the possibilities in a situation rather than the realities which interest them.

In terms of judgement, we tend to prefer coming to decisions in one of two ways. These are called thinking (T) or feeling (F). If we concentrate in judging an idea on whether it's logical or true, we are making a thinking judgement. If we base our judgement on our likes or dislikes, on our values or our perceptions of the needs of others, then we are preferring a feeling to a thinking mode.

In very general terms, we're apt to get:

◆ a clear vision of the future from an intuitive
◆ practical realism from a sensor
◆ incisive analysis from a thinker
◆ interpersonal skills from a feeler.

However, we need to be somewhat more focused than this level of generality; we need to be a bit more specific about roles. When we combine the two ways of perceiving (S and N) and the two ways of judging (T and F), we come up with four types. These represent the way we prefer to make sense of our environment. We can attach role labels to them and describe their characteristics as follows:

◆ *Traditionalists* (ST) prefer to gather all the pertinent facts and consider them dispassionately. They are pretty good at coming to logical, reasonable decisions and at making existing systems run efficiently. They are weak at responding to change (the existing systems won't work), and they tend to avoid situations where subjective and personal factors predominate.

- *Visionaries* (NT), too, like to be analytic and logical, but they prefer situations where there isn't much clear information available. They can see the big picture and devise new systems and projects. However, they are weak at following through on detail, and they tend to avoid situations where the facts are established and where feelings and emotions are involved.
- *Catalysts* (NF) like developing their own and other people's skills and talents. They are good at getting people to work together and at handling people problems. However, they are impatient with routine, and they don't like getting involved in decisions which may cause conflict.
- *Loyalists* (SF) are pragmatists, who will do whatever is needed to help colleagues or clients. They have a compassionate concern for the common good, and are concerned to make things work efficiently and harmoniously. They may fail to notice change, however, particularly in areas where they have laboured themselves; and they don't like taking decisions which can cause conflict.

Our four roles are to be found all over organizations. However, some roles are more likely to be found in particular categories of employee, since they self-select into and are selected for these categories on the basis of what they prefer and are good at; more of which later.

What is important here is to tease out how our four processes relate to these four roles. For if a team needs all four processes to occur, and if different roles are needed for different processes, then it follows that the team needs different roles to be played (Figure 7.2). We are suggesting, then, that:

- Catalysts are needed to enhance the team's motivation and cohesion, and loyalists to keep the momentum going so as to achieve the task.
- Visionaries are required for identifying the issues within the broad picture, catalysts for ensuring that ideas see the light of day.
- Catalysts, with their preference for handling people issues, are useful in managing boundaries. So are loyalists, who will dutifully protect their colleagues from outside threat. But above all, visionaries will define the team's boundaries and point to potential clients.

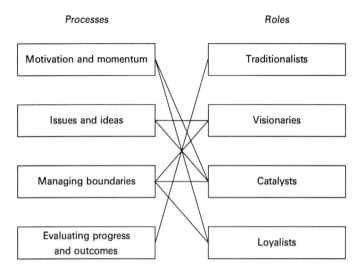

Figure 7.2 *Team processes and their role requirements*

◆ Traditionalists will come into their own when evaluating progress and outcomes, as they direct their unsentimental gaze at the hard realities.

So different processes need different roles; and the under- or over-representation of people willing and able to play these roles will profoundly affect task achievement.

Components and Outcomes

The final relationship we have to consider in the model (Figure 7.1) is that between all its other components and the outcomes:

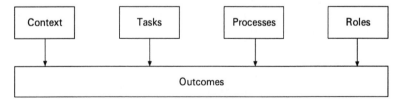

Note the plurality of 'outcomes'. The evidence we have is based almost entirely on primary outcomes – whether or not the task set for the team was successfully achieved. Yet there is always a secondary outcome in the knowledge-based organization: did any learning occur? We cannot go along with the hard-nosed bottom-line argument of Shea and Guzzo (1987): 'We believe that real-world, real-time group effectiveness is what matters, and that it boils down to the production of designated products or the delivery of contracted services, per specification.' This is true, but it is only half the truth. It is quite possible that the successful achievement of the primary task makes it less likely that learning will occur. On the assumption that learning happens especially when failure occurs, this is a reasonable hypothesis. It's likely, though, that we learn from failure because failure isn't usually what we plan for or expect. It's the failure to fulfil our expectations that forces us to reflect on what happened and learn from it. Things may go quite contrary to our plans and expectations, but we may successfully adapt and achieve our task in the end. We've learned from success, but success gained the hard way. So learning as well as task achievement or failure is an outcome; and learning can result from both failure and unexpected achievement.

The second reason for using the plural 'outcomes' in the model is that there are always additional outcomes to the achievement of the task. There are all sorts of unforeseen systemic consequences of action, some favourable, others not. This is why evaluating outcomes is such an important process. It's not a mechanical checking off of outputs against objectives. Rather, it's an intelligent and thorough look at the multiple ripples caused by the team throwing its stone into the organizational pool (see Chapter 11).

But back to the team's primary task. What determines a successful outcome? We started the chapter with two lists of features of successful teams. Now that we have a model, we can be more sophisticated. We would expect:

- context to be crucial, since others in the organization usually set the task, expect the outcomes, and provide the resources
- task to be vital, since task type and task difficulty clearly make task achievement more or less probable
- processes to be important, since all four processes are necessary for the team to approach the task, continue addressing it, and keep their client on-side
- roles to play a part, since tasks can't be undertaken and processes can't be carried through unless people with the right skills and knowledge are prepared to contribute them.

Which of these four components of the model contribute most to task achievement? Perhaps this is a meaningless question, since they are all so closely related. It is probably just as much the quality of these relationships as the components themselves which explains success. However, one thing we can say. The team's organizational context and how the team manages it are more important than we've so far realized (Guzzo and Shea, 1991). After all, others in the organization:

♦ oriented the team towards its task
♦ provided it with its resources
♦ set its final deadline
♦ monitor its progress.

This degree of dependency can make it very difficult for the team to keep the necessary autonomy (particularly important when it's defining issues and having ideas about how to tackle them). How the team manages its boundary relationships is crucial. Recent research (Ancona and Caldwell, 1992) on 45 teams developing new high-tech products showed that senior management rated the team's performance and innovation more highly in various areas when the team took care of several boundary relationships as follows. First, if people in the team adopted an ambassadorial role towards others in the organization:

♦ persuading them of the team's importance
♦ lobbying for support for the team's decisions
♦ reporting progress toward task achievement
♦ watching out for threats, changes in strategy or politics
♦ deflecting interference and excessive demands

then the team was more likely to meet its budgets and schedules and to be considered innovative. Second, if people in the team coordinated the technical task issues and cooperated with other teams, then the team was likely to be rated more innovative. Third, however, if the team spent a lot of time scanning its environment for marketing and technical ideas, then performance was rated lower. Perhaps this is a case of paralysis by analysis, or perhaps a lack of confidence. After all, a history of prior success can boost a team's performance no end (Shea and Guzzo, 1987). Finally, if the team imported other people from its own or other organizations into the team, then it performed better (but it was less satisfied and cohesive) (Ancona, 1990).

So there are a wide variety of team success factors; but perhaps the most crucial are about how the team manages its context. Now we will look at each of the four key team processes in turn, recommending ways of facilitating them and providing case study examples from the different team members' points of view.

Case Study

In October 1987, on Black Monday, the US stock market experienced enormous losses. Almost immediately, the London-based office of a large US finance house received a directive from New York: make 150 staff redundant within three weeks, and to a tight budget. The context and the task could not have been more clearly defined for the personnel department, who had responsibility for the assignment.

A team of four were put together, in a climate of total secrecy. No one outside the team was to know that redundancies were on the agenda, a fact that gave the team an immediate sense of cohesion and responsibility towards each other.

The nature of the task meant that time for acquiring new ideas was less important than maintaining momentum and managing boundaries. They had a job they would have preferred not to do, and if they were to do it effectively they would have to manage a number of relationships. Line managers do not like making staff redundant, and would need support in doing it. Individuals would have to be managed sensitively so that shock and anger were minimized. The team were well aware that the way in which redundancies are handled sends powerful messages about company culture to those who remain after redundancy.

By chance the four people who comprised the team embodied distinct roles, as follows.

Amanda: Employment Relations Manager   In Myers-Briggs terms, Amanda was an ST, a traditionalist who placed a strong emphasis on establishing the facts and looking at them logically. Her value to the team was that she had specialist knowledge on employment law. She was concerned that things were done in a right and fair way. She was also someone who liked to get things done in a planned and timely fashion. Her ability to keep her eye on the task helped sustain momentum when difficulties arose, or targets were in danger of slipping.

Jill: Recruitment Manager   Jill was a catalyst (NF), someone who had an intuitive sense of what to do combined with a strong focus on interpersonal skills and concern for the feelings of others. She knew the individuals who were to lose their jobs, and had built up good relationships with many line managers. The time she had invested in building personal relationships paid off. Knowing that one manager was shortly due to reach the 25th anniversary of joining the company, she was able to ensure that this event did not coincide with his redundancy. Knowing another had serious health problems alerted her to the need to have medical help on hand throughout the period.

John: Senior Personnel Manager As a visionary, John combined N and T. He was strong in analysis and logic, but could also deal with the bigger picture, and lack of certainty. When others were getting bogged down by the immediate pressures, his arrival could bring in fresh ideas and clear thinking. He wasn't the person for dealing with detail, but he was invaluable for injecting energy and offering support.

Rosa: Administrator Rosa, like many information workers, was the team loyalist (SF). She had a strong concern for people's feelings combined with a sound pragmatism and a concern to get on with the job. She was often able to offer information that was unknown to others, because it had been gained from her own internal networks. She also had a concern to get the detail right as a statement of respect to those who were losing their jobs.

This combination of qualities allowed the team to work effectively together. They were bound by a task undertaken in siege conditions. When they could talk to no one else, they could at least let off steam in the pub with each other. The tightness of the schedule removed the possibility of disputes and rivalries, since conflict would have made the task unachievable.

The task was achieved, and the feedback from the organization was that a difficult assignment had been handled well. The team carried out its own evaluation, focusing on what they would do differently if the situation ever recurred.

Not surprisingly, given the economic conditions of the early 1990s, a further round of redundancies was later called for. While the process was performed efficiently, this time Amanda had to carry out the assignment alone. The lack of a team to motivate, stimulate, and support her made the assignment far more stressful.

Summary

+ Teamworking is a way of integrating individuals' knowledge into the organizational knowledge process.
+ Our concepts of teamworking have been held back by two pervasive myths: the 'all good friends' myth and the 'seven ages of team' myth.

- ◆ A new model of teamworking includes the elements of context, tasks, processes, roles, and outcomes.
- ◆ Tasks are taken to include both the specific set task and the task of learning.
- ◆ Different tasks require predominantly different processes.
- ◆ Processes are four in number: achieving motivation and momentum; defining issues and getting ideas; managing the team boundaries; evaluating progress and outcomes.
- ◆ Different processes require predominantly different roles.
- ◆ Roles are four in number, and based on the core types of the Myers-Briggs Type Inventory: traditionalists, visionaries, catalysts, and loyalists.
- ◆ The most underrated predictor of team success is the process of how it manages its boundaries.

References

Ancona, D.G. (1990) 'Outward bound: strategies for team survival in the organization', *Academy of Management Journal*, 33: 334–65.

Ancona, D.G. and Caldwell, D.F. (1992) 'Bridging the boundary: external activity and performance in organizational teams', *Administrative Science Quarterly*, 37: 634–65.

Belbin, R.M. (1981) *Management Teams: Why They Succeed or Fail*. London: Heinemann.

Coulson-Thomas, C. and Coe, T. (1991) *The Flat Organization: Philosophy and Practice*. Corby: British Institute of Management.

Furnham, A., Steele, H. and Pendleton, D. (1993) 'A psychometric assessment of the Belbin Team-Role Self Perception Inventory', *Journal of Occupational and Organizational Psychology*, 66(3): 245–57.

Gersick, C.J.G. (1988) 'Time and transition in work teams: toward a new model of group development', *Academy of Management Journal*, 31(1): 9–41.

Gladstein, D.L. (1984) 'Groups in context: a model of task group effectiveness', *Administrative Science Quarterly*, 19: 499–517.

Guzzo, R.A. and Shea, G.P. (1991) 'Group performance and intergroup relations in organizations', in M.D. Dunnette and L.M. Hough (eds), *Handbook of Industrial and Organizational Psychology*, 2nd edn, vol. 3. Palo Alto, CA: Consulting Psychologists Press.

Katzenbach, J.R. and Smith, D.K. (1993) 'The discipline of teams', *Harvard Business Review*, 71(2): 111–20.

Larson, C.E. and Lafasto, F.M.J. (1989) *Teamwork: What Must Go Right/What Can Go Wrong*. Newbury Park, CA: Sage.

Myers, I.B. (1988) *Myers-Briggs Type Indicator*. Palo Alto, CA: Consulting Psychologists Press.

Peters, T.J. and Waterman, R.H. (1982) *In Search of Excellence: Lessons from America's Best-Run Companies*. New York: Harper and Row.

Shea, G.P. and Guzzo, R.A. (1987) 'Group effectiveness: what really matters?', *Sloan Management Review*, 28: 25–31.

Sundstrom, E., De Meuse, K.P. and Futnell, D. (1990) 'Work teams: applications and effectiveness', *American Psychologist*, 45: 120–33.
Tuckman, B.W. (1965) 'Developmental sequence in small groups', *Psychological Bulletin*, 63: 384–99.

8

Achieving Motivation and Momentum

What's In It for Me?

Think of a team you have recently belonged to which has successfully finished its task and disbanded. When you were asked to join it, did you ask yourself 'What's in it for me?' If you did ask this WIFM question, what did you come up with?

+ Doing something interesting?
+ Broadening my experience?
+ Getting noticed?
+ Helping the company?
+ Anything else?

Now remember the end of the project. What *was* in it for you? How did you benefit from the part you played, and how do you feel about the experience? If positively, why do you feel positively? Because of a sense of:

+ Achievement and completion?
+ Having done something worth while?
+ Having made a unique contribution to the team's success?
+ Belonging to a successful team?
+ Having the team's achievement recognized?
+ Having one's own contribution recognized?
+ A feeling of cooperation and mutuality?
+ Contributing to the organization's progress towards the vision?

How many of these outcomes which you felt were beneficial afterwards even entered your head at all before you started the project? Yet all of them add to people's self-esteem, depending upon which values they prioritize and which of their identities are salient (Shamir, 1990):

+ I am a woman; it was good to be on a working party about the development of women managers.
+ I am an engineer; this team really needed my professional know-how and my contacts in our business sector.
+ I value helping others and being helped by them; we only succeeded because we really helped each other when it mattered.

- It's important to me to feel what we're doing is worth while; saving lives is more important than flogging fizzy water.
- Fairness matters; I want to be fairly treated myself, and I reckon others do too. The remuneration committee is well worth the time it takes.
- I can now say I was in the team that first put the organization into the laser-printer market.

Many of us gain in self-esteem when we express our core identities (for example, as women or as professionals) in action. We also feel better people when we put into practice some of the values we think we hold dear. Often we push ourselves into such team tasks because we think we ought to, rather than being pulled by the promised incentives at the end. Of course, it can be argued that we get the satisfaction of doing what we think we ought to, but the main point remains: all sorts of personal benefits are experienced from working in teams.

These rewards are intrinsic to the work itself. Yet most attention is usually paid to the way in which team members are rewarded financially. So hung up are we on the fear that there will be loafers who leave others to do the work that we hesitate to reward the team rather than the individual. We needn't worry. The team exercises its own sanctions on shirkers. Rewarding the team sends messages of recognition and of the value placed on collaboration.

How can we ensure that team members are motivated? Our recommendations are (Hackman, 1987):

- Show how the task is important for the organization's future.
- Then give people the option of joining the team.
- Give them a whole task, not part of one.
- Give them freedom to define the task more tightly and decide how they are going to achieve it.
- Ensure there are potential roles for all four role types: traditionalists, visionaries, catalysts, and loyalists.
- Show commitment by giving them the resources they need.
- Ask for progress reports and give periodic feedback.
- Recognize and reward them as a team; leave recognition of individuals to the team itself.

What Can I Offer?

The obvious answer is: effort and abilities. The effort depends on the factors we've just listed above. The abilities are something else. Let's start with ability in the singular, implying being particularly able. It goes without saying that the more skilled the team members, other things being equal, the more likely the team is to be successful. Two caveats, though. First, the whole is greater than the sum of its parts. Consider the following research on tank crews (Tziner and Eden, 1985). The ability and motivation of each of the three members of many tank crews were assessed. Those crews where all three members were of high ability performed disproportionately better than crews where one or two members were of lower ability. Where team members are highly dependent on each other's skills, one member's weakness can weaken the whole team.

The second caveat is this: the abilities have to be appropriate to the task. We have argued throughout this book for the value of diversity. A greater variety of skills and abilities is usually an improvement on the grey homogeneity that's often found. Yet variety is better for some purposes than for others. Where problem solving, decision making, identification of issues, and having creative ideas are needed, diversity is a plus. In particular, where people from different functions are team members, there is greater innovation and more of that vital communication with the team's context (Ancona, 1992). So diversity can spark ideas, but it can also lead to lower satisfaction with group membership. The more varied in age and organizational tenure were product development team members, the higher the turnover and the lower the group satisfaction (O'Reilly et al., 1989). What's more, the final overall performance in terms of task achievement of diverse groups is rated lower by their bosses than that of more homogeneous groups (Ancona, 1992). Perhaps the implementation stage of the project was too hard to carry through because of conflict or poor communication.

After all, team members bring identities and values with them from the outside world (Alderfer and Smith, 1982). Such identities and values have often been in conflict in the past (workers and managers, marketers and sales people, specialists and generalists). There's no reason to suppose that conflict will cease just because collaboration is required.

Further, communication is notoriously hard between diverse employees. Private language may be a problem. But a bigger one still is not knowing what the other person knows or doesn't know. To be understood, speakers must formulate their contributions with an awareness of what their addressee does and does not know (Krauss and Fussell, 1990). Speakers may patronize, mystify, instruct, or communicate, depending on what they know about the listener (Figure 8.1).

So there's every reason to suppose that implementation will be

	Speaker is unaware	Speaker is aware
Listener knows	Patronize	Communicate
Listener doesn't know	Mystify	Instruct

Figure 8.1 *Mutual knowledge and ignorance*

hard with a highly diverse crew. On the other hand, you'll get plenty of ideas. Here, then, are our recommendations regarding team composition:

◆ Decide what skills and knowledge the task requires (but don't forget that learning is a task too).
◆ Bring together the smallest number of skilled people consistent with those skill needs (don't pick people to represent interest groups).
◆ Use role types as well as technical skills as criteria; traditionalists, visionaries, catalysts, and loyalists are all necessary for successful teamwork.
◆ If the task needs a heavy input of issues and ideas, go for diversity.
◆ Consider introducing new team members at particular points.

How Do I Fit In?

Much of what is written about teamwork stems from an over-simple idea of task. All we apparently need to do is (Katzenbach and Smith, 1993):

◆ Divide up the task into jobs.
◆ Allocate jobs to those with appropriate skills.
◆ Schedule jobs so that task coordination is achieved.
◆ Set interim targets within an overall timetable.
◆ Monitor progress towards these targets.

Yet our model insists that there is a mediating component between the task and roles. It is the component of *processes*. The organizing

Table 8.1   *Role profile of UK managers*

Role	%
SF (loyalists)	18
NT (visionaries)	22
NF (catalysts)	10
ST (traditionalists)	49

Source: Myers and McCaully, 1985

of the team will not just be about allocating technical jobs to enable the task to be achieved most effectively. It will be about deciding which processes will be of paramount importance and allocating those best equipped to progress them.

So as well as allocating people with the knowledge and skills for the task itself, we need them to be loyalists to keep up the effort, visionaries and catalysts to generate the ideas, traditionalists to monitor progress, and several roles to manage the boundaries. Particular skill is needed in activating each of these roles at the right point in the team's progress:

◆ We need ideas and issues at the beginning, and whenever we change the way we're progressing: bring on the visionaries and catalysts.
◆ Assessing progress at target points is a crucial element of the evaluation process: cue the traditionalists.
◆ Two-thirds through is usually a low point. The end is not yet in sight, but loyalists can see the team through its bad patch.

We need all four roles: loyalists, visionaries, catalysts, and traditionalists. They will all be needed to take the lead in one or other of the processes. What we can be sure of is that we're unlikely to find people for all four roles from among the managerial ranks. Research into the preferred MBTI types of UK managers (Myers and McCaully, 1985) demonstrates a marked imbalance, as shown in Table 8.1. So if we draw our teams solely from managers, we're going to be pretty short of catalysts, and we may have relatively few loyalists and visionaries. Where can we find them? Table 8.2 shows the percentages of various occupations that typify these roles.

Finally, the team needs to make explicit some *rules of the game*. If their organization habitually operates in team mode, this may not be necessary: airline crews or surgical teams take them for granted, and move straight into action. However, different rules may be appropriate for different team tasks: running a campaign may need

Table 8.2 *Occupational distribution of roles*

Occupation	%
Catalysts (% NF)	
Consultants	34
Secretaries	29
Marketing personnel	28
Salespeople	25
Mechanics	20
Loyalists (% SF)	
Secretaries	41
Supervisors	37
Transport operatives	35
Computer operatives	34
Operatives (general)	33
Visionaries (% NT)	
Systems analysts	43
Lawyers	41
Scientists	38
Computer specialists	37
Writers and journalists	30
Engineers	27

Occupational figures are mostly for USA employees.

Source: Myers and McCaully, 1985

an appointed leader who has the last word, for example. Above all, different rules need to be made, and made very explicitly, where there is a wide diversity of members. For example, rule 1 might be that contribution, not status, counts here; so leadership is vested in whoever is best able to manage the process or direct the task at any point in the project.

Our recommendations, then, for organizing teams are as follows:

- Spend time defining the task.
- Discover the knowledge, skills, and role preferences available in the team.
- Understand that all four processes are necessary for task achievement.
- Realize at what points in the project each process becomes of paramount importance.
- Give responsibility for leadership to the person(s) with the appropriate role or task skills for that process.
- Make explicit some rules for this particular game.

Getting Going

The first time a team meets is crucial. So eager are members to start
tackling their task, that they typically spend little time defining
what it is or how they're going to set about it. Rather, in they leap
straight away, making all sorts of assumptions (Shea and Guzzo,
1987). They assume they know:

+ what the task is
+ what are the desired outcomes
+ what each member has to offer
+ who are their clients
+ what are the unspoken rules about how they work
+ how the task is to be subdivided
+ in what order subtasks should be tackled
+ who's going to be working (mostly) with whom
+ what the other members' attitude to the task is
+ whether they're progressing well or badly
+ when they've finished
+ how successful they've been.

Now in some cases, teams may be justified in making these
assumptions. We've already cited two examples. An airline crew
comes together for the first time and is working well within 10
minutes. A surgical team will rapidly get to grips with the patient's
insides, each member (of the team!) knowing his or her role in the
procedure. Yet these are cases of well-defined tasks set within clear
organizational and professional norms. Most project tasks are far
more ambiguous, less practised, and with less well-defined norms
and roles.

Yet people still want to leap in straight away; they have an
uncontrollable urge to act, rather than to make explicit their
assumptions so that they can decide whether they're appropriate for
the task in hand. Failure to address right at the start the issues of
how to tackle the task and manage its processes often results in the
following, usually false, assumptions being made:

+ People in higher positions know more.
+ The person who tasked the team is its only client.
+ Technical task issues are the most important ones.
+ Once an agenda is arrived at, the team should stick to it.   –
+ People who have ideas feel perfectly free to express them.
+ All we need to evaluate is whether or not we're meeting our
  progress targets.

The consequences of these false assumptions for successful task completion are only too clear. The team devotes itself to its technical task, maintaining formidable momentum and congratulating itself on meeting its own deadlines. However:

◆ It fails to notice that there have been changes in the rest of the organization which mean that the task it was originally set has now to be amended.
◆ Or, it adopts a task solution based on the authority and know-how of its senior members, and not upon the capacity to know beyond of its other members.
◆ Or, it suppresses efforts to point out that it may be going up a blind alley and that it needs to go back to first principles again.

So what *should* happen at the first team meeting? We recommend determination of the following:

◆ What really *is* the task? This requires lengthy discussion and agreement, and will involve asking: who all the team's clients are; what each of these clients expects of the team; to what extent these expectations are compatible; to what extent they are feasible; and to what the team can commit itself.
◆ Which processes are going to be of prime importance for *this* task: motivation and momentum, issues and ideas, boundary management, or evaluating progress and outcomes?
◆ What knowledge, skills, and roles do the team members bring to aid *these* processes?
◆ What are the rules of the game for *this* project?
◆ What will be our overall plan of campaign, and how will we fit it into the project's time frame?
◆ Who will be responsible, initially, for what?
◆ How will we monitor progress and evaluate the appropriateness of our strategy?

Keeping Going

How does a team maintain its momentum? The visionaries and catalysts have already enjoyed themselves having ideas about what the task is and how to tackle it. The traditionalists have probably been put down for criticizing these ideas and are feeling distinctly peeved. There's all this boring work to do, and no one wants to do it. The visionaries and catalysts are not interested in it, and the traditionalists are in a huff. There's nothing much yet for them to get their teeth into by way of evaluation. It's the loyalists who at this point gallop to the team's rescue. They perceive their obligations to the team, and contribute their staying power and loyalty.

The technical and tasky people come into their own here too. During these steady state periods in the team's work, they immerse themselves in the details of the task, delighting in the opportunity to contribute their knowledge and skills. Any attempts at this point to redefine the task or bring in new ideas for solution are vigorously sat upon by our loyalists. They're committed to 'what we all agreed'. So the specialists get immersed in the task; they don't need motivating. The loyalists keep the rest of the team's collective nose to its grindstone.

What also helps is confidence (Shea and Guzzo, 1987). If the team has a past record of success in other projects, or it's obviously making good progress in this one, then members can inject some enthusiasm, and a favourable comment on progress from the main client can go a long way.

Our recommendations for helping to keep momentum going are:

♦ Note achievement of goals when they are reached.
♦ Point to the existence of goals which were agreed.
♦ Task individuals with responsibility for subtasks, and hold them accountable.
♦ Support people who are having difficulty before they get terminally discouraged.
♦ Inform the team's client of progress and solicit his or her encouragement.
♦ Bring in an enthusiastic new team member interested in the task itself.
♦ Recognize publicly the contribution of loyalists; they seldom get noticed.

Changing Tack

However keen and eager they are to complete their task, all teams periodically have to stop and take stock. Often, the stimulus to do this comes from outside. For example, the team's client might turn up asking about progress and reminding them of the deadline for completion (Gersick, 1988). Alternatively, the visionaries and catalysts will argue that progress isn't being made because the team didn't define the task clearly, or because there are much better ways of tackling it. 'We leapt straight in at the beginning without thinking about it enough', they will rightly argue. Or perhaps the traditionalist has been monitoring progress, and says, 'If we carry on at this rate, we'll overshoot by six months.'

The problem is the opposite of keeping the momentum going. It's putting the handbrake on the runaway car before it's too late. Loyalists will resist passionately: 'But this is the way we agreed to do it', they will protest. Yet if the task is to be successfully completed:

♦ Patterns of working may have to be changed.
♦ New external contacts may have to be made, or old ones re-established.
♦ New perspectives on the task, perhaps from new team members, may be required.
♦ New agendas may have to be set.

Such team revolutions are difficult. People are engrossed in the task and committed to their ways of working together. 'You can't change the goalposts now', they argue. Cooperative relationships are disrupted, no visible progress is made ('What's the use of all this soul-searching?') and satisfaction with the team plummets. Yet without a revolution, the team would have failed. Relationships between team members are often subsequently difficult, and members may drop out. The team is now kept together by visible progress towards the approaching deadline, and often it's only after it's all over that feelings about the revolution and each other are expressed, and fences mended.

Our revolutionary recommendations are:

♦ Frequently monitor progress in the light of the deadline.
♦ Occasionally reflect on *how* the team is tackling the task.
♦ Specifically, ask the team's visionaries what they think, or get in someone from outside.
♦ Listen to expressed doubts about how the team is presently operating, and encourage suggestions for improvement.
♦ Review the setbacks which the team experiences, and learn the lessons from them.

Case Study

The Clapham rail disaster in 1989, and the subsequent enquiry findings, convinced British Rail that the training of technicians involved in the installation and testing of signalling systems needed a radical overhaul. By the time a project team was put together to design over 200 competency-based training modules, it was clear that the complexity of the task and the resource implications required that external consultants be involved.

The relationship between external consultants working alongside an internal team is a potentially fraught one, because the range of motivations, backgrounds, and approaches can be very different. What may be just another assignment for a consultant may be an issue crucial to the internal manager's future career. An organization previously unknown to the consultant may be one to which the manager has devoted his whole working life. A project which arouses the intellectual curiosity of a consultant may be just a means of escaping from a job that has become unchallenging for the internal manager. The potential for misunderstanding, stereotyping, conflict, and poor problem solving is therefore high, unless the team can rapidly establish rapport and common focus.

The three who initially came together were Rick, an external authority on training design; Bill, an experienced BR engineering manager; and Peter, a consultant project manager. As a trio they immediately brought a diversity of approach. Rick as a visionary (NT) quickly emerged as the ideas person, the one who could always think of another way of doing things, and could rapidly shift in response to changes. Peter also profiled as a visionary, but the demands of project management required that he focus on his analytical skills, and act as a traditionalist. He established himself as the 'rottweiler' of the team, setting deadlines and relentlessly pursuing individuals until they met them. Bill, against all stereotypes of engineers, did not profile as a traditionalist, but instead was the team catalyst (NF). He provided feedback on how ideas would look from the perspective of those outside the team. He was also open to considering non-traditional ideas, even when there was no hard evidence.

A year into the project they realized the need for another member, and recruited Steve from BR. He was an experienced manager who was acknowledged as a networker and fixer. He was someone who always knew how to get things done, and by whom. His Myers-Briggs profile showed him as another catalyst, but he was one whose networks operated at grass roots level. Once the political task of selling the team's ideas to senior management had been achieved by Bill, there was still an important job to be done in selling the ideas on the ground.

There was a fifth member of the team, one who was not a formal member but who had a strong invisible presence. Walter was formally the project director, although his direct involvement was limited. Instead he had a representative role, acting as a visionary uncle in the background. He backed their efforts, and gave them permission to think the unthinkable and to act unorthodoxly. In a project where radical change was needed within a bureaucratic organization, the presence of multiple visionaries was a means of sustaining momentum when the pressure of resistance was heavy.

On Walter's wall hung a cartoon showing two ends of a bridge stretching out into a ravine, with a large gap between the ends. One workman was saying to the other, 'Just keep on bloody hammering.' For the other team members, Walter represented that act of faith, that belief that if you just 'keep on bloody hammering' the two ends would meet.

Having come together, they quickly recognized the contributions each could make, and what they each needed from the others. None of this was articulated, but when they subsequently completed a questionnaire on client/customer working they found they had established and were working on unspoken mutual expectations. How had they achieved this? Partly because the nature of the task defined roles and skill sets which were clearly differentiated; partly because they gave a lot of time to getting to know each other. They did not socialize often, because of geographical distances, but there were lots of late-night phone calls. Early on they established a rule of 'having fun'. This meant that any meeting was frequently broken up with banter and teasing of anyone who was seen as getting over-zealous or over-serious. In a company where the history of the organization has given it a rich language of its own, they developed their own project language as a means of linking them together more strongly.

The task started out as the design, delivery and evaluation of a large series of training modules. As the project got under way, privatization became a political likelihood, and the nature of discussions within BR substantively altered. Where once there had been a guaranteed audience for the training materials, in the future BR trainers would have to compete with external providers to win business. It was possible that business managers would want to use the training modules without necessarily using training school instructors. No longer was the team concerned solely with the production of the materials; they now saw the potential of licensing their use within BR, and even outside to railway systems world-wide. Impending privatization also heightened their awareness that once businesses were directly paying for training services they would place a higher value on student selection. There was, they believed, an additional service that could be developed in pre-course assessment. At a time when many within BR were feeling threatened by the changes, the team members managed to sustain themselves by thinking creatively, and by viewing themselves as comrades against an external environment of turbulence.

Sustaining momentum by supporting each other while ignoring

the outside world could be a recipe for grand self-delusion. This did not happen because Bill recognized the team had to remain both in touch with, and an influence on, key decision makers. It was his role to go out into the wider environment canvassing opinion, testing out ideas and winning support at the most senior level. Gaining that support meant he brought back into the team an additional source of energy, which sustained effort when morale flagged.

Inevitably morale did flag. Workshops to test out customer attitudes to training provision produced numerous criticisms. Production of modules was slower than expected. The lack of early visible outcomes encouraged cynicism amongst those who did not want to see change. Most powerful of all, 18 months into the project Walter died. His death came at a point when overwork by the team was leading to bouts of illness, and the gap between the required end point and progress to date was immense.

How did team members sustain themselves? They actively worked on managing the team's mood, and would work on lifting each other on down days. They took time out to hold informal discussions at the end of progress meetings, to answer such questions as 'Are we making the best use of our time?' When the answer was 'No', they changed the way work was done in order that individuals did not become overburdened with non-essentials. They took time after Walter's death to look at whether they needed to take better care of themselves. They recognized that while intuitive thinking and feeling produced lots of energy and time commitment, there was a real danger in encouraging each other to take on more and more. While this may sound like the workings of a T group, it wasn't. The issues were addressed as part of dealing with project progress, not as a special time for 'process'. There wasn't much talk of feelings, but there was strong feeling for each other's welfare, and commitment to helping others perform to their strengths, in order that the task would be achieved on schedule.

Summary

◆ Motivation to work in a team is often intrinsic, and involves our values and identities.
◆ When organizing teams, both the aptitudes required for the task and the roles necessary for its processes have to be considered.
◆ Working with people of diverse aptitudes and role preferences is often difficult but productive.
◆ First meetings of a team are of crucial importance. The

tendency is to make various false assumptions in order to be able to get down to the task as quickly as possible.

◆ Instead, the team should define its task and how it is to be tackled.

◆ Maintaining momentum throughout the task is not always easy; loyalists often keep momentum going.

◆ Changing tack when necessary is equally difficult; it often follows an evaluation of progress.

References

Alderfer, C.P. and Smith, K.K. (1982) 'Studying intergroup relations embedded in organizations', *Administrative Science Quarterly*, 27: 35–65.

Ancona, D.G. (1992) 'Demography and design: predictors of new product teams' performance', *Organization Science*, 3: 321–41.

Gersick, C.J.G. (1988) 'Time and transition in work teams: toward a new model of group development', *Academy of Management Journal*, 31(1): 9–41.

Hackman, J.R. (1987) 'The design of work teams', in J.W. Lorsch (ed.), *Handbook of Organizational Behaviour*. Englewood Cliffs, NJ: Prentice-Hall.

Katzenbach, J.R. and Smith, D.K. (1993) *The Wisdom of Teams: Creating the High Performance Organization*. Boston: Harvard Business School Press.

Krauss, R.M. and Fussell, S.R. (1990) 'Mutual knowledge and communicative effectiveness', in J. Galagher, R.E. Kraut and C. Egido (eds), *Intellectual Teamwork: Social and Technological Foundations of Cooperative Work*. Hillsdale, NJ: Lawrence Erlbaum.

Myers, I.B. and McCaully, M.H. (1985) *A Guide to the Development and Use of the Myers-Briggs Type Indicator*. Palo Alto, CA: Consulting Psychologists Press.

O'Reilly, C.A., Caldwell, D.G. and Barnett, W.P. (1989) 'Work group demography, social integration, and turnover', *Administrative Science Quarterly*, 34: 21–37.

Shamir, B. (1990) 'Calculations, values, and identities: the sources of collectivistic work motivation', *Human Relations*, 43(4): 313–33.

Shea, G.P. and Guzzo, R.A. (1987) 'Group effectiveness: what really matters?', *Sloan Management Review*, 28: 25–31.

Tziner, A. and Eden, D. (1985) 'Effects of crew composition on crew performance: does the whole equal the sum of its parts?', *Journal of Applied Psychology*, 70(1): 85–93.

9

Setting Agendas, Getting Ideas

Defining the Task

In *Riding the Waves of Change*, Gareth Morgan (1988) argues for the importance of a series of balances. He believes it is vital to manage tensions between present and future, so that one can position for the future while avoiding collapse in existing operations. Creativity and discipline have to be balanced, 'so that imagination and flair are always backed by the disciplined effort necessary to make good ideas good realities'. Richard Pascale (1990) likewise likens organizational life to a balancing act.

Putting these arguments into the language of this book, it's clear that we need the creativity of knowing beyond to be balanced by know-how with its keen grasp of what's feasible. Further, we need our third sort of knowledge, knowing that, in order to scan our environment for the information which supports both creativity and expertise.

Putting it in terms of team roles, teams need their visionaries and their catalysts for the process of setting agendas and getting ideas. However, they also need their traditionalists to help them evaluate and choose between ideas. Visionaries, after all, will get carried away with the sheer beauty of their big picture, while catalysts will preen themselves on having acted as midwife in bringing such a wondrous creation to birth. Visionaries won't have the inclination, and catalysts won't have the guts, to consider and force choices between alternatives. We realize the value of traditionalists at this point, for they are able to come to reasonable and dispassionate choices.

Before we can examine properly the roles team members can play in the 'issues and ideas' process, we need to examine further the process itself. One simple and prescriptive model is as follows:

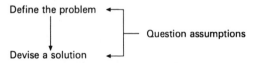

Defining the problem appears simple. After all, the team's been given its task: why don't we just get on with it? Appearances can be deceptive, for the following several reasons (McGrath, 1990);

- There are probably different stakeholders, who each perceive the group's task in a different way.
- These stakeholders are both outside the team and inside it.
- Their different perceptions may be mutually incompatible.

The chief executive, for example, may see the product development team's task to come up with something that will restore the value of the company's shares before year end. The production director wants a new product to be developed, but not so fast as to overload his capacity (he has just extended the life of another product in order to fit in with the marketers' strong campaign to improve its image). The project team manager would like to manage the time-scale and budget efficiently to get Brownie points in her attempt to climb what's left of the managerial ladder. The engineer wants to improve on the quality of the previous best product of this type, while the computer specialist is anxious to find an opportunity to use a new language he's just mastering. External and internal stakeholders have different agendas, and some of them are likely to prove incompatible.

Thus, because of their different motivations and frames of reference, there are likely to be uncertain and conflicting interpretations of what the problem really is. If the team is to succeed, there has to be a mutually agreed interpretation (Weick, 1979). What will this look like, and how will it be arrived at?

The initial multiplicity of definitions of the task is potentially both a strength and a weakness. It is a *weakness* because it may be concealed, and the assumption made that one of the stakeholders' definitions is agreed by all. Such a false assumption of unanimity has to be challenged, as the model above suggests. As Ed Schein observes, 'The checking of assumptions is one of the most critical functions to be performed in a group, especially when the group is silent and in apparent agreement. The leader or consultant must at those times directly ask the group whether the silence means that everyone agrees, and must actively explore alternatives and objections before assuming that consensus has been reached' (1988: 170). If assumptions are not checked, huge efforts will be put by some into solving the problem as defined by one person but not by all. Loyalists will carry on with this definition for as long as they can. But, as we saw in Chapter 8, visionaries in particular will challenge it sooner or later and revolutionize the team's agenda.

Multiple definitions can be a *strength* too, however. For the very need to reconcile different definitions of the problem can generate a novel one. When different definitions are made explicit, the frameworks from which they are derived become clearer to others. Thus a new problem definition can be born from the interaction of different frames of reference.

To continue our earlier example, the team might finally define its product development task as a two-stage one. The first stage would be to put a lot of time and effort into innovative design, so as to create a high-value-added product. Provided the advance marketing was effective, this could bump up share value in anticipation of good sales. The production director won't be swamped, while the engineer and the computer expert can be as innovative and quality oriented as they like.

Our recommendations for defining the problem effectively are therefore as follows:

- Decide who are the stakeholders.
- Discover what they want.
- Isolate and discuss incompatible problem definitions.
- Agree an explicit problem definition.
- Question the assumption that agreement has been reached.
- Don't put down the traditionalists when they query the visionaries' definition.

Getting Ideas

Now on to getting ideas about how to tackle the problem we've just defined. Team members will already have heard the problem defined from a variety of viewpoints. They may each approach the problem from a broader perspective than if they hadn't had the previous discussion. The consequence is, they may individually come up with new solutions because they are seeing the problem from new angles.

Instead of generating solutions together, it's more effective for team members to go off on their own and let ideas occur to them as and when they will. This recommendation goes counter to a great deal of current practice. There's nothing more exciting than a good group brainstorming session. But the evidence is absolutely clear and unequivocal (Diehl and Stroebe, 1987). Fewer ideas are produced by the same number of people working as a group than when they are working alone (although ideas differ not in quality but only in quantity). The reason is a very simple one: only one person can speak at a time! The others who are having ideas may forget them while they are listening; or they may think they are pathetic in comparison with the brilliant products of the group's visionaries and consequently keep them to themselves. This has been realized by ICL (UK), who have instituted an interesting method of pasting up issues and soliciting solutions (Pickard, 1993).

Back come the team members, each bearing a quiverful of ideas for tackling the problem. But some quivers are fuller than others. Visionaries' quivers will be full to overflowing; they will have generated a mass of ideas, partly because they have self-censored very few of them. On the basis that people go into functions which suit their preferred ways of thinking and feeling, many visionaries will be marketers. Consequently, the team runs the risk of being swamped with marketing ideas. It's crucial when considering solutions not to ignore the other role players: traditionalists, loyalists, and catalysts all have good ideas too. They are more likely to have censored them, so those they do bring merit great attention. Some of their reasons for censoring them may be fine: for example, the idea they had was not even feasible in principle, let alone in practice. However, they may have censored other ideas for the wrong reasons, for example:

- traditionalists, because their idea broke with established practice
- loyalists, because their idea might cause conflict
- catalysts, because their idea seemed merely routine.

When the team reassembles, some members should therefore be encouraged to bring forward some of the ideas they had censored internally. Faced with all these ideas, the first inclination of the assembled team is to ignore or dismiss out of hand a considerable proportion of them. An idea may sound ridiculous, or it may have been put forward by someone of low status. Yet before such summary dismissal, ideas deserve to be explored and then evaluated on their merits. The person who had the idea might not have expressed it in 'management speak', or may have failed to see its implications. This does not mean that the idea is not worth exploring; people with different points of view may spot wider implications and potential benefits which its author had failed to see. General managers who have broad-ranging cross-functional perspectives, or professionals with their external information and contacts, are ideal in this role. If by chance they are also catalysts, they will revel in it.

Making a Choice

After exploration comes evaluation and choice. After exciting new lateral thinking, boring old vertical thinking: 'Lateral thinking changes: vertical thinking chooses' (De Bono, 1984: 7). Exit the visionaries, enter the traditionalists. If ever diversity is crucial, it's now. Team leadership is of the essence, for it's easy to go along with exciting new ideas persuasively expressed by articulate visionaries. It's also easy to be seduced by these same visionaries into stereotyping traditionalists as stuffy old blockers of progress. Yet now they are needed, and team leaders have to make sure they get a hearing. The shift is from knowing beyond to knowing how and knowing that: a different balance is needed.

- Those who actually do the core work of the organization can judge practicality: will it work?
- Professionals can assess feasibility in principle: has something like this ever been achieved elsewhere? If not, why not?
- Experienced managers and general managers who know the organization can envisage unanticipated consequences. What are *all* the potential costs and benefits?
- These managers can also anticipate the sorts of obstacles to success that are likely to arise: they are, after all, the repositories of the organizational memory.

A traditionalist should perhaps be team leader at this point. Remember our definition of traditionalists in Chapter 7: 'Traditionalists prefer to gather all the pertinent facts and consider them dispassionately. They are pretty good at coming to logical, reasonable decisions.' Or possibly it's better to have a catalyst as leader, provided that he or she concentrates on the task of getting people to work together and listen to each other. What we don't need is a visionary, since he is likely to be passionately convinced of the benefits of his own solutions.

It's quite probable that what will emerge at the end is a way forward, a general direction to take, rather than a detailed blueprint for action. What seems to be necessary is:

- an overall strategy for tackling the task
- some estimation of how it will fit into the time frame
- allocation of some initial responsibilities to team members
- agreement with and commitment to the proposed strategy
- some account of the strategy and the reasons for choosing it which justifies it both within the team and also to the sponsors.

Yet, as we know only too well from personal experience and from the literature on decision making, these things happen seldom (Koopman and Pool, 1990). The norm is to:

- assume what the task is
- elicit few ideas on how to tackle it
- fail to explore the ideas that are elicited
- choose between them on grounds of power, politics, or persuasion.

Our recommendations for deciding how to tackle the problem as we have defined it are, therefore:

- Allow people time to come up with ideas on their own.
- Make sure all of these are brought before the team.
- Explore as a team the implications of all ideas before evaluating them.
- Ensure traditionalists play a major role in evaluation.
- Check explicitly whether all team members agree with, and are committed to, the finally chosen strategy.

It is certainly not normal to follow these recommendations. What *is* normal is for the absence of some or all of them to necessitate a mid-term revolution. Revolution may well be effective – but it's surely painful!

Case Study

A major UK retail chain approached a management centre to ask for help in designing and delivering a development programme for its middle managers. They asked that the programme should initially be run by the management centre, but that over time responsibility for delivering the programme should pass to its own trainers.

From the client's perspective the aim was to get a high-quality product, whilst controlling costs. From the management centre's perspective the aim was to build a long-term relationship with a potentially important client.

The programme, designed around the company's own identified competences for middle managers, was successfully delivered to 64 of the intended 200 managers. At a point at which full responsibility for delivery of the materials was not yet with the client, it became clear that the task as agreed was not achievable. Many of the company's managers were single parents or had elder care responsibilities. Attendance on a residential programme was impossible for them.

The client's first response was to simply turn the course materials into a distance study pack, and ask managers to complete it on their own. Concepts such as computer-based training and distance learning were not new to the organization, so the client did not think the idea would be rejected.

The management centre could simply have agreed to the idea, since the packaging of exercises and handouts would be a relatively easy, low-cost option. However, Steve Ray, who had tutored on all the programmes, when considering this option recognized that a major strength of the programme had been its participative nature. As a visionary (NT) he was open to questioning assumptions, and to coming up with new ideas, but he was also someone who liked to come to clear decisions. He was also a pragmatist, in that he was not open to investing so much extra time in redefining the assignment that all profit was lost. His combination of attitudes was useful because at this point he invited Gregg Jones in to work on a solution. He chose Gregg because he was recognized as an expert in the design of training materials and an enthusiastically creative thinker. Gregg also profiled as a visionary, but one for whom time constraints and cost considerations were less important than generating creative solutions. Two visionaries together can be a dangerous combination, but the tension between their different inclinations, while creating the potential for conflict, also offered the possibility of successful task resolution. The third member of the team was the client representative, a training manager who assumed the role of traditionalist (ST). Any idea the team put forward would be assessed for its cost, its fit with company culture, and its practical feasibility.

Coming to the task a second time, the team members brought different perspectives:

- For Steve it was important that the strengths of participation should not be lost, and that he should not be persuaded into uneconomical work.
- For Gregg it was important that differences in the way people learn should be recognized. He was also clear that the package should be about learning rather than study. He had enough experience of distance learning materials to know that many were never completed.
- For the client representative, it was important to gain quality materials that would reflect well on the training function. She wasn't certain what they would look like, but she knew they had to be credible.

When the three came together to discuss how the project could be refocused, they each aired their needs and concerns, and from this a new agreed solution emerged. The materials were to be transferred into distance learning materials, but it was not to be left at that.

Instead, the importance of participation was to be captured by linking those 64 who had completed the programme with the 136 who had not. Participants were to become coaches in transferring what they had learnt through group involvement. They were to act as learning buddies. Steve Ray saw this approach as one which would support the momentum to change, rather than one in which momentum would be lost when the residential programme was no longer available.

The training department recognized that the role it could play in the process was through managing the learning buddy system, and controlling the distribution of materials. Their own experience of the failure rate of distance learning persuaded them that giving materials all at once overwhelmed rather than motivated managers. By giving out materials in small bites, and only forwarding the next section when the previous one had been returned, they felt the completion rates would increase. They supported this through suggesting an incentives scheme, whereby timely completion of sections would be recognized in selection for future development programmes.

Gregg Jones was pleased at the training department's ideas, because his understanding of adult learning had shown him the importance of learners only receiving new information when they are ready to deal with it. The additional element he brought to the redefined task was to design the workbooks in a way that would be accessible to whichever preferred learning styles an individual held.

Each module incorporated five elements:

- ◆ Preview   What do I already know?
- ◆ Input   What do I need to learn?
- ◆ Activity   What can I do to practise?
- ◆ Review   What have I learnt?
- ◆ Planning   What am I going to do differently?

For someone who liked to learn through having time to reflect on experience, the preview and review sections of the module would be of interest. For people who enjoyed being given the theory, the input section would hold their attention. For pragmatists and activists, the chance to apply it to their daily work and to discuss its use with their learning buddy would be of interest. For all, the opportunity to discuss what they will now do differently, with their boss, would be a powerful way of integrating the learning into their work.

Once the design was accepted by all three as positively building on their ideas, the training department was able to add another element. Because its staff were the eyes and ears of the client organization, they were constantly evaluating whether the idea could work in practice. Their conclusion was that alone the idea whilst good could still fail, but that success would be more assured if all distance learners and their learning buddies attended a one-day induction course to fully brief them on the scheme.

Out of an assignment which could have collapsed when the original brief proved untenable, a team with very different approaches produced a mutually satisfying solution. The client representative felt that the training department was involved in a pioneering approach which reflected well on its credibility. Steve felt that the benefits of participation were not lost and that time and money were not wasted in reaching the new solution, and Gregg felt that his creative approach to materials design was recognized and well utilized.

Summary

- The task has to be defined before issues can be identified and solutions generated.
- There will be different interpretations of what the task is by internal and external stakeholders.
- Ideas for solutions are generated most prolifically by individuals on their own.
- Some role types should be encouraged to put forward their ideas and explore their implications.
- Traditionalists are best at evaluating different ideas.
- Commitment to the solution chosen is essential, and should be checked.

References

De Bono, E. (1984) *Lateral Thinking for Management*. Harmondsworth: Penguin.

Diehl, M. and Stroebe, W. (1987) 'Productivity loss in brainstorming groups: toward the solution of a riddle', *Journal of Personality and Social Psychology*, 53: 497–509.

Koopman, P.L. and Pool, J. (1990) 'Decision making in organizations', in C.L. Cooper and I.T. Robertson (eds), *International Review of Industrial and Organizational Psychology*, vol. 5.

McGrath, J.E. (1990) 'Time matters in groups', in J. Galegher, R.E. Kraut and C. Egido (eds), *Intellectual Teamwork: Social and Technological Foundations of Cooperative Work*. Hillsdale, NJ: Lawrence Erlbaum.

Morgan, G. (1988) *Riding the Waves of Change: Developing Managerial Competencies for a Turbulent World*. San Francisco: Jossey Bass.

Pascale, R.T. (1990) *Managing on the Edge*. London: Viking.

Pickard, J. (1993) 'How ICL is taking new ideas on board', *Personnel Management*, 25(5): 33-5.

Schein, E.H. (1988) *Organizational Psychology*, 3rd edn. Englewood Cliffs, NJ: Prentice-Hall.

Weick, K.E. (1979) *The Social Psychology of Organizing*. Reading, MA: Addison-Wesley.

10

Managing the Boundaries

No Team is an Island

Paradoxically, the most important process in teamworking doesn't happen in the team – it happens outside it. People who manage teams believe that they have to actively engage with the rest of the world to have a chance of success. Not only so: the evidence supports this belief.

Take a team of high-tech product developers, who have to work together to achieve the necessary high level of creative synergy. Here above all, we might suppose, it's what the team's technical experts know and how they share that knowledge together that determines success. Not so. In one study (Ancona and Caldwell, 1992), 38 managers of such teams were united in putting more emphasis on events outside the team than within it. They were justified, for the more they concentrated on relating to senior management, other teams, and the outside world of suppliers and customers, the higher the ratings they received for performance and innovation.

So were the more successful team leaders heroes to their teams? On the contrary, the more successful teams were *less* satisfied, and *less* cohesive as a group (Ancona, 1990a). In the organizational arena, the message is clear. It doesn't pay to be a happy and contented little club. No team can be an island unto itself. Football teams (Rapaport, 1993) or teams of intrepid explorers are *not* useful models for the world of work. It may be extremely gratifying to add to one's identity by membership of an exclusive club. Adolescents who are developing their identity find it very affirming to attribute macho male (or fashionable female) characteristics to themselves and their mates and rubbish the rest (Sherif and Sherif, 1969). Delayed adolescents continue the habit by belonging to exclusive clubs.

Yet this very cohesiveness and exclusivity, while it enables team members to believe they are doing well, actually militates against success as judged by others. Here's some evidence. Katz (1982) reported that 50 R&D project groups were measured in terms of the average length of time team members had worked together. The more stable team membership was, the less communication occurred both inside the team and with the outside world. Furthermore, the lower the team's performance was rated.

- The team cannot be exclusive: it needs new members with new information and new ideas.
- It cannot be competitive and hostile towards other teams: it needs their coordinated collaboration.
- It cannot have its own insular objectives: it has to relate them to the vision of other teams as to where they want to be.

Roles and the Rest of the World

So, paradoxically, teams are likely to be doing badly when they're feeling good; or, at least, when they are getting too much of their identity from team membership, and consequently erecting ring-fences around themselves. Walking the tightrope between feeling part of the team and engaging with the rest of the world is a tricky task. The team needs all its diverse talents to help it maintain a discernible yet permeable boundary; not so much a frontier, more a membrane. Rather than allocate a powerful team leader to keep the rest of the world at bay while the team has a happy time with its task, everyone must, Janus-like, face both internally and externally. All four of our team roles come into play here, but some more than others.

We need *visionaries*, right from the start. They will be good at:

- defining the boundaries of the team, who's in it, and why
- pointing to relevant domains in the outside world: clients, markets, competitors
- enthusing important others about the team's work and talking up its progress.

Catalysts have a vital role. They can:

- persuade others to support the team with words, deeds, and resources
- relate to other teams, coordinating, negotiating, and collaborating
- bring in outsiders, and help to integrate them.

Traditionalists, with their knowledge of the organization, can spot potential threats on the horizon. With their rational concern for the evidence (ST), they are often skilled at collaborating at the technical level outside the team. *Loyalists* want watching. If they are not brought into contact with members of other teams, they can easily become insular and too fiercely attached to the team. On the other hand, where team colleagues sometimes need some protection against outside threats, pressures, interference, or overload, you can rely on loyalists to take the strain.

Functional Contributions

So it's everyone's task to manage external relations, each contributing according to his or her preferred role. It's not just style of operating that's important, though. Each team member's experience and knowledge is vital for success. Returning to the new product development teams with which we started the chapter, the functional diversity of team members was crucial to success (Ancona, 1990b). The greater the variety of functions represented in the team, the more communication there was outside the team. More contacts were made with marketing, manufacturing, and senior management. Most important, because of the greater number of frames of reference available to them, these functionally diverse teams received higher ratings for innovation.

This is where identities are so important. If a salient component of my identity is my profession of engineer, marketer, human resources, etc., then I will share that identity with other people in other teams in the organization (Alderfer and Smith, 1982). I will belong with them as well as with my team. I will get information from them and do them favours myself. Likewise, if I am a member of more than one team, my loyalties will be divided. Self-definition by team membership is less likely, and the barriers are down. Just as different identities and value priorities help an organization face outward and learn, so it is with a team. Perhaps the group with the most to offer its team in promoting its external relations is senior managers (Finkelstein, 1992):

♦ Because of their *structural* power, they can often acquire resources and people for the team.
♦ As part of their *expert* power, they have contacts with customers, suppliers, competitors, shareholders, and government.
♦ Consequent upon their *prestige* power, they can help the team manage uncertainty.

The Potential and the Peril of Power

People who are potentially a huge asset, however, can be just as huge a liability. They are apt to take over the process of managing the boundaries completely. They have to act as Big Daddy, protecting the children from the threats of the wicked world. Here, they feel, is one way of retaining their position-based power in an organizational world in which teams are replacing hierarchy. With so many team members as specialists, longing to get on with the task and leave the politics to others, the way is open to them to keep the team dependent upon them. This dependency is most obvious in terms of resources. It is but a little step from obtaining the team's resources to allocating them to the team. Greater power hath no man than this!

Perhaps the greatest challenge to the success of teamworking lies in this issue of power. Early optimistic enthusiasts sidestepped this issue. They supposed that focusing on the team's task would mean that those who knew most about how to get it done would assume the leadership role when their knowledge became relevant. This misplaced optimism was derived from a simplistic model of teamworking. Successful teamworking involves a variety of processes and roles, as our model indicates. The successful performance of these involves various sources of power, not just expert power. It's not merely a matter of the person with the knowledge taking the lead. Rather, all the forms of power which team members bring with them are likely to be useful. Given that team members differ markedly in the power that they bring, the danger is clear. Initial inequalities of power make it easy for those with more to start with to enhance it at the expense of the team's interests. What are those interests? Not just to achieve the task objectives (in which case autocratic leadership can sometimes be effective). Rather, to learn from the project and develop as individuals and as a team.

The process of evaluation is therefore crucial, and must involve evaluation of both progress and outcomes. Only a fiercely independent evaluator can focus upon power inequality or misuse as a reason for poor progress. Only a stubborn old traditionalist can prick the feel-good hype that typically follows project completion. We turn to the evaluation process in the next chapter.

In the meantime, here are our recommendations for the management of boundaries:

- Think about whom you have to influence.
- Discover who in the team has influence with these targets, and allocate appropriately.
- Have a regular report-back sessions where intelligence information is shared.
- Exchange members and information with other teams.
- Use senior managers to manage boundaries, but keep checks on their power.

Case Study

In 1989 Linda Kelsey was editor of *Cosmopolitan* – the most successful women's monthly magazine in the UK. After taking maternity leave she returned to the magazine with a strong sense that she had done all she could do for the magazine. At the same time she began to develop an idea for a magazine that would take women on from *Cosmo*.

As a new mother it was apparent to her that while women were marrying later, having children later, and continuing their careers after childbirth, there was no magazine which addressed the issues that come with multiple role juggling. When she looked at magazines aimed at mothers, the focus seemed to be on the stress of parenting. There was little sense of the fun parenting brings, or the importance of retaining one's individuality as a woman. She saw motherhood and individuality as going hand in hand, rather than in diametric opposition. In a very real sense Linda Kelsey was a visionary.

At this stage there was no team; there was only one person's sense that there was an unmet market. As a first step she put her ideas on paper to her managing director, Terry Mansfield. As a traditionalist his enthusiasm for the idea was tempered by the need to provide proof that women's lives were developing in the way she claimed. When market research provided that evidence, he gave the go-ahead to produce a dummy copy. There was now a team of two, joined shortly after by Nadia Marks. Nadia was a former art director of *Cosmopolitan*, and currently on maternity leave. Soon the two women were meeting during lunch hours to put together a dummy of how the magazine could look.

The first test of boundary management came when representatives of the US parent company visiting the UK were given a presentation. They listened, but were not convinced. They were about to launch two new titles in the UK, and were understandably reluctant to increase their financial investment.

At this point the idea could have died, but it was then that the value of having a traditionalist on board came into play. Having been convinced by the data, Terry Mansfield looked for a way of keeping the idea alive. His gaze fell on *She* magazine. A 30-year-old magazine with a falling readership and declining advertising revenue, it was in trouble. Its focus was unclear, its readership age profile was diverse, and its visual presentation was quirkily old-fashioned. It did, however, have a by-line: 'For women who juggle their lives'. The by-line, lifted from an American magazine, made no sense in the context of the magazine's content, but it made perfect sense when linked to Linda Kelsey's idea. Having made that connection, he asked her to take on the challenge of transforming an ailing publication into the magazine she had presented to him.

Her first response was horror rather than delight. She considered carefully, and made a list of conditions that would have to be met before she would accept. That they were accepted was evidence of the structural power she already held as a magazine editor, and the expert and prestige power that her past success had given her. The company agreed to her demand that the changes would be made wholesale, in a complete relaunch, rather than by incremental tweaking. They also accepted her estimate that one-third of existing readers would be lost and that, therefore, strong financial backing would be needed if she was to have any chance of success. As part of her boundary management she was making it clear that some stakeholders would have to be lost, if the new vision was to be achieved.

In taking on the challenge of putting a new magazine on the market in three months, there were a number of boundaries that would have to be managed:

- *She* would rapidly have to gain new readers to replace those that would be lost. This meant that the message of the new magazine had to be communicated quickly and clearly.
- Existing advertisers had to be convinced that there was sufficient overlap between old and new readership to justify their staying with the magazine.
- New advertisers, who previously had ignored the magazine, had to be brought in.
- Advertising sales staff had to be made passionate about the new magazine. Since many of them differed in age and life-stage profile from the intended readership, this could be problematic.
- Magazine journalists had to be convinced that Linda Kelsey was right if they were to give 100 per cent. As one of her first decisions was to drop all but one of the regular features, this might well not be easy.

The process of boundary management began with the advertisers. As people looking for a return on their outlay, the initial approach was to use the magazine's publisher Karen Pusey to provide them with market research data. They remained unconvinced. They had never placed fashion and cosmetics advertising with the magazine, and saw mothers as purchasers of baby products and tracksuits. When data failed, Karen Pusey, as a skilled catalyst, recognized it was time to bring on the visionary. She set up a series of meetings in which advertisers met Linda Kelsey on a one-to-one basis. She was able to communicate her passion and conviction persuasively, helped by a number of contextual factors:

◆ The popularity of the American TV series 'Thirtysomething', chronicling the lives of women who combined families, work, and visible consumption.

◆ A spate of films, most noticeably *Babyboomer*, which showed professional women trying to juggle work, children, and relationships.

◆ An Audi car advertisement, which had been heralded as a breakthrough in the industry because it portrayed male car ownership in the context of caring fatherhood.

◆ The beginnings of a backlash to the 1980s 'greed is good' philosophy, and talk of a more caring decade in the 1990s.

While Linda Kelsey had some reservations about the high-powered elitism of some of these examples, she believed they had a wider applicability, and she could see they were persuasive to stakeholders who were vital to her success. There was an additional way in which boundary management was made easier. The age profile of advertisers meant she would often go into a meeting to find her potential client was pregnant!

Central to the retention of existing advertisers, the winning of new, and the motivation of the sales staff was Karen Pusey. Brought into the new *She* after a successful career with other major women's magazines, she provided an additional team member, and a further perspective. Where Linda could win over individuals with passion, Karen could win over groups with hard facts and *chutzpah*. She shared the passion for the new magazine, but presented it very differently. The two women recognized that though they had different daily concerns, and individual styles, they had a strong mutual trust built on shared conviction.

If advertisers were one key to the magazine's chance of survival, another was the magazine's own journalists. The first edition was produced entirely by Nadia Marks and Linda Kelsey, a tactic which ensured delivery of a clear message, but which was untenable. Magazines are about teamwork, and journalists had to be won over to the new approach. Linda Kelsey saw each journalist individually, in order that she could focus on his or her particular concerns. The task was made easier because many were relatively new to the magazine, and were less committed to the old style than concerned for their continuing job security. Only one senior editor had difficulty in accepting the new editorial line, and she chose to leave shortly afterwards.

Most important of all were the readers. Linda Kelsey was right in her assessment of the likely response. In the first three weeks after publication over 1000 letters of protest were received from outraged loyalists. She chose to manage the readership boundary by making it clear who should leave and whom she wanted to attract in. The readership losses were offset by an overall 20 per cent increase in readership in 1990, which was matched the following year.

The *She* relaunch is a clear example of how one person's idea when sold convincingly can gain a momentum which builds its own team. It shows also the importance of boundary management both in building external support, and in recognizing when former supporters are no longer helpful for successful task outcome.

Summary

◆ Managing the boundaries is probably the most important process in teamworking.
◆ Teams cannot be exclusive in membership or hostile to other teams.
◆ Every member must be concerned both with the task *and* with external relations.
◆ Role types each have particular knowledge and skills which assist boundary management.
◆ So do team members from different functions and levels.
◆ Senior managers, in particular, are a huge asset, but can also take too much power.

References

Alderfer, C.P. and Smith, K.K. (1982) 'Studying inter-group relations embedded in organizations', *Administrative Science Quarterly*, 27: 35–65.

Ancona, D.G. (1990a) 'Outward bound: strategies for team survival in the organization', *Academy of Management Journal*, 33: 334–65.

Ancona, D.G. (1990b) 'Demography and design: predictors of new product team performance', *Organization Science*, 3: 321–41.

Ancona, D.G. and Caldwell, D.F. (1992) 'Bridging the boundary: external activity and performance in organizational teams', *Administrative Science Quarterly*, 37: 634–65.

Finkelstein, S. (1992) 'Power in top management teams: dimensions, measurement, and validation', *Academy of Management Journal*, 35(3): 505–38.

Katz, R. (1982) 'The effects of group longevity on project communication and performance', *Administrative Science Quarterly*, 27: 81–104.

Rapaport, R. (1993) 'To build a winning team: an interview with head coach Bill Walsh', *Harvard Business Review*, 71(1): 111–20.

Sherif, M. and Sherif, C. (1969) *Social Psychology*, New York: Harper and Row.

11

Evaluating Progress and Outcomes

Are We in the Right Ballpark?

Unless a team evaluates its *progress*, it cannot adjust so as to aim more accurately for its objectives. Unless it evaluates its *outcomes*, it cannot learn from its successes and failures since it won't know whether it has succeeded or failed. Evaluation is necessary both for task achievement and also for learning and development.

Many teams evaluate their progress, some informally, some as a matter of regular routine. Almost invariably, what is evaluated is progress towards the achievement of the team's task. This is perfectly reasonable: after all, that is what the team was set up for in the first place. How close are we to attaining task objectives, the team asks, and how well does the progress we have made so far match the timetable we have set?

A moment's reflection tells us that this is not enough. Suppose our evaluation indicates we are not making adequate progress towards task completion. How do we discover why we are falling short? We cannot improve progress unless we understand the causes of our problems and remedy them. A proper evaluation needs to go beyond task. It needs to evaluate the whole process of teamworking. The model of teamworking we outlined in Chapter 7 will provide the framework for such an evaluation, and is repeated here as Figure 11.1. Evaluation should follow a sequence of stages, based on the elements and the relationships of the model.

Stage 1: Context

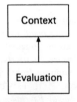

Right at the start, we have to ask ourselves: are we managing the context satisfactorily? If boundary management is the most

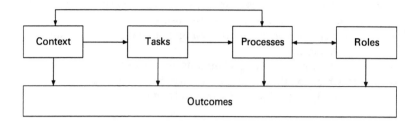

Figure 11.1 *The teamworking model*

important key success factor, as we argued in Chapter 10, then we should focus first on how well we are succeeding in this crucial area. We will be asking such questions as:

◆ Have we clarified who *all* our clients are?
◆ Have we discovered from all of them what they are expecting?
◆ Have we decided whether these expectations are compatible with each other, and with our own?
◆ Have we negotiated different expectations if there are incompatibilities?
◆ Have we informed all clients of plans and progress? Are they happy?
◆ Have we asked them for *their* ideas?
◆ Are they informed and happy about our use of resources?

Stage 2: Tasks

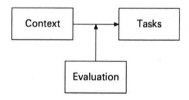

The second evaluation is of the relationship between the context and the task. The basic question to be answered is: is the task we are engaged in still the one that our stakeholders are wanting us to tackle? Or have their expectations changed to such an extent as to require us to change course in mid-stream?

In order to find out the answers to these questions, we will need to:

- keep reporting progress towards current objectives to each stakeholder, and invite their evaluations
- keep a weather eye open for changes in the power or aims of these stakeholders
- watch out for latecoming claimants to a stake in the project
- decide which of these existing, changed, or new claims we need to adapt to, and which we can safely ignore.

It's the *visionaries* who will be best at this stage of evaluation, with their capacity for seeing the big picture and being willing to redefine tasks and have new ideas.

Stage 3: Monitoring Progress

The third stage is the traditional one. It answers the questions: now that we are confident that we are tackling the right task, how well are we doing at it? What sort of progress are we making, and are we up to schedule? To answer these questions, we need to discover the following:

- Do we know what are the various significant staging points on the way to task achievement?
- Do we know at what points within the time frame for the project these should be reached?
- Do we have criteria to establish whether the staging points have been achieved in a satisfactory way?
- Do we have an acceptable way of modifying our original timescales and criteria if experience shows them to be inappropriate?

Traditionalists are the team's best bet here. They can look at the facts dispassionately and see things for what they are, not as we would like them to be.

Stage 4: Monitoring Process

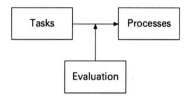

'If it ain't broke, don't fix it', runs the old adage. Adapted, it reads: 'If you're doing OK, don't bother to find out why.' If the team is on course for achieving its task objectives, why bother to look at how it's succeeding in doing so? In order to learn and remember how we did it, is the answer.

Stage 4 asks the question: given the nature of the task we've been set, are we engaging in the appropriate teamwork processes, in the right proportion, at the right time?

As an example, suppose a team has been tasked with running a publicity campaign. This requires a lot of footslogging telephone work, so maintaining motivation and momentum will be continuously high on the process agenda. Once campaign strategy and tactics have been initially established, there will be little continuing need for issues and ideas (unless the campaign is obviously faltering).

So the subsidiary questions we need to be asking at stage 4 are:

- What degree of attention to motivation and momentum will *this* task require?
- How original do the issues and ideas have to be for *this* task to be achieved, and when in the course of the project are they needed?
- How much attention do we need to pay to boundary management for *this* task?

If the stage 3 evaluation indicates satisfactory progress, then we note that our attention to these processes is about right. We thus have a model for future such tasks. If stage 3 indicates unsatisfactory task progress, then we need to ask:

- What are the impediments to progress?
- Which processes need more attention to remove these impediments?

Visionaries are probably the best evaluators for stage 4; they can see the big picture and put their fingers on the problem area. They can also see the general direction which change must take.

Stage 5: Looking Harder at Process

Stage 5 forces us into a more detailed evaluation of what we are doing. After the question 'Is the balance of our processes appropriate to the task?', we are now asking, 'How well is each of our processes working?' If stage 3 is unfavourable, this question will be diagnostic: the reason for lack of progress on the task may well be faulty process. If stage 3 is favourable, it is still worth understanding why the processes are working well.

More specifically, the team will ask such questions as:

- How clear are we about what we are trying to achieve?
- Do we really want to achieve it?
- Do we *all* feel we are contributing?
- Are we each contributing what we are best at?
- Are we all agreed on and committed to an overall strategy?
- Do we all believe that progress is being made?
- Do we know who the stakeholders are?
- Do we know what they expect of us?
- How frequently are we in contact with them?
- How many ideas do we elicit?
- How many different people contribute to them?
- Do we explore them before evaluating them?
- Are they evaluated in terms of whether they will help achieve our objectives?
- Have we got enough resources? Can we get more?
- Have we brought in any new blood recently?

These and other such questions allow us to evaluate the extent to which the motivational, ideas, and boundary management processes are working well. Of course there is the fourth process – evaluation itself. To evaluate evaluation, we have to ask such questions as:

- How frequently do we review how well we are doing?
- How often do we succeed in diagnosing a difficulty and putting it right?

Catalysts are likely to be good at spotting the feelings and identities involved in the motivation process. Visionaries can see beyond the boundaries and how well they are being managed. They are probably useful for looking at the ideas process too, though the occasional beady-eyed traditionalist might not go amiss here.

Stage 6: Are We Playing the Right Roles?

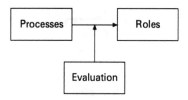

The real issue here is one of membership. Just as the team took a lot of care that people with the requisite task knowledge and skills were coopted, so with process. Stage 6 of the evaluation asks: do we have people who can play the roles in all the processes which this task involves?

The further questions are therefore:

- Which processes are most important in *this* task?
- Which roles do these processes require?
- What are the preferred roles of the current team members?
- Do they fill the bill, or do we need to recruit new members?
- Alternatively, are current team members prepared and able to play non-preferred roles?
- Suppose we do have people with the roles needed: do we let them take the lead when the process requires it?
- How well do those with other roles collaborate with the temporary leader role?

The greatest difficulties in teamworking often concern roles. When people who strongly prefer a particular role take the lead in a process where that role is not appropriate, trouble follows. Not merely does the process work badly, but conflict arises with those who do prefer the appropriate role. Traditionalists, for example, are the wrong people to lead the generation and exploration of ideas. Visionaries often get very cross with them when they try to do so. The trouble is that a leader may be appointed from above (or be self-appointed) who assumes he or she has to lead all the time. It's a matter of chance whether they are the appropriate role type at any particular point.

Again, visionaries are probably the best people for stage 6 of the evaluative process; they can take a broad view of whether the right people are taking the lead at the right time. Unfortunately they are quite likely to have assumed an overall leadership role themselves!

Stage 7: Are We Playing Our Roles Well?

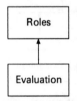

This stage is much more straightforward. We simply ask: are the roles of traditionalist, visionary, catalyst, and loyalist being performed well enough? This is not the same as asking: how good a traditionalist is Fred? The question is about how well a role is being played. It is a question for the team to answer together, since it concerns how the team works, not an individual's performance. The team may have an extremely skilled visionary who is always swamped by a surfeit of traditionalists.

Detailed questions might include:

- When, recently, did we really need traditionalist, visionary, catalyst, or loyalist skills? (Think of specific occasions.)
- Did we have the skills we needed in the group?
- If yes, did we use them to the full?
- If not, why not?

Such questions as these raise issues about mutuality. There might be a particular occasion when the team is desperately in need of a new idea. A visionary in the team might be capable of producing it; but it might take a catalyst to drag it out, a traditionalist to bite her tongue and withhold judgement for a bit, and a loyalist to encourage the visionary to keep going.

Catalysts, with their skills at getting people to work together and handling people problems, are ideal for stage 7 of the evaluation process.

Stage 8: What's Come Out of It All?

Last of all comes the final wash-up. 'How well did we achieve our task objectives?', is the first and obvious question. But as we argued in Chapter 10, there is another, equally important question: what *other* outcomes resulted from our work? We might further ask: are these outcomes good or bad (from whose point of view)? Could we have anticipated them? Why did they happen? Can we gain any benefit from them next time round? But perhaps the most important question of all is: what have we learned from our project?

With their highly activist orientation to their work (Honey and Mumford, 1982), many British and American managers believe that we learn by doing. Simply by engaging in this project, we have learned something new. This is true – and false. *Taking action* is normally a necessary condition for learning: but it is certainly not a sufficient one. We also need to *observe and reflect* on what we are doing or have done and its outcomes (Kolb, 1984).

Know How and Know Beyond to Learn

In our model of teamworking, the evaluation process forces us into the observation/reflection mode. We have to observe our own behaviour and its consequences in order to evaluate it. And the very act of evaluating, of applying criteria, necessarily involves reflection. For we are comparing our behaviour and its outcomes with some standard or objective. This is the essence of knowing how.

However, there is a third element of the learning process which David Kolb (1984) and many others believe to be necessary too. Our observation of and reflection about our actions is still not sufficient for learning. I might observe meticulously my performance in making a mechanical watch, and reflect endlessly on how I might improve my already near perfect performance. But if I cannot change my basic conceptualization of how watches might be made (faster and cheaper electronically), then I have failed to learn. Learning implies continuous adaptation to and of our environment.

We have to allow our *frames of reference* to change, and therefore, among other things, our criteria of excellence. We have to know beyond.

Perhaps the most fundamental benefit to come out of teamworking is its stimulus to learning. We can best engage in action, observation, and reflection, and reframe our ideas, in the context of the team. For in that arena, we engage in *social learning*. (Bandura, 1986).

◆ We do not have to perform every action ourselves in order to learn from it; other team members may do things too.
◆ We do not have to rely on our own keenness of observation alone; others spot different things.
◆ We are not reliant on our own reflection and evaluation; everyone applies criteria.
◆ We cannot keep a fixed frame of reference; others continuously demonstrate the advantages of alternative points of view.

Learning is social. It can even be sociable too!

Case Study

When we looked to find a real-life case study to illustrate the points we were making about the evaluation of teamworking, we knew we had a difficult task on our hands. Our own experience tells us that evaluation is often only seen as necessary when things have gone wrong, in order that blame can be attached to individuals. When the task has been achieved, consideration of how it was done, whether it could have been done better, and what has been learnt, can be seen as self-indulgence or an unnecessary use of time. The following case study does not attempt to mask stages which were missing from the evaluation, because that is the reality of most project work.

An IT consultancy practice was invited by London Underground to help them in developing an information systems strategy. The project was defined as lasting five months, and was carried out by a project team of external consultants and internal IT specialists.

The problem from the client's perspective was the present fragmentation of the IT system, which had simply grown in response to demand. This meant, for example, that rather than there being one time attendance system there were several, each having developed from particular conditions operating in one part of the business at a particular time.

The client's expectation was that the consultants would, after interviewing a number of managers, understand the nature of the business, and so be able to make recommendations as to how IT could be used more effectively. The project leader took a different perspective. His concern was to understand both how the business was, and how it was moving forward. The consultancy team interviews with senior managers paid little attention to current IT systems, a fact which both surprised interviewees and gave them a sense of relief. While most managers can happily talk about their business, they have great difficulty talking about IT. The client assumed IT consultants would want to make information technology the basis of the business, whereas the interviewers wanted to understand where the business was developing, so that they could understand where IT should support it.

The outcome of 50 interviews was captured in the preparation of a business model, which was presented to the client in feedback sessions. These sessions formed stage 1 of the evaluation process. The team was sounding out with the stakeholders whether the task they had been addressing was the one the client expected. At first sight the answer was 'No'. Giving 40 per cent of the assignment time to establishing the business context was not what the client would have expected, but when it was done the value was recognized. For many of the client audience it was the first time that they had understood the interconnections between different parts of the business, and in particular the customer's perspective of business systems. Systems which made sense in terms of an internal focus on the organization's structure often made little sense from the point of service delivery. The project team were able to give the stakeholders a different context for viewing their future business. They provided a bigger picture. Once that context had been presented, the client was able to reframe its expectations of the assignment, and to start asking different questions.

Stage 1 had used the skills of both the visionary and the catalyst in building the picture and selling it to senior managers. The outcome of stage 1 evaluation was agreement by the client in moving forward to an agreed scenario. The need now was to build up a portfolio of possible IT solutions, and to assess the benefits of each against the business model. Now was the time to broaden the team to involve London Underground staff more closely. They could be expected to act as traditionalists in evaluating ideas, and loyalists in their commitment to getting a quality outcome for an organization they were part of. The project team also identified four key groups within London Underground who could help in defining the benefits of suggested IT solutions, and assessing their value to an information system.

The portfolio of ideas that emerged dealt with everything from the need for document imaging in order to facilitate the planned move to Canary Wharf, to geographic information systems to ensure staff knew where all drainage equipment in the system was located. Having defined the list, the team met the four key groups to ask for their feedback on the priority that had been given to each of these ideas by the project team. Key users were encouraged to challenge the ratings, in order that the team could show how the ratings had been reached. This process could be seen as an extension of stage 1, but with a new aim of building client ownership of the solution. By the end of the workshops, few of the priority ratings had been changed, and the users were fully committed to the outcome.

It was at this stage, after the writing of the strategy document, which laid out the priorities against the needs of the developing business, that the project ended. While further work is hoped for, financial constraints have so far delayed progression of the strategy. So how can we judge the project's success in terms of the model of evaluation we outlined earlier?

Stages 1 and 2   This was clearly addressed, and the value of using visionary, catalyst, traditionalist, and loyalist roles was proved in the level of support that the strategy gained from the client.

Stage 3   The project leader, whilst he facilitated the vision stage, was at his personal best in a more directive traditionalist project management role. He ensured that the time frame was clear from the start, the staging posts were laid out, and no excuse for missing a deadline was acceptable. When the workings of a large bureaucracy clashed with the time demands of the assignment, he made greater use of external consultants. He did this because as outsiders and non-company loyalists, they could far more easily make unreasonable demands on senior managers' time.

Stage 4   A decision was made at the outset as to how the time should be allocated, and that a seemingly disproportionate amount should be given to business context setting. This allocation, based on previous consultancy experience, was not revised during the course of the assignment.

Stage 5   There was little open discussion within the team of whether each of them was doing what they were best at, but this was an aspect that was consciously monitored by the project leader. He was able to recognize when additional team resourcing was needed.

Stage 6 Again, discussion of whether they were playing the right roles was not explicit, although the balance of external consultants with their known preference for visionary and catalyst roles, and company managers with their known preference for traditionalist and loyalist roles, made for a useful combination. There was no question of shifting leadership responsibilities, and the project leader remained in charge throughout, although in formal status terms there was no difference between the consultants. Having been assigned the leadership role, he defined it as making sure team members knew where they were against their own and the project's schedules, and giving credit to work well done. He saw himself as both encouraging the opening up of ideas, and knowing when ideas had to be closed down in order to keep moving.

Stage 7 The question of whether individuals were playing their role well was only implicitly assessed, in that all deadlines, however unreasonable they seemed, were met. It was the project leader, rather than the team as a whole, who assessed whether the roles were being well played, and if the skills balance needed to change.

Stage 8 In evaluating projects, three commonly used consultancy criteria are time, cost, and quality. On all three criteria, the assignment was judged a success. The project was completed to time, to budget, and to the stated satisfaction of the client. For many assignments this is the end of the process, but in this instance the project leader took it a stage further. He called his colleagues together (although not the London Underground team members) to discuss what they did well and what they could have done better as individuals, and as a team. Such an event was unusual since, in a task-focused company culture, to ask the question 'Could we have done things better?' invites the response 'Then why didn't you?'

The evaluation process in this project was no different and in many ways better than that undertaken by many project teams. Elements of all the stages were addressed, but responsibility for much of the evaluation lay with the project leader. If we are genuinely talking of evaluating teamworking, then responsibility for managing all the stages would be recognized as a shared one. In order for this to happen we need to break the time–cost link as the justification for minimal evaluation, and see time investment in learning as a means of adding quality to task outcome.

Summary

- Evaluation is necessary to achieve the task; it is also required for learning.
- The monitoring of progress within the timescale is not enough. It can tell us something's going wrong, but not what.
- Evaluation of each element and relationship in the teamworking model is necessary for diagnostic evaluation.
- In particular, it is important to monitor whether processes are occurring and roles being played satisfactorily.
- Monitoring and evaluating require reflection, which can lead to learning.
- However, the learning which leads to knowing beyond requires evaluation and reflection *by the team together*.

References

Bandura, A. (1986) *Social Foundations of Thought and Action*. Englewood Cliffs, NJ: Prentice-Hall.

Honey, P. and Mumford, A. (1982) *A Manual of Learning Styles*. Maidenhead: Honey.

Kolb, D.A. (1984) *Experiential Learning*. Englewood Cliffs, NJ: Prentice-Hall.

12

Frameworks, Roles, and Organizing

Stereotyped Jobs

Our discussion of diverse people in Part One focused on the different knowledge frameworks which people in different organizational jobs bring to their work. In considering joint practice (Part Two) we have discussed teamworking, largely in terms of the different role preferences people have as individuals, regardless of the nature of their job. However, we also saw that some jobs tended to attract people with one role preference, other jobs those with another: 49 per cent of UK managers, for example, are traditionalists; 43 per cent of systems analysts are visionaries; 34 per cent of consultants are catalysts; and 41 per cent of secretaries are loyalists. This is hardly surprising: people with preferred roles seek jobs which allow them to play those roles. Their subsequent successful development within their job probably leads them to prefer that role still more.

The danger is obvious. Because the most frequent preferred role amongst secretaries, for example, is loyalist, stereotypes develop. We categorize them as loyalists, and place them in the loyalist role whenever teams form and work together. The same goes for general managers and professionals, who are type cast as strategists and boffins, visionaries all. Middle managers, with the traditionalist tag, are put into that role with monotonous regularity, while the operatives can always be relied on to be loyalist supporters, like the secretaries.

Stereotypes like these prevent people from exercising roles other than that with which they are stereotyped. Information workers and operatives aren't expected to be visionaries and have big ideas, or catalysts and manage people processes, or traditionalists and be rational. No, they are expected to be good loyalist helpers, there to support the others. This is despite the fact that the second most frequently preferred role for information workers is catalyst. Some 29 per cent of information workers are catalysts by preference, a pretty scarce resource one would have thought, given that only 10 per cent of UK managers are catalysts. Yet secretaries' catalyst lights are likely to be hidden under their loyalist bushels.

The same goes for all the other stereotypes. Much current management theory suggests middle managers should be helping their subordinates and supporting them, rather than controlling and directing them. Yet their favoured role is traditionalist, which tends towards the latter sort of behaviour. If they are stereotyped as traditionalists and always expected to act in a traditional way, the chances of them engaging in roles which few of them prefer are slim indeed.

For a final example, look at the boffin stereotype, the professionals with their heads continuously up there amongst the visionary clouds. Yes, their single biggest role preference is NT (visionary). But consider the increased requirement for the catalyst role in today's multi-disciplinary project teams: facilitating co-operation between people from different backgrounds.

So stereotyping results in roles being allocated by job and not by suitability. To force the point home, consider a team of which you are currently a part:

- Who arranges meetings?
- Who takes notes?
- Who sums up?
- Who passes judgements?
- Who sees new possibilities?
- Who deals with clients?
- Who manages controversies?
- Who monitors markets?
- Who encourages everyone?
- Who checks things are done?

Information Loss

One consequence of stereotyping is therefore that many people who prefer and are good at certain roles don't get the chance to play them because they are 'in the wrong job'. This is both sad for them, and also a waste of potential. But there is another equally dangerous consequence. It is that the actual knowledge that people get from their jobs isn't used either. We are not only missing out on role-playing skills; we are missing out on all sorts of useful and important information.

Consider again our information workers. In Chapter 5, we saw that secretaries frequently played roles other than loyalist in the course of their daily work. They often managed events or projects;

Table 12.1 *Non-stereotyped roles for job holders*

Job role	Knowledge	Knowledge role	Stereotype role
Information worker	Organization climate and politics	Catalyst	Loyalist
Operative	Manufacturing or business process	Traditionalist or Visionary	Loyalist
Experienced manager	Organizational memory	Catalyst	Traditionalist
Professional	Professional network	Catalyst	Visionary
General manager	Evaluating outcomes of actions	Traditionalist	Visionary

found things out about sensitive organizational issues; established relationships with clients, customers, allies, and suppliers; negotiated with colleagues to get things done; established and maintained office systems; and made sense of the data that comes from those systems. Indeed, we concluded Chapter 5 by pointing to a part of secretaries' loyalist role itself which was potentially hugely informative: all those salespeople whom the boss never hears about because she protects him from them.

There is, then, knowledge to which information workers have sole or main access. It is knowledge which could be crucial to a team's success. It might contribute vitally to any one of the four processes underpinning teamworking. Take just one example: the process of managing the boundaries (Chapter 10), perhaps the most crucial process of all. The team needs to relate to other teams and clients inside the organization, and probably to external clients as well. Information workers have precious and unique information about current organizational climate and politics. Yet will that information be used? Unlikely: it's usually managers who manage the boundaries, in their visionary or catalyst roles. It's only if information workers can emerge from their stereotype role of loyalist that their knowledge will be used. Otherwise, things will carry on as usual: 'It's only managers who understand the politics, isn't it? After all, that's how they've got to where they are!'

Table 12.1 gives some more examples. For each type of job, we give an example of an area of knowledge to which the job holders have more or less privileged access. There is a role associated with the exercise of that particular area of knowledge; in every example in the table, this role is different from the stereotyped role of that job. So for example, in the case of the operative, knowledge about the manufacturing or business process may be used in a traditionalist role to evaluate how effective that process is; or in a visionary role to imagine better ways of doing things. Both these roles are not the stereotyped roles of the operative-loyalist.

Prizes will not be awarded for spotting the close link between the power and prestige of jobs and the power and prestige of the roles with which each job is stereotyped. Those with position power, managers and professionals, get the leading roles; those with little position power, secretaries and operatives, get the support role. So it is not merely the existence of stereotypes which puts a brake on diversity. It is also the power which individuals bring with them based on their position in the organization. The challenge, therefore, is to learn how to undertake and allocate roles and tasks according to skills and knowledge, rather than according to prestige and power. How can we learn this hard, hard lesson?

It is the organizational context as a whole which will permit such learning. Only if the fundamental design principle of the organization is that of learning will every employee have the context in which to exercise his or her skills and knowledge. And only when people exercise their skills and knowledge together will they learn from their individual contributions and from each other.

Acting Knowledgeably

If we truly believe that knowledge is the real asset, then we will have to completely revise our ideas about organizing. This will be no easy task, for our current models will be hard to give up. In a period of continuous change, it is very comforting to hang on to something with a nice, tangible feel to it. Strategic business units, or market niches, or families of products and services, or divisions of the corporation give us reassurance. They make us feel there's something there, something tangible, something to fall back on.

Knowledge, on the other hand, is terribly abstract. We can't lay our hands on it, we don't know how to produce it, and we're baffled when we seek to translate it into practice. In what deserves to be one of the most influential articles of the decade, Prahalad and Hamel (1990) indicate the importance of knowledge to the survival and success of organizations. They propose that each currently successful major organization has a few core competences. These are elements of know-how which give it competitive advantage, and which are very hard to imitate. Sony's capacity for miniaturizing electronic goods is an example of one such core competence.

Prahalad and Hamel go on boldly to argue that organizations should organize on the basis of their core competences. Since knowledge, rather than products or markets, is the basis for their competitive advantage, then it should also be the basis for their structure, process, and function too. Organizations should develop around each of the core competences; they are the roots and trunk of the tree of which specific products are but the leaves and fruit on the branches.

The recognition that knowledge is the key asset to organizations, and that the way they organize should be based upon that knowledge, is a huge step forward in our thinking. We argue, however, that it is not far enough, for the following reasons:

- Knowledge is not just about knowing how; it's also about knowing beyond. How, we may ask, do new core competences emerge?
- Talking about knowledge as if it were a thing, a substance, a competence, has some unfortunate consequences for the way we think.

Let us consider this second point first. When we use 'knowledge' as a noun, we imply that it's an abstract something, locked away inside people's brains or in books or systems. When we use it as a verb or as an adverb, on the other hand, we are recognizing that it is expressed in action and derived from it. Knowledge isn't a substance, but a process; and the processes of knowing how and knowing beyond necessarily involve acting knowledgeably.

Let's put some flesh on this highly abstract argument. Consider some of the knowledge people we looked at in earlier chapters. All of them were seen to be acting knowledgeably:

- General managers often take action in order to decide whether their analysis of the situation is correct (Chapter 2).
- Professionals are continuously trying out their solutions on colleagues or clients.
- Operatives can operate on the data from their control systems so as to act more knowledgeably in the future.

All of our knowledge people, then, were involved in learning through action. They were concerned not so much with the *content* of knowledge as with the *process* of acting more knowledgeably. It is this *process* of learning how to act more knowledgeably that our model of organizing is about. We believe it to be entirely mistaken for us to recommend particular modes of organizing. It may be appropriate to pay especial attention to markets, products, or business units for a particular organization at a particular juncture. What we are arguing is that these are surface manifestations of the process of organizing. What matters is that they all encourage and enhance the knowledge process. For it is the continuous process of learning to act more knowledgeably which will enable organizations to survive and prosper.

Organizing, not Organization

Our emphasis is on organizing as a social *process* – the process of adapting to change and creating change through our actions. Again, the benefits of thinking in terms of verbs rather than nouns are clear. If we talk of 'the organization' having to adapt and catch up with the pace of change, we are implying continuous painful transformations, and the distant dream of a blue beyond where at last the organization is 'itself' again. However, when we talk of organizing rather than of organization, we are construing ourselves as part of that process of change. Change is not then outside 'the organization', to which 'it' has to adapt or perish. Organizing is process, and process is change, and it is we ourselves who are changing.

This new way of thinking is going to be very difficult, though. After all, our use of language forces us all the time to think of 'the organization' as an entity, an actor who does things to us. We ourselves have used the word in this way throughout the first six chapters. Ask yourself: when do I use the phrases 'the organization', 'the company', or 'the business'? What am I talking about when I do so? Why am I talking like this?

Here are some possibilities. We usually use such phrases as the subjects of sentences: the organization did this, that or the other, or the organization feels this way or that way. For example:

- The organization has decided to go into a new market.
- The organization has formulated a vision and a mission statement.
- The organization values profitability above all else.
- The organization is introducing yet more bureaucracy.
- The organization isn't sticking to its agreement with me.

Or even:

- The organization is busy getting into bed with one of its customers.

Strictly speaking, only people do these things. When we create a person out of an organization, we may be meeting one or several of the following needs:

◆ The need to attribute blame or responsibility for something we don't like. However, we aren't prepared to be specific about exactly who is responsible. We may not know, or we may not be willing to find out and do something about it.
◆ The need to belong to something much larger than ourselves, with which we can identify.
◆ The need to pretend that what we want to happen is what everyone else wants to happen too. We can then impose it on them more easily, provided that they swallow our definition.
◆ The need to understand and make sense of what we do at work, to impose meaning on complexity.

The consequences of thinking about the organization as an actor are profound. We often contrast 'the organization' with 'the employee' or 'the individual'. Many of us have enjoyed talking about the spoken or unspoken contract between these two 'parties' (Herriot, 1992). Yet both are figures of speech. Neither individuals nor organizations really do things. It is people in relationships with each other who do things (Hosking and Morley, 1991). It is not organizations which change. It is people who change their working relations with each other.

We are arguing, therefore, for a model of organizing which expresses the *process* of learning, the process of acting more and more knowledgeably within the business environment. To this extent, we are in sympathy with the idea of 'the learning organization'. However, rather than think of organizations encouraging learning by their members, we want to identify organizing with learning. Organizing means, in our book, people collaborating in learning to act more and more knowledgeably. *Organizing is the repeated occurrence of the knowledge process.*

Our other hesitation about Prahalad and Hamel's (1990) idea of core competences related to the problem of where new core competences are going to come from. The basic element of their idea of competences is knowing how: how, for example, to miniaturize electronic goods. It's only by making knowing beyond the core of organizing that new competences can develop, new products and services be erected. For knowing beyond enables us to imagine desired activities and outcomes into which we can then put effort and creativity. Knowing beyond is the central feature of our model of the knowledge process as the basis for organizing.

A Model of the Knowledge Process

Our organizational model is not, therefore, going to be a model of structure. Functions, markets, products, strategic business units, lines of reporting are nowhere to be found. Our model is not of organization but rather of organizing; not of structure but of process. It is a model of a highly abstract nature which outlines a process of learning together through action and reflection. We will build up the model piece by piece, examining each of its relationships in turn.

Relationship 1

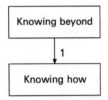

Relationship 1 assumes that the central element of the knowledge process is knowing beyond. With knowing beyond as the driver, we will be wanting to realize the vision we derive from it. Yet to do so, we need to work out what know-how we'll need to get us there. So often, our skill and knowledge resource is based solely on what we've got already. Sometimes, we think ahead over a short period, and realize that we need new skills to undertake a planned project. Seldom do we take a really strategic view and ask: what know-how do we need to be able to achieve our vision? Yet according to Prahalad and Hamel (1990), the development of such core competences of the corporation is the basis for the success of international organizations.

Relationships 2 and 3

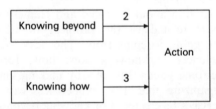

Relationships 2 and 3 imply that both knowing beyond and knowing how guide and inform action. Knowing beyond does so by envisaging possible longer-term activities and the conditions in which they might be undertaken; actions anticipating and leading up to these activities are implied as a result. Knowing how is equally necessary, though, since many of these intermediate actions require skills which have been acquired in the past. Every possible future has to be built from the present.

For example, the Prudential Assurance Company's directors envisaged their deregulated future as a market prospector. Their immediate acquisition of a large number of estate agencies, however, was not built on existing know-how. Only the courage of an individual rescued them from the worst consequences of trying to know beyond without knowing how.

Again, a software company has launched a smart card for shoppers. Shoppers are expected to see a single sample of a product displayed on a shelf. They will then swipe their card if they want that item, and the product will be added to their order. All items chosen will then appear packed at check-out. The software house has known beyond; it has envisioned an entirely new mode of shopping. However, those with retailing know-how argue that people want to see, touch, feel, and smell before they want to buy. Perhaps in this case knowing beyond wasn't supported by knowing how.

Relationships 4 and 5

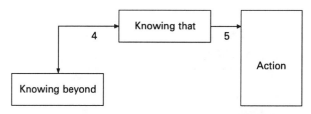

Relationships 4 and 5 are more controversial. We can find out all sorts of things about our present situation. Knowing that is not a matter of passively receiving data; it involves actively searching it out. The question then arises: on what basis do we search it out? What information do we look for? Typically we look for information about the consequences of our past actions. For example, a business school or management centre will ask clients how satisfied they are with the training and development which has been provided. The benefits of such feedback are seen in terms of doing better what is done already – improving the senior management programme, for example. Yet the training and development needs of client organizations are changing so rapidly that this may well not be the sort of information that's most required. Instead, knowing that should be informed by knowing beyond. The business school should be speaking to potential rather than existing clients. It should be asking them how they would respond to new services which they might not have previously considered, but which the business school itself had envisioned as a future possibility (Hamel and Prahalad, 1991). The present may be examined from the perspective of knowing beyond more fruitfully than from the perspective of knowing how.

Note that arrow 4 is two way. Suppose we find something out about our present situation in the light of what we would like to be doing in the longer term. Suppose, for example, that using the example on p. 6 we analysed the recent recessionary situation in the light of where we would like to be. We might then be looking at those organizations in our sector which might buy our non-core businesses, or those which offer complementary knowledge and skills to help us penetrate new markets. Suppose our searches revealed no such organizations existed. In that case we would have to know beyond in a different way, since our original vision would no longer by feasible in the light of the evidence. Vision isn't static, etched in stone when the board came down from the mountain. It's developing and changing in the course of the knowledge process.

Relationships 6 and 7

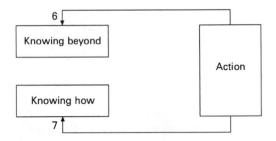

Relationships 6 and 7 represent the standard feedback loops which occur in any model which relates thinking and action. Without reference to the consequences of action, knowing beyond becomes mere utopian idealism. We stick to our vision of nirvana despite all evidence that it is unattainable. Yet if the intermediate actions implied by our vision fail to achieve their anticipated outcomes, we should be thinking beyond again. Of course, the gap between our vision and where we are now is the dynamic tension that motivates us. It will be dangerous to modify our vision too easily, but if we continuously fail to make any progress towards it, we have to think again. Perhaps we're trying to reach it the wrong way, or perhaps it isn't attainable as it stands.

Likewise, if we carry on applying the same old know-how skills to new situations without noticing that we're failing, the knowledge process grinds to a halt. For example, British Airways and British Rail continued for some time to concentrate solely upon their excellent skills of running planes and trains. They assumed that it was sufficient for the passengers to finish their journey on time and safe. They failed to realize that passengers' expectations had changed. People wanted now to get there in comfort and have various services provided. Many would argue that British Rail have not yet got the skill mix right, while it took BA near financial disaster, a new CEO, and a customer-first programme to turn things round. These organizations took a longer time to acquire customer service skills because they failed to notice new expectations, and they failed to pay attention to the evidence that the old skills weren't enough.

Or to move from the prosaic to the exotic, consider women's fashion. Such designers as Christian Lacroix are extremely skilled at dressing anorexic socialites so that lots of people look at them. They have been exercising these designer skills for some long time, and now they know precisely how to turn heads. Yet a major requirement of *haute couture* is that it is capable of being adapted and sold in mass outlets subsequently. This the puff-ball skirt signally failed to do. The designer had failed to adapt his skills to new market requirements.

What's implied is more than simple learning, however. We are not only set on doing something differently or better. We are also concerned with how we think about our actions and their consequences. What can we learn about our learning (Argyris and Schon, 1978)? For example, do we see ourselves and others as succeeding or failing as individuals; as learning together; or as affecting a wide range of other people by our actions? Do we reflect on *how* we are doing things as well as on *what* we are doing?

Relationships 8 and 9

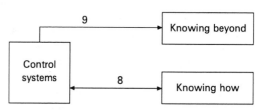

Relationships 8 and 9 refer to the systematizing of know-how into means of controlling processes, regulating finance, integrating the product cycle, maintaining stocks, and so on. Much of what were the tacit and unexpressed skills of people has been transformed into explicit computer programs.

This explication is a continuous process. It started with F.W. Taylor, and there's no reason to suppose it won't continue in the future. In one sense it is a way of making the know-how of a few available to others. Arrow 8 is bidirectional, suggesting that know-how in turn can be increased as a consequence of paying attention to the recorded output of the control systems. Arrow 9 indicates that we may change our view of what's possible as a result of such information.

Relationships 10 and 11

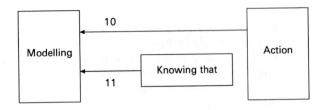

Relationships 10 and 11 make the point that computer or conceptual models depend on the knowledge process. Our ongoing actions lead us to consider the possibility of adding new parameters to our models as well as adjusting the ranges of the old ones to accord with experience (arrow 10). And our continuous analysis of our present situation forces us to take current environmental as well as organizational information into account (arrow 11).

Many marketers, for example, have failed to add additional customer parameters to their statistical models. There is a new customer – the businesswoman who travels and who has a high disposable income. Or consider credit rating systems. Many models of credit-worthiness assume that people who live at the same address share financial liabilities. Yet mere flatmates do not; nor do many who are partners yet who nevertheless keep their financial affairs entirely separate. Projections of future financial service products may be in error if such social trends are not incorporated. Certainly, potential customers will be alienated.

Relationship 12

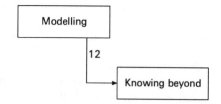

Finally, with relationship 12, we are making the point that modelling impacts upon our knowing beyond. Specifically, by playing with the modelling facility we can create new possibilities which we would not have thought of unaided. Modelling can generate new visions. For example, when the required knowledge competences were added to the financial parameters of a business game, the outcome indicated the need for training.

Modelling has a complementary function, however. It can bring our visions down to earth with a bump. By attempting to quantify the outcomes of an envisioned activity, a model can demonstrate knock-on consequences and implications which we might not have considered. For example, we may come to realize that an apparently successfully marketed product won't succeed because it's under-capitalized.

All of these relationships are brought together in the model, shown in Figure 12.1. This model represents a continuous process, in which knowledge informs action and is informed by action's consequences.

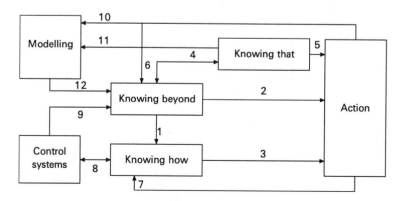

Figure 12.1 *The knowledge process*

Summary

- Types of job are often stereotyped with particular roles, e.g. secretaries as loyalists.
- Such stereotypes prevent skills and knowledge being exercised.
- The only way to overcome such problems is by designing organizational contexts to aid learning.
- Knowledge is expressed in action and derived from it. It is a continuous process, not a static product.
- Organization, too, is better understood as a process rather than a product.
- Any model of the organizing process should be based upon the way in which knowledge informs and is informed by action.
- Knowing that is a necessary component of the model, since it is the activity whereby information relevant to achieving our vision is acquired.
- However, knowing beyond and action are the core components of the knowledge process model.
- Organization is seen as the repeated occurrence of the knowledge process.

References

Argyris, C. and Schon, D.A. (1978) *Organizational Learning*. Reading, MA: Addison-Wesley.

Hamel, G. and Prahalad, C.K. (1991) 'Corporate imagination and expeditionary marketing', *Harvard Business Review*, 91(4): 81–92.

Herriot, P. (1992) *The Career Management Challenge*. London: Sage.

Hosking, D.M. and Morley, I.E. (1991) *A Social Psychology of Organizing*. Hemel Hempstead: Harvester Wheatsheaf.

Prahalad, C.K. and Hamel, G. (1990) 'The core competence of the corporation', *Harvard Business Review*, 90(3): 79–91.

13

Innovating and Learning

We don't apologize for the abstract nature of our model for organizing. The whole point is that any model for organizing has to be abstract, because it has to allow for a wide variety of concrete expressions. Organizations may structure themselves in a wide variety of ways. They may differ profoundly in the number of markets they address, or in the allies or enemies they make. They may have product functional, market, or project structures, or a mixture of these. However, if they are engaging in the learning process they are similar to each other in the most important dimension of all.

Instead, therefore, of peddling specific solutions, we will attempt to show how some organizations have succeeded in innovating and learning. While this hopefully puts some flesh on to our bony model, it does not imply that their particular methods are appropriate elsewhere. Rather, what their examples demonstrate is that knowing beyond is at the core of the learning process; and that reflection upon the outcomes of actions is a necessary condition for learning to occur. First, let's consider how people organize to innovate.

The business management mythology is full of entrepreneurial heroes and heroines – business geniuses who, single-handed, had a brilliant idea and carried it through to completion. They weren't merely creative geniuses; they were tough as old teak with it. Tireless, committed, inspirational, they persuaded others to buy into their project. Overcoming bureaucratic obstruction and market resistance, they became legends in their own time. Steve Jobs, Anita Roddick, Ross Perot – the roll of honour is trumpeted from the popular management texts.

A different sort of myth comes by way of counterblast from the big corporations. Pointing to the subsequent downfall of many of the entrepreneurs, they argue the solid achievements of their R&D professionals. IT&T and IBM, Unilever and ICI, GEC and BT, SmithKline Beecham and Glaxo, can all boast a long series of technical innovations which have originated in their laboratories and emerged as successful new products. Here the hero is more abstract: science and technology marching ever onwards and upwards, rather than the awkward individualists bucking the system and winning out.

We all need myths; they help us put meaning on to our experience. If we need the hero archetype to bolster our flagging faith in the importance of the individual, so be it. Or if we want to believe we are making steady and rational progress towards a better world, then there are probably some worse places to look than to science and technology. But myths are self-serving: they meet our need for optimism more than that for understanding. If we really want to understand innovation, we have to take a far more complex reality on board.

First, though, we need to check out the very idea of innovation. Analysts have distinguished two forms: technical innovations and administrative innovations. The former 'occur in the technical systems of an organization, and are directly related to the primary work activity of the organization. A technical innovation can be the implementation of an idea for a new product or a new service, or the introduction of new elements in an organization's production or service operations' (Damanpour, 1987). Administrative innovations, on the other hand, are concerned with new relationships between people at work. They involve 'those rules, roles, procedures, and structures that are related to the communication and exchange between people and between the environment and people' (Damanpour and Evan, 1984). The distinction is between doing new things and doing them together in new ways. We'll start by looking at technical innovations, but we will conclude that administrative ones may actually be more important in the long run.

Critical Success Factors

So what makes for a successful innovation? We need to unpack the mythology and get down to the realities. Thorough research based on many hundreds of organizations from all sectors and many countries of the world has given us some clear answers. In order to discover what makes for successful innovation projects, we have to compare them with unsuccessful ones; this analysis was first carried out in the UK in the 1960s (Rothwell, 1972), and resulted in the following five major predictive features. The 43 successful projects in the study demonstrated:

- a full understanding of customers' or clients' needs
- careful attention to marketing and publicity
- efficient development of the original idea

Table 13.1 *Critical success factors for innovative projects*

Product or service advantage
- offered unique selling points
- was of higher quality than others
- reduced customers' costs
- was innovative in concept and design
- was perceived to be superior to the competition
- solved a problem that the customers felt they had

Proficiency of pre-development activities
- initial screening of the idea
- preliminary assessment of the market
- preliminary technical assessment of the idea
- detailed market research
- a business analysis

Protocol definition
- of the target market
- of customers' needs, wants, and preferences
- of the product concept itself – its benefits and positioning in the market

---

Source: Cooper and Kleinschmidt (1987)

- effective use of technology and technical advice from outside the organization
- senior and authoritative managers responsible for the project.

A thorough review of the subsequent research literature (Cooper and Kleinschmidt, 1987) came up with three critical success factors. These were: product advantage, proficiency of pre-development activities, and protocol. Table 13.1 indicates what each of these factors refers to. And all of these three critical success factors have to be properly assessed *before* charging ahead with product or service development. No wonder eager entrepreneurs get impatient with the system! Yet if most of these features are not present in a project, it will probably fail; and they are all features which people can do something about.

Here is an example of a project which failed because one or another of these factors was ignored: Clive Sinclair's C5 electric car. The C5 certainly offered unique selling points, reduced customers' costs, and was innovative in concept and design. It had certain very strong product advantages. However, the market research was inadequate or non-existent. Sinclair believed that people wanted something like the C5 but hadn't been able to afford it until he invented an electric trike which they could afford. He certainly succeeded with the pricing, but only 8000 were sold in the first three months. People didn't want them; or, as Sinclair preferred to explain the débâcle, they were 'resistant to change'. The contrast with Japanese organizations is painful; there, the sales department and customers themselves are frequent sources of ideas (Kono, 1988).

Kodak were so concerned that good ideas should not be lost that they established an 'office of innovation' (Rosenfeld and Servo, 1990). This proceeded as follows:

- ◆ X has an idea.
- ◆ X takes it along to Y, a facilitator.
- ◆ Y questions X about the idea, and they explore it and its implications for the organization.
- ◆ If X wishes to continue, he/she describes his/her idea and its benefits on two pages.
- ◆ X and Y choose a group of colleagues who each comment in writing in terms of the idea's novelty, marketability, feasibility, improvability, etc.
- ◆ X may remain anonymous.
- ◆ X and Y meet to review colleagues' feedback and help X decide whether or not to proceed.
- ◆ If the decision is to proceed, then X seeks more advice and help from colleagues. X may engage in some preliminary market research or experimentation at this stage.
- ◆ If this proceeds well, X seeks a powerful sponsor and some resources. Until now, everything has been done on the side. From now on, extremely selective and hard-nosed criteria will be applied, since proper resources are being committed.

The Kodak process moves from the nurturing of the seedling through to the ruthless weeding out of all but the strongest saplings. Of course, for all the ideas which are passed through such a formal process, many others survive and develop or fall by the wayside more haphazardly. The point is that there are all sorts of bad reasons why ideas which would have become sturdy saplings and stood up to the sternest winds of criticism died as seedlings. These reasons include:

- ◆ The ideas were not expressed because their originator thought no one would listen.
- ◆ They *were* expressed, and no one *did* listen.
- ◆ They were expressed and were immediately evaluated rather than explored.
- ◆ The evaluation was not made on the basis of the critical success criteria.

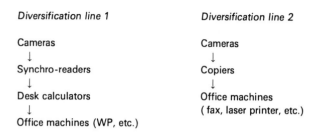

Figure 13.1 *Dynamic synergy at Canon*

If a formal process can help initial survival, there are many more ideas left to select from when the time does come for rigorous assessment.

There is another success factor, however, which is much broader than the consideration of individual projects. It is how projects fit together – their *synergy*. If we take the knowledge process seriously, then we will engage in projects which derive from the knowledge we have in common. If we know beyond towards an envisioned future, we will be developing only the particular know-how we need to get us there. What's more, we will be knowing that as well – acquiring information about markets and technology which helps us towards our future aim. Our knowledge will not be haphazardly gained, therefore. Rather, it will be structured; it will build upon itself.

If we look at some of the outstanding Japanese companies, we can see how they have built upon one core competence to develop others. Take Canon, for example. In line 1 in Figure 13.1, one technology built on another to produce the product sequence. The knowledge/technology line was:

Precise metal fabrication technology
↓
Electronics technology
↓
LSI technology

Or, to take a non-manufacturing example, Marks and Spencer used their core retailing competence to market and sell credit facilities and other financial services. Customers buy their credit to buy their products! Of course, neither Canon nor Marks and Spencer had the later stages of their development in mind when they entered upon the earlier ones. The point is, however, that they went into projects which built upon existing knowledge.

So innovation is usually based on existing knowledge. How is

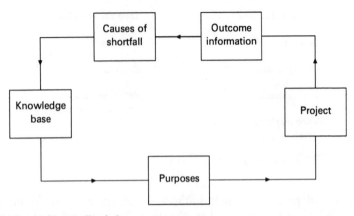

Figure 13.2   *Feedback loop*

that knowledge acquired? How do people organize themselves to learn?

Purposes and Outcomes

As we argued in Chapter 11, evaluating process and outcomes is a powerful way to learn. We have, therefore (Figure 13.2):

♦ To discover what our purposes are for our projects
♦ To obtain the information which enables us to evaluate how far we succeeded
♦ To infer the causes of the gap between fully realizing our purposes and what we actually achieved
♦ To incorporate this information into our knowledge so we stand more chance of achieving our purposes with our next project.

In the knowledge process there are three sorts of purpose for every project which we undertake. They are:

♦ How can we better satisfy (or indeed, delight) our customers with this product or service?
♦ How may we move closer towards achieving our envisioned future?
♦ How can we improve and develop the knowledge process itself?

For some, these three purposes may not all be distinct. In some organizations, for example, the vision *is* to delight the customer. In others, it is simply to continue learning and developing the knowledge process – to learn, change, and survive.

The point is, though, that the criteria for deciding to go ahead with a project will always include customer satisfaction, coherence with vision, and knowledge enhancement. It is informative to examine the way in which strategy is formulated at Rank Xerox:

1 The economic, political, technical, and commercial aspects of the environment are scanned. In terms of the knowledge process, knowing that is attempted.
2 Their vision is reiterated, as are prominent values, previous strategic priorities, and the quality principles of TQM. Knowing beyond is reinforced.
3 A strengths, weaknesses, opportunities, threats (SWOT) analysis is carried out: more knowing that is required.
4 A market map, with scenario models for alternative strategies, is drawn up.
5 A situation analysis reveals the desired outcome, the current situation, the distance from here to there, and the barriers likely to be in the way.
6 A vital few projects are chosen as the way to progress and achieve these strategic objectives.

Inherent in this strategy process are the three key purposes for any project in the knowing process: the 'vital few' projects are intended to delight the customer, move towards the company's vision of beating the competition world-wide, and improve systems and processes. This is clear from four criteria by which Rank Xerox evaluate the success of any project (in the following order of importance):

◆ customer satisfaction
◆ employee satisfaction
◆ market share
◆ return on assets.

Rank Xerox would not be searching out information on customer satisfaction if their purpose was not to satisfy customers. They would not be canvassing employees' satisfaction if they were not wanting to help them work more effectively. They would not be looking at market share and return on assets if they did not want to achieve their vision of becoming the best document company in the world. Their feedback information is thus based upon their fundamental purposes; they want to see how far they are getting towards achieving them. Note that Rank Xerox *never* discover that they have achieved all their purposes; there is always a gap. Therefore, there is always learning to be undertaken. Instead of assuming a steady state as the norm, with deviations as 'problems' to be addressed and solved, Rank Xerox assume that the knowledge process is like a journey, at the end of which they never arrive.

So the content of the feedback loops 6 and 7 in Figure 12.1 is information which is actively sought out to assess whether purposes have been achieved. And 'actively' is the word. Jim Havard, Director of Quality at Rank Xerox (UK), speaks of 'dragging the information out of customers'. Not satisfied with questionnaires alone, he encourages colleagues to phone and visit to ensure that customers' expectations are being met. Wisely, he includes customers in the design process so that their expectations have been anticipated and can be managed and met more effectively. Perhaps most important of all, he checks time and again that the performance indicators are not those which suit Rank Xerox but those which concern the customer. It is of little use to discover that customers are highly satisfied with the frequency of visits when this matters little to them compared with length of downtime.

Further, Havard finds that it pays to spend some time working out who the customers really are. Are they the machine's users, or the office manager who pays the bill? If both are considered customers, then it's quite likely that different things will matter more to each of them. Among the other forms of customer satisfaction data obtained by Rank Xerox are questionnaires about the quality of the relationship with the service engineer, and about how the company is regarded relative to its competitors (Main, 1992). This 'benchmarking' is carried out for different aspects of their products and services, so that they may compare themselves with the best in each aspect.

This extended case study has demonstrated the trouble to which a world-class organization goes in order to obtain feedback. It also demonstrates that there are organizations for whom the knowledge process is a reality.

Feedback Problems

Yet for every organization which demonstrates the knowledge process in action, there are hundreds for whom it breaks down. And the most common point of breakdown is in feedback; few indeed concentrate on obtaining information on the outcomes of their actions, understanding it, and acting upon it. It's worth summarizing once more the enormity of the learning task; then it's easier to understand why so many fail. We have to:

- have explicit purposes
- choose our projects in accordance with these

- build modes of evaluation into their design
- acquire valid information about outcomes
- acquire it before, during, and after the project
- infer causality, that is why the project had these outcomes
- draw out the implications for subsequent projects.

There are all sorts of reasons why we might find such a demanding activity difficult. We have no difficulty in dredging up perfectly valid excuses, especially recently when survival is the sole priority for many. In *recession*, short-term outcomes such as year end profit are paramount. Consequently projects are geared towards achieving these objectives, rather than moving towards a longer-term vision. Unfortunately, short-term outcomes may actually militate against longer-term ones (Senge, 1990). Cutting training and development costs or graduate recruitment, for example, may result in longer-term undermining of the knowledge base. Another victim of the recession has often been the obtaining of outcome information itself. To start with, obtaining information is costly in time and money. Moreover, if the sole feedback is the state of the bottom line, people are in effect turning in upon themselves. They are failing to look outside and discover what their customers think and feel. Yet it is upon these thoughts and feelings and the actions that flow from them that the bottom line ultimately depends.

A second problem with the idealized picture of the knowledge process is its *rationality*. In reality, we engage in projects for all sorts of reasons, or indeed for none at all (Daft and Weick, 1984). Consider a project in which you are currently engaged. Why are you doing it?

- You don't know?
- Because it furthers your own or another group's interests?
- Because it naturally followed on from the previous project?
- Because you had to spend some money fast before the end of the financial year?
- Because a consultant sold it to you?
- Because it made use of your existing skills and resources?

In sum, the reasons why a project has been undertaken are many and varied: political, inertia, reactive. As a consequence, objectives are likely to be *post hoc* rationalizations. They are justifications produced during and after the event in self-defence (March, 1981).

Given that projects often go wrong, there is frequently a self-defensive screen erected by those involved. Such defensive motives often distort any information and learning that might come out of the failure. It is extremely difficult to evaluate negatively the outcomes of a project for which one was responsible. Through self-interest one is apt to:

+ justify one's championship of the project
+ interpret outcomes favourably and selectively
+ attribute unfavourable outcomes to others' shortcomings
+ claim unintended but favourable outcomes as planned
+ claim unintended and unfavourable outcomes as unforeseeable
+ manage information about outcomes so that only one's own interpretation gains exposure
+ fail to ask the customers whether they are satisfied with the outcomes.

Think back to the last occasion when you sought to evaluate what you had done:

+ On what basis was the project evaluated?
+ Who decided what those criteria were?
+ Who decided which information was sought?
+ Were any unfavourable outcomes revealed?
+ What causes were inferred for these unfavourable outcomes?
+ Was anything learned from them?

Of course, on reflection, we realize that learning from difficulty is likely to be far more beneficial then learning from success (Smith and Morphey, 1993). Success only indicates that what we did worked (though we may not know why). Difficulty demonstrates that we need to change, and often points to the specific area. Here are two markedly different examples of learning from difficulty.

In the first, Amanda was made account manager for a small telecommunications company, with a brief to set up a marketing department. Having only previously worked with a large public sector organization, where she had received very thorough training, but had been given little real responsibility, she was suddenly thrown in at the deep end. She succeeded in her task, because the ethos of the organization allowed for learning through doing and making mistakes. It's OK to make mistakes, as long as you tell us, and don't try to cover up or surprise us later, was a clear message given to her by her boss. She recognized early that her credibility rested on winning over engineers within the company – people who believed products sold themselves, that only they understood them, and that marketing was simply 'glitz'. She listened to their viewpoint, learned how to understand and influence them through getting to know them as individual customers, and recognized which areas were unencroachable, and which could be changed.

She looked to her boss the sales director for support, and he offered it. Not only would he act as coach, he would also give open feedback. This was acceptable because it was put in the context of a company commitment to helping everyone get it right for customers, and helping everyone to learn. It was safe to take risk, responsibility and initiative.

In the second example, Anne worked in personnel in a large nationalized industry. As both a woman and a young person she was visibly different from the male engineers who shaped the environment of the organization. Having only recently come into the job she was unsure when a line manager asked her if he could dismiss an employee whose performance was unsatisfactory. She sought out advice from a more senior colleague at headquarters, and advised the manager that the employee could be dismissed. The issue was taken up by the employee's union, and at a subsequent hearing the decision was reversed.

Anne was left shaken and embarrassed by her mistake, but she was even more surprised by the response of colleagues. No one mentioned the issue to her. The line manager ignored the subject; her own boss explained the error away through dismissing it as an administrative mistake of a clerical worker. In an organization in which it was openly stated that mistakes cannot happen, when they did happen there was no mechanism for learning from the situation. The learning she took was that she was inept, and she left the job shortly after.

As these two examples show, the impact of recession and the victory of self-defence over organizational rationality are two powerful reasons why the feedback element of the knowledge process isn't so easy as it looks. There are two more difficulties to deal with as well. The first is the nature of the *information* we obtain. It's obviously a huge advantage if we can obtain quantified feedback which is hard to distort. This decreases the possibility of those self-serving interpretations which we have just discussed. On the other hand, there are some outcomes which it is very hard to quantify reliably and validly. 'Reliably' implies that the same result or something very near it would be obtained if the measure was taken a second time closely afterwards. 'Validly' implies that the measure actually measures what it claims to measure. For example, a feedback questionnaire at the end of a training course might be an index of relief and anticipation at the prospect of getting back home rather than a measure of satisfaction or learning. We seem easily seduced into believing, first, that numbers mean what they appear to mean; and second, that if it can't be measured, it doesn't exist. We are only too aware that words don't always mean what they appear to mean: why should numbers be any different? And numbers are only one way of looking at things: words and pictures are others. The history of business is replete with senior executives who failed to see the qualitative wood for the quantifiable trees. Recent examples include many of the property developers of the 1980s. So numbers have their problems!

Inferring Causes

In chaos theory (Gleick, 1988) it is recognized that tiny differences in input can quickly become overwhelming differences in output. Putting it poetically, a butterfly stirring the air today in Beijing can transform storm systems next month in New York. The butterfly effect is a nice instance of our final and most crucial difficulty in learning from feedback. This is the difficulty of discovering why or indeed whether the observed outcomes followed from our action projects. This step in the knowledge process is so crucial that we were tempted to put a fourth form of knowledge into steps 6 and 7 of Figure 12.1: 'knowing why'. It is crucial because unless we have some sort of theory about why a project had the results it did, we have no way of adapting our knowledge and acting appropriately. All we can do is trial and error tinkering with what we currently do until outcomes are better. And then we don't know whether the improvement is due to what we've done or to something extraneous.

So a causal theory is essential. Unfortunately, it's not so easy as Rank Xerox made it appear in our case study above. As far as they are concerned, their desired outcome is complete customer satisfaction, if not delight. They design a product and its associated services on the basis of various evidence and assumptions about what makes customers satisfied. They design, produce, install, and service their new machines and deal with any initial difficulties experienced by the customer. Then they assess the extent to which customers are satisfied in terms of each feature of the product or service which they believe contributes to satisfaction. They can then infer what feature(s) specifically contribute most to overall satisfaction, and, ultimately, to customer retention, market share, and return on assets. They can also notice those features with which customers are less than perfectly satisfied, and act accordingly. On the other hand, even Rank Xerox are struggling to establish how much *each* of their few projects contributes to their purposes.

However, it is seldom so straightforward, for a variety of reasons. All of these reasons relate to the nature of organizations as social systems: extremely complex sets of interrelationships in which a spreading of social wings in one subsystem can indeed result in cataclysmic storms elsewhere (Scott, 1987). It's worth listing the possible mistakes that we can make when we try to infer the causes of events:

♦ The outcome is the one we wanted, so we attribute it to what we did rather than to its real cause.

♦ The reasons we attribute it to our own actions are twofold. First, there is a self-serving bias whereby we credit ourselves with the responsibility for good outcomes. Second, there is a universal bias in our thinking (certainly in the West) which leads us to attribute outcomes to ourselves rather than to situational causes (Eiser, 1986). We all thought that our temporary advantages in the late 1980s were because we could do no wrong, whereas they should rather be attributed to aspects of the situation, such as Chancellor Lawson's expansionist policies.

♦ There are all sorts of additional unintended knock-on consequences of our action. We fail to notice them because we only evaluate the extent to which what we intended actually happened. We didn't look around for additional outcomes, perhaps because we didn't even try to anticipate them when we planned our project (Rogers, 1983).

♦ We concentrate too much upon *what* we do as a cause of subsequent outcomes, and too little upon *how* we do it. Process can be much more powerful than content.

Let's put some flesh and bones on these difficulties by looking at the introduction of performance-related pay into a large mature organization in the financial sector. Performance-related pay (PRP) was introduced with two main aims: first, to improve performance by making reward contingent to some extent upon performance; and second, to change the values of the organization so as to increase the emphasis upon personal accountability. On the first annual appraisal after the introduction of PRP, ratings of performance improved considerably overall on the previous year; and in an attitude survey, employees tended to agree with statements to the effect that they valued being held accountable for their own performance.

The installers of PRP inferred that its introduction had succeeded in achieving their objectives: people were working harder and were more accountable. The carrot had succeeded in motivating the donkey. Yet they were possibly making all or nearly all of the mistakes we have listed above. First, the outcome measure may not have been valid. Instead of measuring performance, it may have been measuring bosses' desire to boost their subordinates' salary.

Second, the installers of PRP failed to look for other possible consequences of PRP:

- There was an increase in self-aggrandizement and self-promotion at the expense of teamwork.
- There were feelings of injustice and demotivation in those who obtained little or no PRP.
- The annual appraisal was now devoted to assessment of past performance, to the exclusion of the discussion of development. Employees were disappointed at the loss of this opportunity, which they valued.

These were immediate or short-term consequences. Had the installers of PRP looked at the longer-term consequences, they might have discovered that the introduction of PRP was the initial impetus towards an overall focus of HR systems on performance management. The selection, appraisal, reward, and training systems were all integrated by the use of a common set of competency terms, and the emphasis throughout was on individual performance improvement. Yet the business needs of the organization changed radically over this period. A far greater variety of service products and a continuing emphasis on innovation and time, to market put teamworking and supportive skills at a premium. Yet at precisely this point, the emphasis on individual performance had finally produced a culture in which the most valued achievement was to excel over others rather than to support them. A single new system had played a part in a subsequent dissociation between HR strategy and business needs. Such a dissociation could result in the organization failing to survive; an increase in individual competitiveness had reduced corporate competitiveness. It's worth noting that the action project in this example was an internally oriented process intervention. We noted earlier in this chapter that such 'administrative innovations' were more likely to have profound long-term effects than product or service innovations (Daft, 1982).

Or, take an example of an intervention at the level of the sector rather than of the organization. In order to help the UK textile industry compete against cheaper foreign imports, the UK government of the day subsidized UK fabric production; better-quality cloth was available as a consequence at the same price as Eastern imports. Eastern clothing manufacturers then bought the UK cloth, and produced higher-quality garments for the same price as before. They started selling these products in the UK, undercutting UK clothing manufacturers, who went out of business. Their equipment was sold to Far Eastern manufacturers, who were able to increase volume and quality as a result. As a final irony,

UK textile workers were in much demand in the Far East to train local labour in using the machines!

Perhaps we are seduced into a simple-minded view of causality by our linear, cause–effect action orientation. If we believe that we can act upon a process and change it to accord with a desired outcome, this fits in with current 'can-do' philosophies. Yet simple cause–effect theories of this nature fail to do justice to the complexity of organizational systems. Organizations are extremely complex sets of interrelationships between people and groups of people. The picture is much more of a constantly changing ebb and flow of action and interaction, of information and knowledge. Instead of demonstrating cause–effect relationships, a more frequent activity is making some sort of sense of what is going on. Since what is going on is invariably complex, only a complex picture can do justice to it. Consequently, only a diverse set of viewpoints can help compose such a complex picture. By way of an analogy, throw a stone into a still pool: the ripples will travel all over, and sometimes bounce back from the side, meeting the more recent ripples near the edge. Throw five stones in simultaneously and there will be a multiplicity of ripples, colliding and interacting. Which stone caused which ripple is impossible to ascertain. Add the effects of stones thrown in before these five, and of the wind which has just got up, and the complexity makes it a ridiculous undertaking to even try to guess. Yet most organizations have at least five major projects on the go at any one time; they have engaged in previous projects which are still having effects; and they are blown upon by competitive, economic, and political winds.

So complex then is the nature of organizational change, and so difficult is it to establish cause–effect relationships on the basis of specific outcomes, that a more forward-looking mode of evaluation is appropriate. The emphasis should be more upon knowing beyond than upon knowing how; and more upon the knowledge process than upon meeting specific objectives. This change of emphasis might require us to address the following sorts of question:

1 Are we moving towards our envisioned future?
2 If not, is this because the external situation renders that future unattainable?
3 Is it because the sorts of projects we engage in are not capable of moving us in that direction?
4 Or is it because the knowledge process operates so poorly that we are not capable of learning from our actions?

These are big questions. They can only be addressed from a variety of perspectives. What is clear, though, is that we only learn if together we reflect upon and seek to understand our activity and whether it is taking us towards what we would like to be doing.

Summary

- There are various critical success factors for innovation to succeed in organizations.
- Innovations tend to be derived from existing knowledge within the organization.
- The learning from action projects is based on careful monitoring of the extent to which they have achieved their objectives.
- These objectives are always likely to include favourable customer response, achieving an envisioned future, and improving the knowledge process itself.
- There are major difficulties associated with obtaining accurate feedback of project outcomes. One such is admitting to unfavourable outcomes, that is learning from difficulty.
- More fundamentally, it is extremely hard to establish specific cause and effect relationships in complex organizational systems.
- A more useful approach may be to seek to monitor general progress towards the envisioned future.

References

Cooper, R.G. and Kleinschmidt, E.J. (1987) 'New products: what separates winners from losers?', *Journal of Production Innovation Management*, 4: 169–84.

Daft, R.L. (1982) 'Bureaucratic versus non-bureaucratic structure and the process of innovation and change', in S.B. Bacharach (ed.), *Research and Sociology of Organizations*. Greenwich, CT: JAI Press.

Daft, R.L. and Weick, K.E. (1984) 'Toward a model of organizations as interpretative systems', *Academy of Management Review*, 9: 284–95.

Damanpour, F. (1987) 'The adoption of technological, administrative, and ancillary innovations: impact of organizational factors', *Journal of Management*. 13: 675–88.

Damanpour, F. and Evan, W.M. (1984) 'Organizational innovation and performance: the problem of "organizational lag"', *Administrative Science Quarterly*, 29: 392–409.

Eiser, J.R. (1986) *Social Psychology: Attitude, Cognition, and Social Behaviour.* Cambridge: Cambridge University Press.

Gleick, J. (1988) *Chaos: Making a New Science.* London: Heinemann.

Kono, T. (1988) 'Factors affecting the creativity of organizations – an approach from the analysis of new product development', in K. Urabe, J. Child and T. Kagono (eds), *Innovation and Management: International Comparisons.* Berlin: de Gruyter.

Main, J. (1992) 'How to steal the best ideas around', *Fortune*, 19 October.

March, J.G. (1981) 'Decisions in organizations and theories of choice', in A.H. Van de Ven and W.F. Joyce (eds), *Perspectives on Organization Design and Behaviour*. New York: Wiley.

Rogers, E.M. (1983) *Diffusion of Innovations*. 3rd edn. New York: Free Press.

Rosenfeld, R. and Servo, J.C. (1990) 'Facilitating innovation in large organizations', in M.A. West and J.L. Farr (eds), *Innovation and Creativity at Work*. Chichester: Wiley.

Rothwell, R. (1972) *Project SAPPHO – A Comparative Study of Success and Failure in Industrial Innovation*. Brighton: SPRU.

Scott, W.R. (1987) *Organizations: Rational, Natural, and Open Systems*, 2nd edn. Englewood Cliffs, NJ: Prentice-Hall.

Senge, P.M. (1990) *The Fifth Discipline*. New York: Century.

Smith, B. and Morphey, G. (1993) 'Learning from difficulty', paper presented at AMED research conference, Bromley, Kent.

14

Information Technology and the Knowledge Process

Information Technology is Dynamic and Social

Figure 12.1 could have contained only the first seven connecting arrows, and been much less complex. Five years ago, this simplicity might have been justified; today it cannot be. Information technology is now being used to enhance the knowledge process in three fundamental ways. Two of them, *control/informating* and *modelling*, are included in Figure 12.1. The third, *communication*, is so pervasive throughout the knowledge process that to include it at any one point of the model would have been to underestimate its impact.

The image many have of information technology is in stark contrast. For many, IT isolates people from each other. They see individuals sitting at VDU terminals cocooned in a world of their own, and very cross indeed when someone else interrupts their reverie. The argument of the present chapter seeks to erase this image. We argue not only that IT is a major contributor to the knowledge process in knowledge-based organizations, but also that this contribution is dependent upon people using it together. The *whole* of Figure 12.1 represents a recurring *social* process.

The first function of IT that we will discuss, that of *control*, seems at first sight to contradict both of these assertions. The control process seems neither a process of continuous change, nor a social activity. The archetypal control model is of a steady state, with deviations in output being corrected by the feedback mechanism. The whole point of control is to maintain equilibrium within fixed parameters. Similarly, control technology in its most advanced form removes the need for people entirely, we are led to believe. Labour saving devices pass through a phase when they are labour enslaving, but end up as labour replacing (Carlopio, 1988). So at first glance, control processes using IT are steady state rather than change processes, and they are asocial.

When we think of all the ways in which IT is used at work for control purposes, these impressions are reinforced. Computer-aided design and manufacturing come instantly to mind, but of course control systems are far more widespread than this. Stock control, financial control, salaries, sales, HR procedures and many more are automated. In some sectors, for example retail (Ford, 1990), the relation between systems is automated too, so that the sales/orders/distribution/stock/price/display cycle is integrated. All of these systems are so programmed as to trigger action when certain parameters are exceeded, certain dates reached, etc. Sometimes this corrective action is undertaken by machine, sometimes by individuals; but either way, we feel constrained along predetermined lines.

If we feel that information technology does things to us, however, we are succumbing to an unfortunate determinism. Just like our use of the word 'organization' as a 'thing' outside of us, so with 'technology', 'information', and 'knowledge'; all these words are nouns when they should be verbs. Fortunately, we can speak of organizing, informing, and knowing, thereby making it clear that these are all activities in a social context. But it's hard to think of a verb from technology! Yet, just as information only has meaning and use when someone is informing either themselves or someone else, so it is with technology. Technology is not set apart from people; it is a social product with a social use. The following quotations express the point we are making far more clearly than we can ourselves:

> Human use makes a technology what it is ... the social technology shapes the user, but the user likewise shapes the technology, exerting some degree of control over its use and meaning in social action. (Poole and De Sanctis, 1990)

> It is here in the realm of choice that technology reveals its indeterminacy. Though it redefines the possible, it cannot determine which choices are taken up and to what purpose. (Zuboff, 1988: 388)

> To fully grasp the way in which a major new technology can change the world ... it is necessary to consider both the manner in which it creates intrinsically new qualities of experience and the way in which new possibilities are engaged by the often-conflicting demands of social, political, and economic interests in order to produce a 'choice'. To concentrate only on intrinsic change and the texture of an emergent mentality is to ignore the real weight of history and the diversity of interests that pervade collective behaviour. However, to narrow all discussion of technological change to the play of these interests overlooks the essential power of technology to reorder the rules of the game and thus our experience as players. (1988: 389)

Or, to put it more crudely, we can in principle use technology to increase our knowledge in new ways, but in practice others might not let us do so.

For example, decision support systems have options permitting contributions to the discussion to be anonymous; they also allow for anonymous votes to be taken. This offers new choices of ways of conducting discussions and coming to decisions. It provides a mechanism for minimizing power differentials and the differences in political influence which stem from them. If used, these options can enable team members to appreciate how important it is to evaluate contributions according to their quality rather than their origin. But they may not be used. The most powerful team member may have taken control of the technology and ignored these options.

Our example depends, however, upon the decision support system being in place and available for use. In most organizations, only sufficient systems are in place to encourage improvements in know-how and control. Five levels of information technology use in organizations have been distinguished (Venkatraman, 1991):

1 Localized exploitation, where IT is used within business functions such as marketing, or only in isolated activities within functions. These IT applications usually improve the efficiency of specific operations, but have no impact on other areas.
2 Internal integration, where IT is applied in all business activities. Both a common technical platform integrating systems and applications, and a common organizational platform of roles and responsibilities, make this possible.
3 Business process redesign, where the business process is so redesigned as to maximally exploit the IT capabilities.
4 Business network redesign, where integration occurs across the business partners of a changed business network involved in the creation and delivery of products and services.
5 Business scope redefinition, which involves using IT to redefine the mission and scope of the organization.

Most organizations are at level 1. Levels 3, 4, and 5 offer clear opportunities for knowing beyond.

- An example of level 3, business process redesign, is a firm of fund managers which devised a new business strategy based on cutting staff and concentrating on stocks and shares little known to other fund managers. This strategy utilized the firm's large and integrated IT capabilities to give a competitive edge.
- Level 4, business network redesign, is exemplified in a just-in-time arrangement where a supplier's shipping department was electronically connected to the buyer's purchasing department. In a sense, this is shifting the boundary of the organization to

create a 'virtual organization'. It implies a new and closer tie between supplier and buyer.

♦ Level 5, business scope redefinition, is often exemplified when organizations succeed in making their own IT system a business in its own right which they sell as a service to other organizations. Reader's Digest's main business is now its data bases, not its magazines. Similarly, credit control companies capture data from multiple sources and combine it to permit lending decisions to be taken.

Control and Information

There are, then, clear examples of IT being used to aid knowing how and knowing beyond. However, we have now to support our argument that it is used *socially* and *dynamically*.

First let us consider the control function (Figure 12.1, arrow 8). Here are some examples:

♦ Quality control, fault-finding and equipment malfunctions systematized.
♦ Useful external sources of information and supply gathered together into a data base from people's diaries.
♦ Computer-aided design and manufacturing systems.
♦ Customer support systems.

In all these cases, people with know-how were persuaded to surrender it to the system designer or the data base compiler. It cannot have been easy to persuade someone to hand over their precious list of contacts, for example, or to elicit from a craftsman or a professional their own skills. Such a task is doubly hard. Individuals perceive themselves to be surrendering the tricks of their trade; and they find it difficult to be explicit about skills they have seldom been required to explain before. It is however, clearly a social process.

So is the adjustment which the craftsman or professional has to make subsequently. Shoshana Zuboff quotes the reactions of a process worker at a paper mill who used to adjust the process on the basis of touch and smell:

> With computerization I am further away from my job than I have ever been before. I used to listen to the sounds the boiler makes and know just how it was running. I could look at the fire in the furnace and tell by its colour how it was burning . . . there were smells that told you different things about how it was running. I feel uncomfortable being away from these sights and smells. Now I only have numbers to go by.

I am scared of that boiler, and I feel that I should be closer to it in order to control it. (1988: 63)

So getting the know-how out of experts into systems isn't easy:

- They may find it hard to make it explicit.
- They may be unwilling to surrender trade secrets.
- They may find it hard to work with the new systems.

However, they may benefit enormously. They may lose some of their craft skills, but if they adjust to the more abstract mode of work, they may understand the system far better. Not only have they had to explain how they do the job; they can also gain information from the data which the new system provides.

People can use the record of the control process to try to understand it and indeed to improve on the system. As the context in which the system operates changes, these adjustments will be all the more important. So the feedback arrowhead on arrow 8 indicates that people can adjust their understanding of the system from its output. Unfortunately, we can only go so far by these means. The situation might change so that the identity of the system parameters themselves needs changing. When incontrovertible evidence that smoking can kill became available, calculations of life insurance risks had to include a new variable. No amount of simply looking at the effectiveness of the old model would help. So making sense of control system data *and* scanning the environment could result in increased know-how and a better model. The point is that the model itself and hence the system is repeatedly changed; there's little time for a steady state.

So large is the amount of data which comes off control systems that it's often a major task to cope with it all. One response is to retreat to the status of button-pusher – keeping the system going as it is. However, an alternative is to ask others what sort of sense they make of it. Very often they will know about output from other systems, and explanations may emerge from comparisons of different sets of data. Different perspectives can provide an overall integrating explanation which one individual could never have reached.

It's even possible (arrow 9) that these efforts at understanding what's going on can feed into our ability to know beyond. For example, a group of salespeople suddenly realized, when mutually comparing patterns of hit rates, that the hit rate of sales to customers from one business sector was far higher than that for other sectors across all geographic areas. They hadn't previously analysed by sector, just by area, although sector had actually been available in their data base. On further analysis, they discovered that the manufacturing process in the sector concerned was changing, and their product – a software system – was highly appropriate to the new technology in addition to its existing office use. This discovery made them change their longer-term vision of what they would like to be doing; they started exploring and colonizing what was for them a new market.

Modelling and Communication

Another input, arrow 12 to knowing beyond in Figure 12.1, comes from the box entitled modelling. Computer modelling enables us to try out possible projects without actually carrying them out. Decision trees, for example structural modelling, simulations, and risk analysis programs, suggest what might be the outcomes of alternative courses of action (Andriessen, 1991). Delphi techniques pool expertise to arrive at an estimate of what will happen in the future and when. All of these decision aids are accessible to multiple users at the same time, and they can be communicated through electronic messaging, teleconferencing, and store and forward facilities (Poole and De Sanctis, 1990). Graphics facilities enable visual or statistical models to be communicated too; and the whole electronic meeting can be recorded for future reference.

Modelling isn't therefore an isolated activity in the knowledge-based organization blessed with an integrated IT facility. It is highly social, and social processes such as interpretation and negotiation have to be taken into account. Indeed, some decision support systems suggest which social rule might be appropriate for particular purposes: open idea generation, for example, but anonymous evaluation of those ideas. Participants are thus learning new ways of working together.

The two arrows 10 and 11, feeding into the modelling box in Figure 12.1, indicate that many models have parameters which benefit from current data. Again though, as with the control box, the danger is to limit the model to those parameters which have been chosen and have data available. We need to distinguish between managing change and taking charge of change. 'Managing change means reacting to the environmental factors that signal change. Taking charge of change involves looking ahead across the discontinuity and making very basic decisions about business, organization, and technologies without relying on extrapolations from the status quo' (Keen, 1990). Models of the future cannot be based solely on parameters from the present. We need to know beyond as well as to know how.

While modelling is a social process and can be communicated using information technology, *the whole of the knowledge process* can be hugely facilitated by making use of these methods:

♦ People can network to persuade others of the desirability of a project.
♦ They can use the know-how and the knowing beyond of a range of people separate in time and place to carry it through.
♦ They can share information about outcomes and reflect upon what it means.
♦ They can also use the outputs of control and modelling systems to add to their knowledge.

They *can*, if they have the technology. But whether they *will* or not is another matter. If a club has power, it will seek to own information and use it for its own projects. It will try to control the use of the technology by choosing which sorts of data are gathered, and then filtering out whatever it wishes others not to see. It will also direct the data only to those it wishes to receive them, by using the privileged access capability of the system. As a consequence, learning on the basis of feedback from action projects is highly unlikely, since the data have already been preselected. Whatever sense is made of them by the recipients will be strongly infected by the club's own theories (by which it selected what the rest should see). Ironically, the club itself is also unlikely to learn; but then we already know that that is one of the characteristics of clubs in the first place.

Other club abuses of communication systems include:

♦ using the voting systems in decision aids to identify non-compliers for future reference
♦ spying on members of an electronic mail conference by reading the record of their discussion (Zuboff, 1988: 378)
♦ using control system data to evaluate the performance of individuals without their knowledge
♦ setting up a compulsory electronic diary system, but not entering their own engagements.

In sum, those with most power can use IT to concentrate knowledge in the managerial domain and reinforce managerial control. Note that the centralization of information at corporate HQ does not necessarily imply these motives. Recently, several major organizations (e.g. Unilever, Toyota of America, Citibank, Xerox) have realized the benefit of both decentralized and centralized information. If the centralized information is available to its peripheral contributors, they can relate their own business's information trends to what's happening in the rest of the corporation.

Share and Learn or Retain and Control?

In summary, it takes little imagination to understand the strong feelings of injustice which can be aroused. If I, as a craftsman, have surrendered my skills and knowledge to a system or program, thereby making it available to all, I am going to expect the same of others. If a club of middle managers prevents me from making sense of my own system data or comparing it with the data of others, it is hanging on to information and therefore to power. Perhaps the absence of the emperor's clothes would otherwise become too apparent. Or if the board retain for themselves data regarding company performance, they too are refusing to relinquish a source of personal power whereas I as an operative have already done so. Sharing of information has to be mutual.

The consequences of sharing information by communication technology have been shown by recent research to be as follows (Andriessen, 1991);

- Reductions are made in telephone calls, letters, and memos.
- There is faster and easier information exchange.
- There is an exchange of new information.
- More people receive information.
- Senior people are more reachable.
- There is an initial increase in the connectedness of existing groups.
- There is more communication between members of different organizations.
- Organizational boundaries are overcome.
- New groups are formed.
- Status differences are reduced, and participation is more evenly distributed.
- Influence is based more on competence and less on position.
- Consensus is harder to achieve.
- Messages are harder to understand than in face-to-face communication.
- Rules and roles improve outcomes.
- Planning and decision tasks are more facilitated than issues and conflict resolution.
- Coordination across space and time is improved.

Alternatively, those with power can exploit the new technology so as to elicit and share amongst themselves the knowledge of a wide variety of people inside and outside their organization. The lack of availability of information has limited people's contribution in the past, rather than inadequate cognitive ability or motivation. To quote Zuboff yet again: 'Organizations must provide performance opportunities; that is, conditions must exist that require, invite, and nurture these new skills. Such conditions are likely to involve relationships of collaboration and mutuality, where the emphasis is on achieving the best interpretation of shared information rather than on gaining personal advantage on the basis of private knowledge' (1988: 216).

Incredibly valuable information about outcomes of past projects is potentially available to help with planning and choice of project. We might discover how long projects of this sort typically take, rather than relying on our rosy memories and optimistic projections. Perhaps still more important, immediate feedback from a currently ongoing project allows us to learn on the job and improve its outcome. Feedback on the project's overall success after outcomes are known is also necessary for general learning about how to do projects. Yet such information could be retained rather than disseminated; it could be used for evaluating subordinates' performance rather than being given to them to help them learn; it could retain power for oneself rather than empower others.

However, perhaps we have not taken a sufficiently deterministic view of the impact of information technology. Perhaps, as we hinted in the previous chapter, we may not have to rely solely on the good sense and goodwill of those with power. Perhaps the immense power to communicate which information technology offers will result in networks being developed in spite of, rather than with the help of, the club currently in charge. What is certain is that if technological tools are used to impede the flows of information in the knowledge process, that process will atrophy and the organization will cease to be knowledge based. If, however, the amazing speed, capacity, and flexibility of information technology is used to facilitate the process at all points, people will learn faster and gain competitive advantage.

Yet ultimately, the successful use of this immensely powerful tool depends on relations. If relations are collaborative, with the achievement of a successful learning outcome to a project as the aim, and trust in and respect for the others' knowledge as the means, then the opportunities are there. To quote a product development manager in an organization which used a sophisticated electronic communication system to connect its R&D laboratories world-wide: 'All things considered, however, the most effective communication, especially in the beginning of a project, is a handshake across a table to build mutual trust and confidence. Then and only then can the electronics be really effective' (De Meyer, 1991). Perhaps it is hopelessly naïve to expect mutually collaborative relations purely on the basis of personal relations,however. Recent research suggests that the politics of IT dominate its use (Keen, 1990). The same differences of interest operate when information is in question as when other resources are sought. A more realistic option is to negotiate the definition, use, and ownership of information between the interested parties. Such parties may consist of the divisions of businesses in a corporation. This federalist approach supports both autonomy and coordination. Accomplishing it, of course, requires negotiating skills and the willingness of managers to take the time to negotiate.

Clearly, the knowledge process can be facilitated by IT; but equally clearly the profitable use of IT is most likely to occur in the context of the knowledge process. Knowledge and IT are complementary.

Summary

♦ Information technology can be used to enhance the knowledge process as a whole.
♦ If it is to do so, it has to be used dynamically and socially.
♦ However, in many organizations its use is limited to the control function.
♦ The modelling and communication functions of IT are capable of facilitating learning.
♦ However, vested interests and the exercise of power may prevent usage to this end.
♦ A 'federalist' approach to IT within the corporation may be a solution.

References

Andriessen, J.H.E. (1991) 'Mediated communication and new organizational forms', in C.L. Cooper and I.T. Robertson (eds), *International Review of Industrial and Organisation Psychology*, Vol. 6. Chichester: Wiley.

Carlopio, J. (1988) 'A history of social psychological reactions to new technology', *Journal of Occupational Psychology*, 61: 67–77.

De Meyer, A. (1991) 'Tech talk: how managers are stimulating global R&D communication', *Sloan Management Review*, Spring: 49–58.

Ford, R. (1990) 'Managing retail service businesses for the 1990s: marketing aspects', *European Management Journal*, 8(1): 58–62.

Keen, P.G.W. (1990) 'Telecommunications and organizational choice', in J. Fulk and C.W. Steinfield (eds), *Organizations and Communications Technology.* Newbury, CA: Sage.

Poole, M.S. and De Sanctis, G. (1990) 'Understanding the use of group decision support systems: the theory of adaptive structuration', in J. Fulk and C.W. Steinfield (eds), *Organizations and Communications Technology.* Newbury Park, CA: Sage.

Venkatraman, N. (1991) 'IT-induced business reconfiguration', in M.S. Scott Morton (ed.), *The Corporation of the 1990s.* New York: Oxford University Press.

Zuboff, S. (1988) *In the Age of the Smart Machine.* Oxford: Heinemann.

15

Developing People for Knowing Beyond

Developing Everyone

So far we have highlighted how diverse groups of people in the organization are used, and the limitations placed on the ways in which they can contribute. We have also argued that all those individuals could contribute to the knowing beyond process within teamworking. In force field analysis terms there is still a gap. We have defined a desired end and noted the status quo, without addressing the drivers and restraining forces acting on the desired end.

For an enlightened organization the drivers may be:

♦ a belief that the ability to innovate doesn't only lie in the brains of the most senior and highly qualified
♦ a reduced workforce, with fewer managers, where it is recognized that contributions have to be maximized
♦ the knowledge that keeping ahead of the competition demands the total brainpower of the organization
♦ a real commitment to developing people as the most important business asset.

Against these commendable drivers the list of constraints may be longer:

♦ In reality, people are trained and developed according to the demands of their present job and job title.
♦ Formal development is avoided by those employees who failed in the school system.
♦ Any notions of development are abandoned once middle age is reached or promotion falters.
♦ Development is seen as a symbol of organization valuing, but the link with desired outcomes is unclear.
♦ Outcomes are not reviewed in terms of how they were achieved and what was learnt, but only in terms of whether they were achieved.
♦ Training and development are synonymous with time spent away from work.

◆ Learning is associated with individual activity even though all work involves others.

In the list of constraints the words 'training' and 'development' have been used interchangeably, when in reality they are not synonymous. The *Oxford English Dictionary* defines the terms in the following ways:

> *Train*: to instruct and discipline in or for some particular profession, occupation, practice; to make proficient by such an instruction or practice.
> *Develop*: to unfold more fully, to bring out all that is potentially contained within.

Within organizations these distinctions are clearly understood. Operatives and information workers are trained, while managers are developed. When the UK government set national training targets (Department of Employment, 1994) the language was of training and development. Yet the benchmark of national vocational qualifications (NVQs) reveals that the prime focus is on individuals showing that they can display specific competences, rather than on a broader development of their potential to contribute. The concern is to ensure we can do to the same proficiency those things which our competitors can do. While it is encouraging that even in recession, employers in 1993 trained more workers than in 1992 (Department of Employment, 1994), our message is that this is insufficient for an organization which wants to know beyond. The focus has to be on development, and this does not necessarily require formal programmes. Indeed formal programmes may hold back the development process because they share learning from what is already past. The design of many management development programmes draws heavily on case studies, where the outcome is known. The assumption is that we can learn from past experience. Clearly such methods do have value. Managers need know-how, and the less experienced the managers the more they are anxious to speed up their own learning, by learning from the actions of those who have gone before.

Within our model, however, there are limitations to this approach. It sits divorced from knowing that and knowing beyond, and draws attention away from the changing balance between the three sources of knowing. Since environmental change is increasing its speed and is often discontinuous (Handy, 1989), we have to act more in terms of where we want to go and less in terms of where others have been. We choose what we need to take from our present situation in the light of where we want to go. This does not mean an unaltering path towards a fixed star, but a path which makes adjustments to the vision in the light of learning.

The current emphasis in training and development on increasing know-how makes development lop-sided. When secretaries complain that their working lives are less satisfying now that they are working for five bosses instead of one, they are indicating that the know-how skills they acquired at college are inappropriate when the demands of the role have changed. The know-how they value is being able to understand and provide the services required by another. The know-how they may now need is how to negotiate, how to manage time, how to delegate and how to work outside the hierarchy. But even learning these new skills will be insufficient if they do not stand back to consider how the changes that are happening to them are part of business change as a whole. Taking a broader perspective could enable them to look beyond the immediate to what may be required of them in five years' time, and the knowing that which follows. Or consider the HR professionals who have acquired extensive industrial relations skills and knowledge. Such know-how is largely irrelevant to devolved business units who want HR to take a strategic and business-related perspective (Cooke and Armstrong, 1990).

While knowing how and knowing that are developed in the light of knowing beyond, attempts to develop the skill are largely confined to senior managers alone. It is they alone who are expected to explore uncharted territories and report back the results of their endeavours. Given that what we notice is based on our previous experience, it is an unreasonable burden to place on senior managers. Ask an ornithologist, a doctor, a fashion designer, and an educator what they learned from a trip to Kenya, and you will receive reports that may have no point of contact. Yet, we expect senior managers to be able to scan the horizon and pick up all that is relevant to the future needs of the business.

If we want to develop an organization which can grow its whole knowledge process, then we need to challenge the constraints which we identified in our force field analysis. We can do this by acknowledging the following:

- All those inside and some outside the organization are involved in the knowledge process and are necessary to its success. All therefore, need to be developed.
- The knowledge process is social in nature. Development should therefore be socially rather than individually based.
- Social relations in organizations do occur between people at different levels. Learning should both encourage the growth of

those relations, and structure learning so that it acknowledges them.

♦ The knowledge process is related to action, and therefore development involves learning through action.
♦ All the elements in the knowledge process are necessary for success.
♦ The knowledge process is a continuously recurring cycle. Learning how to better operate the cycle is a development objective.

Having identified markers for a knowledge process in action, we need to apply those benchmarks to the diverse groups we looked at in Chapters 2–6. We need to identify how each could be developed to know beyond in terms of our 3P model of people, practice and process (see the Introduction to the book).

General Managers

This group is likely to have received more attention to their development than any other. They may have had their career initially propelled by selection on to a fast-track scheme. Such schemes identified the know-how skills needed to move up the organization, and gave the opportunity to test them out. What fast trackers often missed was that part of the learning process which gave them feedback on outcomes, since they were quickly moved on to the next assignment. If the most effective learning comes from difficulty (Smith and Morphey, 1994), they may have been protected from that learning by the organization's career management systems. The difficulty was bequeathed to those left behind after they themselves had moved on.

They will also have been beneficiaries of prestigious management programmes, run externally to the organization. The organization may have rationalized the decision to send them to Harvard or INSEAD by the thought that they will be learning from people in different organizations, when in reality learning is limited by the similarities amongst those who are sponsored. They may return with knowledge learned from lectures, discussions and case studies to guide their future actions, but without having learnt how to learn. McGill et al. (1992) call this 'learning disadvantage'. The learning may be mechanistic and deal with change as discrete problems to be addressed. They contrast this with 'generative learning', which encourages continuous experimentation and feedback in an ongoing examination of how organizational problems are defined and solved.

Generative learning, they suggest, will come from meeting the following four learning conditions.

Openness

There must be a willingness to suspend the need for control and to adopt cultural-functional humility. Managers need to be able to see their own values, background, and experiences as not necessarily better or worse than those of others. In action, this means that BP now operates upward appraisal where managers are judged by their subordinates on their openness of thinking.

Rather than development being focused on contacting those most like themselves outside the organization, managers need to be actively seeking contacts which encourage their exposure to difference. This could mean asking to be part of in-company development activities for more junior colleagues, meeting customers, choosing to mentor subordinates who do not remind them of themselves, going to a conference they would not normally choose, or attending the company's women's network. There is more ammunition for knowing beyond in openness than in staying within one's comfort zone. Argonaut Insurance Company in San Mateo, California, offers an example of such a move outside comfort. A divisional manager in the company has established a forum at which employees can bring complaints and suggestions. The committee comprises the manager, the HR manager and three non-managerial employees randomly chosen. While the divisional manager acts as a traditionalist informing the committee of the limits of its remit, he sees his prime reason for being there as learning (Jamieson and O'Mara, 1991).

Systemic Thinking

Managers need to be able to make connections between issues, events, and data. General managers are already rewarded for doing this, but McGill et al. (1992) suggest that their learning is limited by the tendency to whitewash history. Real learning is lost when a manager cannot accept a difficult truth, or discuss failure without looking to blame. Systemic thinking means encouraging input and review from those functions with which he feels least comfortable.

Creativity

General managers who know beyond have to be capable of thinking creatively and flexibly without fear. This means freeing themselves from using the lessons of the past as their prime source of learning. 'Be creative' is an impossible injunction to consider alone. It requires the sanction that actions which increase learning are to be encouraged even if success cannot be guaranteed. It requires longer-term reward policies, and the support of others. Telling a general manager who has been rewarded for his ST traditionalist skills to loosen up and become an NT visionary is a cry in the dark unless the manager is exposed to a different way of thinking and is supported in making a shift. It's one of the pay-offs of action learning that, through their questioning, learning partners open up new ways of thinking to the problem holder and make a new way of being more comfortable.

Personal Efficacy
A feeling that managers can influence the world, and are not simply victims of change, requires them to be self-aware and proactive in their approach to problem solving. Self-awareness means that their development comes from encouraging feedback from 360 degrees. Successful managers have often engaged in upward focused perception management. Knowing beyond managers seek multiple feedback as a source of learning for future actions. Paradoxically, they may need to work on their own self-confidence. Knowing that one's rewards have come from working with the prevailing culture does not necessarily build confidence for working with uncertainty. That confidence can be built by learning from actions which move outside comfort, as well as by learning with people with whom they may not instinctively feel at ease.

Table 15.1 offers guidelines for the knowing beyond development of general managers.

The Professionals

Claims for exclusive competence, for protected expertise, for controlled entry, and for separation from the business mainstream are incompatible with knowing beyond, at an individual or an organizational level. Those tactics which have protected professional status are incompatible with the conditions necessary for a knowing beyond context, namely:

- working with and understanding functions different to one's own
- listening to others rather than offering expertise
- being able to communicate with and influence people different to oneself.

Traditionally professionals have associated development with escape from the organization. Learning takes place with other professionals at conferences or in networks, because development is

Table 15.1 *Developing the general manager*

Current development	Knowing beyond development
Selection for a fast track which links speed of movement with speed of learning	Early responsibility on assignments which have to be seen through and where learning is reviewed
Learning how to rationalize and deny setbacks in order to manage perceptions of ability	Openess about what has been learnt when the outcome is unexpected
Sponsorship by a mentor who identifies with the individual and teaches him how to walk in his shoes	As great a concern to learn and gain feedback from all those with whom they work, regardless of rank
Attendance on high-prestige programmes with those of similar status	Development primarily within the workplace, or on programmes which are tailored for the organization and use projects as the basis of learning
Development is a career propellant	Development is a prerequisite for coping with the demands of a changing environment separate from any link with promotion

associated with increasing depth of specialist knowledge. Knowing beyond can and does take place when the professional moves outside. Colin Hastings (1993) noted how when scientific researchers meet together there is often a new 'igniting idea' that emerges from the discussion between two or more researchers. The professional may be able to take the idea back into the organization, but given that the context in which the idea emerged is not replicable, she may find that selling the new idea back is difficult. How much easier if the idea had been developed in concert with others inside her organization. Kreiner and Schultz (1990) found that professionals networked very effectively outside their own organizations, establishing codes of conduct as to what sorts of knowledge could be entrusted to others, levels of discretion, and degrees of cooperation. Yet within their own employment professionals often have very limited networks, and do not apply the same networking skills they apply elsewhere.

If professionals are to be able to know beyond and to contribute fully to the knowledge process within their organizations they need to overcome a number of barriers:

♦ a belief in their own autonomy set against the reality that their sphere of influence is limited

- ◆ a need for individual recognition which goes against notions of teamworking
- ◆ a reluctance to explain their thought processes to non-professionals, and a preference for simply offering conclusions
- ◆ a lack of experience in listening to others.

The basis for developing professionals' ability to know beyond lies in their developing internally the skills of effective external networking (Hastings, 1993).

Cross Boundaries

They need to be helped to cross functional and organizational boundaries, to be at least geographically close to other functions, and preferably to have opportunities to spend time understanding the demands placed on the function and the skills involved. More radically, a knowing beyond organization would regularly second professionals to other departments and to customers, in order to facilitate the ignition of new ideas.

Exchange and Reciprocity

To exchange ideas is easier when one understands the needs and expectations of the other party. When scientists at Unilever saw the link between the fat emulsions technology used in a foods division of the company and the lipstick technology of a cosmetics division, they did so because they were in regular contact with the divisions. As organizations split into smaller units, there is a danger that such learning links are lost. Exchange and reciprocity are easier when the profession is close to the core of business activity. For many professionals this is not the case, and consequently accountants, lawyers and personnel professionals can feel their ability to contribute to the knowledge process is limited.

Lucas Engineering is challenging this view with its engineering for non-engineers programme. Staff who are not technical felt they lacked credibility and self-confidence working within an engineering culture. A modular 12 month programme combines university-based input on engineering concepts with experience on site. The aim is not to produce quasi-engineers, but to give participants the tools of enquiry, so that they can ask informed questions that challenge the engineers' ways of thinking. The scheme is a recognition by Lucas that talk of cross-functional teamworking is meaningless if people in those teams do not feel capable of contributing on an equal basis.

Alliance Building and Conflict Management

In professional ghettos, there is an established alliance of professional interests, and a hierarchy of established expertise may well be used to manage conflict. In a knowing beyond environment, both the alliances and the means of conflict resolution have to be renegotiated. A solo professional in a project team can feel without allies and unsure how to deal with differences of viewpoint. A developing professionals and specialists programme at Sundridge Park Management Centre attracts professionals from a wide range of disciplines. They come because they feel threatened by the new expectation to earn their right to be listened to. Learning how to listen, to negotiate, to assert themselves, and to sell ideas gives them the confidence to contribute to the knowledge process.

Personal Management

A professional joining an external network does so after considering what her needs are – whether these be support, knowledge, career contacts, or personal development. A professional inside an organization needs to make a similar analysis of what skills she needs if she is to contribute to knowing beyond. In some organizations this will mean acquiring skills held by others in the team; in others, simply understanding the skills of others will be enough. In either case it is clear that knowledge alone is not a qualification for being part of the knowledge process.

Table 15.2 gives guidelines for the knowing beyond development of professionals.

Experienced Managers

Developing experienced managers is an organizational oxymoron. Stay around the organization long enough and people assume you don't need to be developed. At best the performance model for long-serving managers assumes that performance maintains itself until decline sets in, shortly before exiting (Ference et al., 1977). The assumption behind the practice is either that long-serving managers don't like learning, or that the organization doesn't believe an old dog (*sic*) can learn new tricks. The first interpretation has been challenged in several studies of older managers (Industrial Society, 1990; IPM and KPMG Peat Marwick, 1991). The second, if true, presents the paradox that those with the most organizational experience are judged the least capable of learning.

Table 15.2   *Developing the professional*

Current development	Knowing beyond development
Focus on acquiring the qualifications necessary to establish professional identity	Knowledge gained in professional training is one source of a professional's contribution; it is not her sole means of development
Periodic injections of new professional knowledge	Constant learning which frames professional knowledge within the emerging context
Management skills acquired once professional skills are established	Management skills are developed alongside professional skills from the beginning, because those skills are seen as aids to contribution, not career markers
Contact with non-professionals is through giving advice and expertise	Contact with a wide range of functions and levels does not assume that the professional is always expert; she may be there to learn from them
Networking is external	Extends the range of their internal networks

Leaving long-serving managers to sink or swim whilst the business context changes is a recipe for ensuring that their ability to contribute to knowing beyond is minimized. What is important, as Feldman and Weitz (1988) highlighted, is to recognize that their development needs will be diverse:

♦ The individual who feels she lacks the skills and abilities for the new demands does need know-how training if she is going to have any stake in the knowledge process.
♦ The individual who is bored by a job he has been left in too long needs a new project, a job move, or an expansion of his role if he is going to have a personal stake in the future.
♦ The individual who is doing a good job, and seeks only continued employment, needs to be aware that he has a responsibility to contribute to the knowledge process. He may be skilled at knowing how to get things done, but his development challenge is to apply those skills in a more demanding context.
♦ The individual who has been through so many changes that she has developed organizational cynicism will have a survival

strategy of doing nothing and hoping the maelstrom will pass. Her need is for an injection of freshness. Her development may come from working on client-based projects, rotating jobs, or even attending an external development programme.

As experienced managers increasingly disappear from organizations, it can be hard to believe that the learning has been worth while. One multinational company, aware that managers who had reached their most senior grading had not received development for several years, designed an older managers' programme in the hope of revitalizing their learning. The experience was a disaster. The participants felt they were being patronized. The ideas they were given were already known to them and they took them as evidence that they were seen as remedial. The programme degenerated into defensiveness. Some while later a new management development manager tried a new approach. He set up a problem-solving programme in which the participants were carefully selected to balance experience and youth. The problem they were presented with was a real one: how to launch a US premium price food brand into a UK market which did not associate a high price with the product. The programme design allowed participants to solve the problem whilst allowing time for debriefing to identify both learning and development needs. Older managers found there were aspects they found easier than younger colleagues, but also that their ideas were challenged by less experienced managers. Rather than being labelled mentors – a resource for those on the way up – they began to recognize that they had things to learn, and that through learning they could contribute to new solutions. They were able to be open about their need to learn because it helped them to deal with a new challenge.

Table 15.3 gives the factors in the knowing beyond development of experienced managers.

Information Workers

Ask a secretary or clerk what training she has received and she will list the courses which qualified her to work in an office, and the software packages she has subsequently learnt. She may even add the customer care training course she once attended. Ask her what development she has received and she will look blank. Certainly, within the UK secretaries do not expect to be developed. According to an Industrial Society (1994) report, three out of four secretaries expressed dissatisfaction, and a desire to contribute more, yet they

Table 15.3 *Developing the experienced manager*

Current development	Knowing beyond development
Organizational concern stops when promotion stops	Experience is seen as valuable but also limiting if it is left unattended
Experienced managers are seen as good developers of others	Experience can support others' learning, but will be more effective if they also have the opportunity to identify where new lessons need to be learnt
Hives off experienced managers into special programmes	Believes that learning is maximized in a diverse environment where ages are mixed and assumptions are challenged
Sees motivating older employees as a problem with a solution	Recognizes the diversity within the group and finds individual ways of unleashing their willingness to learn
Looks to extract the lessons they have learnt	Does not believe that problems are replicated, and acknowledges that experience has to be able to recognize what is different as well as what is the same in problem solving

rarely received help to do so. When frustration overwhelms her, she simply takes her know-how to a new employer and hopes things will be different. They rarely are. It seems that secretaries are passive in asserting their claim to development, and take flight rather than fight. From an organizational perspective it makes sense to take a hand in the process rather than lose their potential for knowing beyond.

At United Distillers secretaries are being visibly grown beyond know-how in a Secretarial Development programme. The impetus came from secretaries themselves. The company had developed a set of values, 'The UD way', which were translated into specific behaviours that were capable of assessment. The behaviours included:

- open and honest feedback
- pursuit of excellence
- sensitive approach to the implementation of decisions.

The scheme was being cascaded amongst managers, but secretaries, seeing information on 'The UD way', started to ask questions as to why it did not apply to them. In response, Management Consultant

Sally Watson was called in to look at how the ideas could be spread outside management.

Sally Watson's solution was to offer a learning process which secretaries and their managers would attend together. For secretaries to grow beyond their role, it was important that the learning was not exclusively with other information workers. As predominantly loyalists (SF), the learning challenge for secretaries was to move outside that role and to be comfortable in a different dynamic with their boss. For their bosses, the challenge was to test how far they would go beyond simply espousing their secretaries' abilities towards actively supporting their development.

When secretaries spoke with each other about their working life, they were able to talk about wanting access to more information, and of feeling they could do more for clients. However, they were not used to expressing such thoughts to their boss. By the end of a one-day programme they had been helped to express such thoughts. As a result they were able to agree joint action plans for improving the efficiency of the secretary–boss relationship. They had also established their ability to move outside the normal limits of their contribution.

The first event proved a catalyst to the design of a full learning process for the development of secretaries within a technical function. Here managers and secretaries have negotiated perform-ance contracts based on what each wants the other to do more or less of, and to start or stop doing. A second outcome has been the setting up of mixed secretarial and managerial groups to work on real projects. Initial follow-up has shown that redefining the one-to-one relationship is an essential prerequisite to operating as equals. Secretaries now have increased confidence in making demands of each other and their managers. This growth in confidence has helped ensure that the development is ongoing. It is not a development programme where, if the skills are not learned on the day, there is little hope of their growing. Here there is a commit-ment from both sides to carry on learning together.

Already differences of contribution have emerged in the group. During a Force Field Analysis session secretaries made more pragmatic, concrete suggestions and were keen to follow up on actions. Managers took a broader view and asked the 'what if' questions. Over time, shifts in contribution have occurred as each group has become more willing to let go of their normal expectations of the other. Already secretaries can identify benefits they have experienced:

- A bigger picture helps understanding.
- Making time for each other helps learning.

Table 15.4   *Developing the information worker*

Current development	Knowing beyond development
Training is acquired before entering the workplace, and is then intermittently updated	The organization recognizes that, in applying those skills, large amounts of valuable organizational and customer information are acquired. Development means helping them recognize the value of what they know
Training is with other information workers	Getting the benefit of that intangible knowledge means being developed with others
Learning how to understand and respond to the needs of their boss(es) is their prime need	Learning how to be comfortable in questioning and challenging their boss(es) is a key criterion for making the working relationship more productive
Learning how to access and input information is a major objective	Being able to analyse and make new connections with information is a major objective
Development is seen as unnecessary if there is no career route out of the role	Development is essential in order to ensure they can respond to the changing context of their role

- ◆ Understanding each other's styles helps each to contribute.
- ◆ Making time to learn together is worth while.

United Distillers' innovative programme highlights the fact that development beyond is unlikely to be an individual activity for information workers. When a role is defined in terms of service to another, unless that role is mutually explored there is no basis for encouraging the service provider to contribute in a different way. Knowing beyond can mean challenging the established dynamic of working relationships.

Table 15.4 shows factors in the knowing beyond development of information workers.

Operatives

In some ways the development route for operatives seems the most obvious. The popularity of TQM and quality circles has highlighted the fact that operatives can contribute when they are given an opportunity to do so. There are still, however, limits on their contribution. The focus is often on reducing faults, on getting it right every time, rather than on encouraging innovation. A further limitation is the dynamics of the process. Being close to the product means concern for the details of design and production, but this may be a concern that operates in a vacuum. How much does the operative know about customers, competitors or the finances of the business? Giving the operatives a bigger picture enables them to widen their contribution to the knowledge process.

The operatives' prime development need may be information, but information may be the last thing management provides. When Land Rover undertook an employee attitude survey 10 years ago they discovered that the first source of information was the grapevine, followed by the trade unions. Management limped in at 12th place. In 1994 the grapevine still rules, but management has risen to second place. Management now realize that there is a business case for providing rather than withholding information from workers, and the success of Land Rover over the period has justified the decision.

The question then is: what sort of information do operatives want? US company Security Pacific offers a daily newsletter to all employees giving details of what's new in the industry, the economy, the marketplace, and with their competitors (Jamieson and O'Mara, 1991). Tandem offers a 'First Friday' monthly talk show which shares information on new products, programmes, and strategies. Diversity consultants David Jamieson and Julie O'Mara believe: 'Keeping people informed shows respect for them and provides them with more information to use in carrying out their jobs, thereby enhancing their capability to be effective' (1991: 123).

Swedish consultancy Villa Bonanza argues that helping operatives understand the company's finances gives an added perspective to their learning process. They have devised a board game that shows the direct impact on the financial strength of the company of its activities in buying, selling, and financial management. They use the game with whole organizations, in order to reinforce the importance of everyone's contribution to the bottom line.

Put out a suggestion box and you'll collect ideas. Give people a context for their ideas based on a bigger picture and the ideas will be even better, is the logic of these ideas for developing operatives.

If providing a bigger picture is one framework for growing knowledge, another is feedback. Extracting ideas without feedback is a recipe for revisiting the same learning loops. In 1985 a pharmaceutical company set out to become the lowest-cost, highest-quality provider of ferro-alloys and silicon metals. As part of the process they set up a company-wide improvement scheme. The scheme elicited lots of ideas from operatives. Each idea that was implemented was tracked so that successes and failures would be made public. The aim was not to identify heroes and villains but to aid organizational learning.

If operatives learn from information they also learn from widening their world. Going out to meet customers is not just a means of understanding customers' needs and reducing their complaints. It is also a means of experiencing oneself differently. Within the workplace the dynamics of the operative/management relationship are well established. In the UK, the manager is most commonly traditionalist to the operative's loyalist. An individual operative may be uncomfortable with the role but have no awareness that she could offer any other, until faced with a customer who expects something different of her. Customers may view the operative as a visionary, there to come up with new ideas on how the product could be improved, or a catalyst who can ease their difficulties with the company. Exposure to different expectations develops new learning muscles.

'Operatives don't like learning' is a common response to the idea of operative development. One major public utility had enormous difficulties persuading operatives to attend programmes once financial incentives to do so were removed. Training implied having failed and having to be tested. The organization approached the resistance as a barrier to be battered by building systems that demanded training be attended. Companies such as Ford UK and Land Rover have taken a different approach. Their sponsorship of leisure learning for operatives seems at first sight like a sop to those who cannot qualify for 'real' courses. Land Rover Managing Director Terry Morgan sees it differently. On his factory floor he sees men in their 30s bored with their work, but frightened of formal learning. Give them a chance to learn something they enjoy, and an internal barrier to their ability to learn has been broken, he believes.

The ability of operatives to know beyond is based on a sense of confidence that they can learn and a sense of inclusion in a wider picture. When infertility expert Professor Robert Winston faces a new ethical issue in his work, he calls together the whole unit to reach consensus. The departmental cleaning staff have as much right to contribute as the embryologist, because he recognizes that they will offer a perspective that may be missing from a medical viewpoint.

Table 15.5 *Developing the operative*

Current development	Knowing beyond development
None: operatives are trained	Recognizes that operatives are constantly learning, but that learning has more value if it is supported with new sources of information and self-knowledge
Acceptance that operatives are resistant to training	Recognizes that people learn differently, and looks to find ways to overcome resistance which will unlock willingness to learn
Ideas are welcomed that relate to shop floor practice	By making other sources of experience available to them, the organization believes it will broaden the scope of their ideas
Learning is focused on the acquisition of competences	Encouragement of learning beyond competences, so that they can contribute to organizational decision making

Table 15.5 gives guidelines for the knowing beyond development of operatives.

References

Cooke, R. and Armstrong, M. (1990) 'The search for strategic HRM', *Personnel Management*, 22(12): 30–33.

Department of Employment (1994) *Labour Market Trends*. Skills and Enterprise Network.

Feldman, D.C. and Weitz, B.A. (1988) 'Career plateaux reconsidered', *Journal of Management*, 14(1): 69–80.

Ference, T.P., Stoner, J.A. and Kirby Warren, N.E. (1977) 'Managing the career plateau', *Academy of Management Review*, October: 602–12.

Handy, C. (1989) *The Age of Unreason*. London: Business Books.

Hastings, C. (1993) *The New Organization: Growing the Culture of Organizational Networking*. London: McGraw-Hill.

Industrial Society (1990) *Valuing Maturity: a Report on the Employment of Mature Managers*. London: Industrial Society.

Industrial Society (1994) *Typecast*. London: Industrial Society.

IPM and KPMG Peat Marwick (1991) *Age has its Compensations*. London: Institute of Personnel Management.

Jamieson, D. and O'Mara, J. (1991) *Managing Workforce 2000: Gaining the Diversity Advantage*. San Francisco: Jossey Bass.

Kreiner, K. and Schultz, M. (1990) *Crossing the Institutional Divide: Networking in Biotechnology*. EUREKA Management Research Initiative, Copenhagen Business School.

McGill, M.E., Slocum, J.W. Jr and Lei, D. (1992) 'Management practices in learning organizations', *Organizational Dynamics*, 22(1): 5–18.

Smith, B. and Morphey, J.M.G. (1994) 'Tough challenges – how big a learning gap?', *Journal of Management Development*, 13(8).

16

Developing Practice and Process
for Knowing Beyond

Developing Team Practice

In looking at how each of our individual contributors can be developed to know beyond, it has become clear that no one can develop in isolation. General managers can learn more by changing their expectations of who they can learn from; professionals need to listen to non-professionals; experienced managers can learn from those whose experience has been built over a shorter time frame; secretaries learn with their bosses; and operatives can learn about themselves from their customers. Put all these changes in place and we will have a group of people capable of contributing more, and with greater confidence. So they are brought together to work on a project. At this point regression can occur. Individuals revert to role type, censoring what they can and can't say and reinstating a hierarchy of thinking. What does the team need to do to help them develop together?

A clue to the dangers has already been outlined in Chapter 1. A vindaloo team may still emerge where contributions are offered and accepted so long as they can be boiled down into the one pervading flavour that has been determined by those perceived to have most power. A *nouvelle cuisine* team may emerge, where those who clearly differ from accepted team membership are given particular attention. Their ideas are placed on the side of the plate as kiwi fruit decorations – decorations which are not expected to add to the flavour. Instead we have argued for the Sunday lunch team, where each flavour remains distinct but adds to the whole. How can it be achieved?

A clue lies in the management of diversity as increasingly practised in US organizations. Procter and Gamble have been leaders in developing employee programmes for the valuing of biological diversity. On one such programme participants are asked to make assumptions about whites, blacks, disabled, men, and women. Such assumptions could include:

♦ The white person will carry more authority.

- The black person will resent being managed by a white person.
- The disabled person will need a lot of help.
- The woman won't be comfortable being the leader.
- The man will assume he should lead.

Having elicited the assumptions, participants take on a role different to their own and act out the assumptions. In doing so they experience some of the discomfort of having those assumptions placed on them, and can be open in challenging assumptions. The white male can admit he doesn't like feeling he has to take the lead and would prefer to take a back seat. The black woman can admit she wants help in gaining the management skills which she sees her white boss use.

Let's apply the Procter and Gamble model to a hypothetical team that has been put together specifically in order to learn. Our organization, having realized that managing diversity is a key to innovation, wants to support the process of learning within the organization. It wants to help diversity work, but it has previously discovered that simply putting a group of people who appear different together is no automatic recipe for success. From previous attempts at diversifying teams it has learnt that:

- The greater the differences, the more time spent in discussing issues, often with no usable outcome.
- Those with most formal authority still tend to dominate the group.
- Those who see themselves as most different from the norm will form cliques in order to defend themselves.
- Those who are used to working in the same type teams will get irritated by the slowing down of decision making that difference can bring, and take the message that it's easier when you know who you are dealing with.

Not dissuaded by these criticisms, the company's development manager has persuaded senior management that an opportunity for learning lies in the implementation of a new project. The aims are twofold: both to come up with solutions, and to learn how a diverse team can be developed to work effectively together. The team will consciously use processes used in diversity awareness training, in order to develop the ability of diverse teams to work together.

The team that is put together is invited to join, both because they have valuable and varied knowledge, but also because they have expressed dissatisfaction with the limited way in which they feel they are used within the organization at present. The team comprises:

- Joe, a general manager
- Ann, a supervisor in the claims department
- Andrew, an accountant
- Jane, a personnel manager.

The team meets for the first time, and on the advice of the development manager spends some time discussing the assumptions they hold of each other and of themselves.

- *The team assumes*: Joe as a vocal visionary will offer up lots of ideas but won't be able to distinguish between them.
- *Joe assumes*: as the most senior person in the team he'll get more speaking time than the others.
- *The team assumes*: Ann as a loyalist will bring us down to earth and keep us focused on getting through things.
- *Ann assumes*: as an efficient administrator she will get stuck with the job of tidying up their work.
- *The team assumes*: Andrew as a traditionalist will interrupt the creative flow with points of detail.
- *Andrew assumes*: that as he has been around the organization a long while, they'll think he's out of touch with new ideas.
- *The team assumes*: Jane will make sure everyone is involved and will be happy so long as the team is working well together.
- *Jane assumes*: they will expect her to smooth out differences, and won't be interested in her ideas because she isn't closely involved with the business.

By taking time to make explicit the assumptions each is holding of others and of themselves, team members feel freer to contribute more fully. We have previously challenged models of team which focus on getting things right with each other as a prerequisite for quality outcomes. The managing diversity model starts from getting things right for each team member as the prerequisite for working together to add value.

Having shared assumptions and stated their needs, the team has offerings that look somewhat different:

- Joe wants to operate as a traditionalist, evaluating ideas, rather than feeling pressured to always take the lead on creative thinking.
- Ann wants to use her people rather than her paper skills.
- Andrew wants to be able to use his knowledge of the organization but without it being simply seen as a sign of age.
- Jane wants to experiment with being a visionary.

The establishment of assumptions and the stating of expectations do not exist out of context; they still need to be related to task. It's valuable to know that Jane wants to offer more than her catalyst abilities, but what does the task require? In Chapter 7 we suggested that different types of task and different team processes require different balances between the roles. Our team has been brought together in order to help to introduce business process re-engineering into the organization. This may look like an open door for visionaries to think of new ways of doing and organizing things, but this work has already been done. External consultants have analysed the system and its blockages, and have made recommendations as to what needs to be done. The team's task is to find ways of making those changes happen in an organization which is exhausted with change and has a demotivated workforce.

Identifying the demands of the task highlights some issues for the team. The task's prime demands are:

- evaluating the consultant's ideas against the current and emerging demands of the business and establishing priorities
- evaluating the outcomes of any project they implement so that the task is redefined in the light of feedback
- maintaining momentum and energy in what will be a long process
- managing boundaries so that they can identify areas of support, and find ways of influencing those most likely to be resistant.

Against this agenda the needs of Joe and Ann can be met, since the nature of the task gives them an opportunity to develop new aspects of themselves. Andrew will be able to use his organizational knowledge, but will also have to reframe it against the demands placed on the team. For Jane there is difficulty. She wants to operate as a visionary when the greater need is for skills in managing boundaries.

By setting needs against task demands the team is anchoring its development, so that it does not become an end in itself. Jane cannot on this assignment fully meet her agenda, but she can see a rationale for her contribution, rather than viewing it as an imposed responsibility. By raising others' awareness of her needs she also increases the likelihood that she will look to contribute ideas when the opportunity is there. Alternatively, she may feel so strongly about not acting as catalyst that she withdraws from the team.

Having given time to establishing their development needs, they recognize that if they are to behave differently they each need to contract with the team:

- Joe contracts to reflect before throwing out ideas, since too many ideas will deflect the team from its focus.
- Ann contracts to take more responsibility for helping get things done via people outside the team, and to take less responsibility for paperwork.
- Andrew contracts to use his knowledge of the organization to find ways of getting things done, but to listen to others who will have found alternative ways of doing things.
- Jane contracts to remain in the team until the first project is implemented, acting as a support catalyst, and then to review her contribution. If she does not feel that the team is encouraging her development as a visionary, she will bring it into the open, and may decide to join another team.

Monitoring

Exultant with having got so far, they come to their second meeting enthusiastic to get on with the job. Very quickly the difficulties of behaving differently surface. It feels more comfortable to do those things they are used to doing. After each has silently observed the others breaking the learning contract, Andrew suggests that they should monitor their behaviour, give feedback on how well they are each doing, and discuss what each of them could have done differently. He suggests bringing in an outside observer to help them, but the group decides they want to take responsibility as part of their development for managing diversity. Monitoring time becomes an important link between their own development and ensuring their inputs are helping movement towards rather than away from the goal.

Team development will come not from a sequential progress through team stages, but from visiting and revisiting five activities:

- clarifying assumptions
- checking individual needs against task needs
- negotiating, where possible, the gap between the need for individuals to develop their range and the needs of the assignment
- contracting on contributions
- monitoring and adjusting roles as necessary.

Table 16.1 summarizes knowing beyond development for the team.

Developing Organizational Process

We have developed the people, we have developed the team, but we have not yet considered how the organization can create the conditions in which knowing beyond will flourish.

Table 16.1   *Developing the team*

Current development	Knowing beyond development
Take people away from work, perhaps even outdoors, and give them a task which does not relate to their work but which does amplify processes	Use a real assignment within work and include in the resource allocation, time for addressing development issues
Spend a lot of time at the beginning of the team's project getting relationships right within the group	Spend time identifying the development needs of individuals in the team, and make explicit how these match against the demands of the task
Look to fill a range of team roles	Concentrate on those roles which meet the demands of the task
Focus on the value of all team roles as being of equal merit	Acknowledge the difficulties that differences bring and address those difficulties openly
Performance as a late stage of team operation	Expectation of performance from the beginning, so that learning comes from action and review

It should by now be clear that what we are proposing is a business change in which the knowledge process is a business asset, and has to be managed as such. How this can be done is suggested by the conditions for successful business change identified in the research undertaken for Opportunity 2000 (Hammond and Holton, 1991). By looking at culture change programmes world-wide, the research team identified four conditions that need to be met:

- top-down support
- the identification and reward of required behaviours
- the availability of resources
- the building of ownership.

Top-Down Support

If people throughout the organization are to believe that growing the knowledge process depends on valuing differences, then this valuing needs to be modelled at the most senior level of the organization – the board. This isn't just a case of tweaking membership so that a woman and a foreign businessman break up a monoculture of men of similar age, with similar education, similar business experience and the same club memberships. It could be that the woman and the foreign businessman were chosen because they were known to hold similar attitudes to the chairman. What the board needs to establish are the skills, experience, and role preferences held by existing members, in order to identify knowledge gaps. A woman should not be invited to join because she is female, holds a title, and would at least break up the grey suited monotony of the board photograph. She should be there as a positive source of difference. She asks questions that otherwise would not be asked. She is able to analyse situations using intuition as well as sensing, and can make connections that others on the board would miss. A chief executive who talks of valuing diversity, but cannot live with it, sends a clear message to the organization. The board also needs to expose itself to difference from outside. When Grand Metropolitan's board (itself more diverse than most) invites in a black female store manager to provide her perspective on a business issue, the board is stating both that it wants to learn from others, and that its own range of experience is insufficient to make an informed decision. Contrast this with boards where the employee who holds an issue close to his heart, and has spent long periods of time preparing a report, is not allowed to present his argument to the board because of his grading. Instead the case is presented by a board member, filtered through his perspective, and the real flavour of that different knowledge is missed.

Boards need to challenge their own homogeneity of thinking if they are serious in wanting to know beyond. They also need to make visible statements that the desire for a different way of learning is genuine by making clear gestures of support. There is no stronger gesture than identifying important business projects which are managed by teams which visibly embody difference. Projects with business relevance are motivating to those involved and also signal to those outside the team that the organization believes that difference adds value. This doesn't mean just one project which can be dismissed as the CEO's quirk, but a series of projects spread across the organization which validate the importance of new ways of learning and of learning with others.

Identify and Reward Behaviours

To create business change you have to make explicit how people now need to be, or else they assume that how they are is good enough. The same is true for developing the knowledge process. If the organization is serious it needs to identify OK behaviour:

- Establish means by which task teams are selected.
- Establish criteria for inclusion which focus on match of roles against task, not match of individuals against roles assumed necessary.

- Challenge those teams where membership is too narrow to ensure diversity of thinking.
- Provide development in how to operate within the new model of teamworking, so that required behaviours are quickly embedded.
- Legitimate time given to reviewing learning through making that review an expected outcome of every assignment. A team that can only report that the goal was achieved, without being able to report what was learnt and how that could be used for the future, will be judged to have failed.
- Celebrate success. Projects which achieve an outcome which exceeds expectations because they have been able to unleash the power of diverse thinking should be heralded. The added value of that difference should be identified so that it can be used by others to move learning forward.
- Encourage networks to be inclusive rather than exclusive. Discourage the development of *nouvelle cuisine* groups which sit apart from the mainstream. Mainstream networks need to listen to what those who are not natural members can tell them, if they are invited in.

Invest Resources

Any change programme will talk of the cost of implementing change: the new logos, the mass training programmes, the corporate communication literature. There will be costs in growing the knowledge process, but they will have a different focus:

- Awareness training, so that all employees understand that learning is a critical business issue, and is a business differentiator that everyone has a part in.
- Development for those individuals who lack confidence in their ability to contribute. A secretary may ask for a course on financial management; an operative may need training in presentation skills; a professional may want help in listening effectively; while a general manager may feel unskilled in facilitation. If these are prerequisites for learning together, then they are a justifiable expense.
- Alternatively, resource time may be used in sending out a team member to spend time working alongside a customer or supplier, in order to better understand their needs and complaints.
- The most important resource cost will be time. Conventionally, a week spent away from work on a course has been legitimated time for learning. Time to discuss how the team is working, how well roles are being filled, and how learning is being managed

has been viewed as indulgence time. In an organization committed to knowing beyond, projects will be resourced on the basis of an inclusion for conscious learning time. Review will not be an optional task at the end of the assignment, but will be part of the core assignment activity.

♦ At an organizational level, there will be resources to evaluate results. The learning benefits will be as important an aspect of evaluation as the financial benefits. The questions of what the blockages to learning were and how they can be overcome will be as valid as how the learning gained can be used elsewhere in the business.

Building Ownership

In contrast to the imperative that top-down visible support is vital, it is also true that change occurs from the bottom up. The BA 'Putting people first' culture change initiative gained its momentum from focusing on those people who interfaced most directly with customers, i.e. non-managerial staff. This inversion of most approaches to change was supported by a critical review of change programmes (Beer et al., 1990) which concluded that they worked best when:

♦ The change started at the periphery of the organization.
♦ The initiative was focused on tackling the organization's most important competitive task.
♦ The initiative was specially adapted to particular units rather than being monolithic.
♦ The initiative was primarily focused on roles, responsibilities, and relationships.

An organization which sees developing the knowledge process as a challenge will not start with creating a multi-functional senior management team to divine the company's vision for 2010. That activity will impinge little on the learning processes of those distant from the top of the organization. Indeed, a vision which only captured the perspectives of those in senior management would undermine the knowledge process we have outlined. Instead a bottom-up process, where a number of important business projects are addressed by groups which cut across levels, functions, and experience, will send out messages that learning is best developed by difference. That message, cascaded upwards, will make it easier for those most threatened by diversity, the senior monoculture, to open up to different ways of thinking.

Table 16.2 summarizes knowing beyond practice for developing organizational processes.

Table 16.2 *Developing organizational processes*

Current practice	Knowing beyond practice
Use systematic means to ensure equity in selection procedures. As a by-product, replicate homogeneity in organizational thinking	Develop means by which difference can be recruited and allowed to retain its distinctive voice
Quickly assimilate employees into the prevailing culture of how people think and learn	Encourage different ways of thinking provided that individuals accept the concerns of the organization
Appraise and reward individuals for their ability to accept and work with the 'ways things are done around here'	Appraise and reward people for their ability to make a valued difference
Select out high-potential individuals at an early career stage	Resist labelling high-flyers, since it both acts as a self-fulfilling prophecy, and places limits on the contributions others can make. Look to recognize all those who have made a difference at whatever career stage
Establish formal and informal networks which separate out	Open up networks and encourage links between them, so that differences can ignite ideas
Select board members for their comfort fit with existing members' groups	Select board members for the gap they fill, and the learning grit they provide
Assume learning is best left to trainers and development experts	Make talk of learning a normal part of business conversation. Action taken without being able to identify learning will become culturally unacceptable
Assume success means learning has occurred, and failure means it hasn't	Conscious and open discussion of learning outcomes which does not whitewash failure or ignore the need to dissect success
See learning as a cost defined in terms of the training budget	Assess the cost benefits of learning in terms of team time against the quality of outcome
See major changes as being top down led	Look to find where the push of the knowledge process will gain greatest momentum, and place the energy and commitment there

References

Beer, M., Eisenstat, R.A. and Spector, B. (1990) 'Why change programs don't produce change', *Harvard Business Review*, 68(61): 158–66.

Hammond, V. and Holton, V. (1991) *Towards a Balanced Workforce?* Ashridge Management Research Group.

Epilogue

As the train started to draw out of Brighton Station, Tom hurled himself into the first-class compartment. As he sat back and drew breath, he saw Mike opposite. The two had first met 15 years ago when, as new recruits straight from university, they had joined Xylon's company trainee management programme. Five years ago, feeling frustrated at talk of change, which seemed only to mean constant restructuring and redundancies, Mike had left to join Apton International.

The two men smiled at each other in recognition.

Mike: Tom, I don't believe it. Good to see you. What are you up to, you old rogue?

Tom: I'm on my way to Gatwick for a flight to Lausanne. God, it must be five years since you left Xylon. Funnily enough we were only talking about you the other day, and laughing about how you always managed to keep one step ahead of disaster. A career which rose without a trace of the mayhem you left behind. I could never figure out why you left; with your track record you were destined for great things.

Mike: Maybe, but I came to feel that we were getting it wrong at Xylon. That worrying about changing the culture, when what we needed was to change the products, seemed the wrong way to be approaching things. I was becoming cynical about yet one more restructuring, which would provide the answer, and never did. In the five years since I've been gone, how many management reorganizations have there been?

Tom: Lost count, but you wouldn't recognize the place if you came back. All the old hands gone, and our generation looking like old hands now. Sometimes makes me wonder how much longer they'll want me. At least there are still development courses, so when the pressure gets too much, I get myself signed on one for a week or two. That's where I'm off to now, an international programme in defining strategy at Lausanne. Don't suppose I'll learn much, but I should make some useful business contacts. What about you, where are you off to?

Mike: Oh, nothing so exotic, I'm *en route* to Northampton for a learning review meeting.

Tom: Mike, you've lost your touch. In the old days, if you did any learning, it had to include a minimum of a three-hour flight from London. Budgets a bit tight, are they?

Mike: No, nothing to do with budgets. It's just the way we do things at Apton. The project is based at Northampton, so we are having a meeting to look at what we are learning from the work so far.

Tom: Oh, I see. A bit of an end of project beano.

Mike: No. We've only been working on it for a couple of months, but we want to be sure that we are in touch with all the issues impacting on the project, and are using the right people in the right roles. It's something we do regularly.

Tom: Sounds a bit off the wall to me. I thought your job was to manage projects, not to act as nanny to them. Can't imagine our lot having the time to spend sitting around talking about learning. Unless it's gone wrong of course, and then we can always find time to discover whose fault it was.

Mike: I'm not nannying the project, no one is. Although if I'm honest, the best person at ensuring we are not losing sight of what's being learnt, while we are doing it, is probably the departmental secretary.

Tom: You mean you have a secretary to take minutes on what you are learning? Now that's a waste of time if ever I heard of one.

Mike: No, she's not there to take notes, she's there because the project involves a lot of customer contact, and over the years she has probably had more contact with the customer than most. She's great at remembering all sorts of aspects of the customer's business and of the people involved that I tend to forget, so it made sense to invite her into the project team. Along the way, I've found out that she is good at forcing us to take time out to look at how we are doing, so that we don't lose sight of the need to change when it's necessary.

Tom: So you've become a bit of a champion of women, have you, Mike? Never saw sight of that at Xylon. Always saw you as an unreconstructed chauvinist. Good at handing over the box of chocolates at Christmas, and keeping the support staff sweet, but no friend of the feminists.

Mike: It's got nothing to do with supporting the cause of women. She's there because she contributes things that other people don't. One of the production workers is also in the team for that matter.

Tom: What! Are you trying to undermine the role of management, as the brains of the organization? I suppose you are keeping this social experiment quiet, so that no one else finds out about it – or it'll be the end of your career.

Mike: It's not a social experiment, Tom, it's how things are done at Apton. We think it's one of the reasons why the company is going from strength to strength. You must have seen the latest profit figures: they were all over the *FT* last week.

Tom: Of course I saw them, but you are not telling me it's got anything to do with having secretaries and production workers doing management's work. Anyway, how can you possibly get that sort of thing going? It would undermine the whole social fabric of Xylon, if secretaries stopped making the tea at meetings, and started seeing themselves as experts on customers.

Mike: Well, I suppose it started with the CEO. He made it clear that he was unhappy with the make-up of the board, and that it needed to have a more diverse make-up.

Tom: You mean he put a woman on the board, and called it diversity.

Mike: Yes, there are women on the board, but that wasn't the rationale.

He identified that the only differentiator we could hope to have from our competition was our ability to think quicker, and more creatively. When he looked at the board, as the leading source of strategic decision making, he realized that the types of people on it were too similar in their backgrounds and experience. It wasn't that they were all men; they had all had similar corporate careers, and tended to think the same way. It made for harmonious meetings, but it didn't necessarily make for great thinking. He brought in some consultants to look at what were the sources of knowledge and skill in the team, and where there were gaps. Having done that he realized that there was a lot of skill available to evaluate financial data, but there were few people who were innovators. So he actively recruited new people who could offer different things.

Tom: Well, given the amount of publicity Apton has received in the business press recently, he may have something. I suppose. But what has the board got to do with your project team?

Mike: Well, once he had seen that different sorts of outcome and different sorts of discussion took place when the board's make-up was different, he decided that the model should be extended everywhere else in the organization.

Tom: I can't imagine that went down very well. All this equality stuff is fine when things are going well, but we all know it goes out the window when times are tight. Let's face it, things have been difficult for all of us in the last few years. We've had to hold on tight, not start taking risks.

Mike: That's precisely why we had to buy into it. Once it became clear that we no longer had guaranteed markets, we had to be able to generate new sources of revenue. All the restructuring and downsizing in the world is pointless, if there are not new sources of ideas to generate the revenue for the future.

Tom: Of course, and that's what management is supposed to do. And those boffins we have to employ. Though sometimes I wonder why, they seem so out of touch with reality.

Mike: No, Tom, it's more than that. Just think of all those people who worked for Xylon for years. Knew the business back to front, saw customers regularly, and yet we never asked them to contribute their ideas because they weren't in the right grade.

Tom: Yes, we did, we put out suggestion boxes – and the suggestions were often accepted. They weren't earth shattering, I'll grant you. Offering visitors herbal teas as well as coffee was one, I seem to remember. Fine – but hardly going to change the balance sheet.

Mike: Yes, Xylon had suggestion boxes, but we didn't help people produce better ideas. If a receptionist only sees her world in terms of how she treats an individual customer, then of course her ideas will be based on how she can make things better for that customer. If, however, you give her a wider world from which to see things, she may come up with ideas that could significantly help the business.

Tom: Like what?

Mike: Well, at Apton, everyone is kept informed not just of how things are with our business, but of who the competition is and how things are going for them. Because our receptionists now know more about the business sector, they have become very good at listening to what our customers say in reception about us and our competitors. They note those things down and feed them into the system. Or clerical staff, who input data into their terminals, will now identify trends that previously would have been lost. Because they would have assumed that no one would be interested in their views. They would have assumed that if it was important, management would have spotted it. I now know that if you want to innovate ahead of the rest, you have got to bring everyone into the decision-making process.

Tom: Sounds like you spend all your time sitting around talking. Who's doing the work?

Mike: You don't understand, Tom. All this goes on while we are doing our normal work. It's just that instead of seeing learning as something that managers do when they go on courses, we have been helped to see that learning is what we all have to do as part of our daily work. Our CEO says, 'We know all we need to know, but the person who knows it mightn't be you, and they may not realize they know it, unless they have the opportunity to find out.'

Tom: So now you are talking quality circles. We've done those.

Mike: Well, quality circles are a part of it, but it has to go beyond that, because quality circles may simply perfect what is, rather than being able to make the jump forward to the next innovation.

Tom: So all your operatives sit around forecasting do they? It's bad enough getting operatives to work, without trying to get them to star-gaze.

Mike: Our workers are no different from those at Xylon. The only difference is that since they have been encouraged to work more with customers, and since they started being given much more information on the outcomes of what they do, the sort of ideas they come up with have changed.

Tom: You'll be showing them the balance sheets next, and inviting them into the executive forum lunches.

Mike: Well, actually we do make public financial data each month, and there's not an executive club any more. The CEO decided that networks should only be there if they were open to everyone, and were concerned with making the doing of business easier. They were not to be means of some people getting a career boost at the expense of those excluded.

Tom: For someone whose career did pretty well out of networking, that's rich coming from you. You mean to tell me you don't network any more?

Mike: Of course I network. But it's a different sort of networking. Now that we can't rely on hierarchy as the way of getting things done, I have to be able to influence a much wider range of people if the project is going to get done. So my network now extends much more widely across the organization. It means I find out a lot more than I ever did before. It's more useful than just meeting with people who joined at the same time, or inviting my boss to dinner.

Tom: Well, I think you've become naïve, Mike. Everyone knows that the only point of networking is to manoeuvre your next promotion.

Mike: And when was your last promotion?

Tom: Five years ago. But that's not the point. We all know times have been difficult at Xylon. Promotions have all but disappeared. That's why I've got myself on this course at Lausanne. An input on strategic management, learning from world experts, will make me poised to strike when the opportunity comes.

Mike: And what do those experts know about Xylon?

Tom: They don't need to know about Xylon, they can tell me what other companies have done. They have the know-how.

Mike: It's not enough, Tom. If know-how was enough, Xylon and many other companies wouldn't have suffered as they have in the early 1990s. It's precisely because know-how doesn't have all the answers that Apton has changed the way it learns.

Tom: Seems to me, you've just been conned because the training budget has been cut. You are not telling me if you were offered a week in Lausanne, you wouldn't be there like a shot?

Mike: Well, if it involved all the people in Apton who I think can contribute to strategic thinking, then perhaps yes, but if it was just for me, then no. There wouldn't be any point, because I'd only be learning from people who have probably got similar views to me.

Tom: Are you sure you are not about to be eased out of the organization, Mike? You know the signs. Doesn't get sent on courses any more. Gets asked to help a bright-eyed youngster learn the ropes. I've seen it a lot at Xylon.

Mike: Well, if there are plans to get rid of me, it's not because of my age. We've got rid of all those schemes which simply lifted out the over 50s. Now, so long as people have useful experience, and are willing to work with and learn from others, age doesn't matter. There's a woman of 60 just heading up a new initiative to launch our products in Israel. She's got a lot of knowledge of the Middle East, and she's put together a really innovative approach as to how we can make an impact quickly. She didn't do it alone of course, but because she listened to the ideas of the rest of her team and added her own perspective, we think she's got a winning project.

Tom: So Apton is going to become a haven for wrinklies. That's a bit of information I'd keep quiet if you want to keep your younger staff motivated.

Mike: Well, seeing some of the mistakes Xylon has made in recent years, I'm not sure that focusing on youth is a recipe for success, or for guaranteeing anyone's job. It can't make it comfortable for you, now that even people like us are moving into middle age.

Tom: There'll always be room for people who know how to play the system, and if there's one thing that Xylon has taught me it's how to make sure those above me think I am doing OK. I've got no worries. Anyway, must leave you, Mike. This is Gatwick. I'll think of you *en route* for Northampton, as I settle down with the first gin and tonic on the plane. Hope I haven't unsettled you?

Mike: Not at all. Nice to see you again, Tom, and to hear that nothing's changed.

Author Index

Subject Index

power, *cont.*
  of minorities 14
  and roles 148
  and secretaries 63
problem definition 115–16
processes 88–93, 104
  and context 89–90
  evaluation of 135–6
  and roles 90–3, 104
  and rules 104–5
  and tasks 88–9
Procter & Gamble 205–6
professionals 35–6, 40–7
  broadening of 45
  development of 192–5
  formation of 41–2
  and innovation 41–7
  vs managers 41–2, 44
  mental frameworks of 41–4
  organizational commitment of
      45–6
  practice and theory 39–41
  and team roles 145–6
professions 35–9
  and academic theory 39–41
  empires 35–6
  enemies of 36–7
  and systems 37–8
protection of minorities 15–16, 205
Prudential Assurance Company 153
psychological contract 50–2
Pusey, Karen 129–30

Rank Xerox (UK) 165–6, 170
rationality 167–9
Reader's Digest 179
recession 6, 154, 167
redundancy
  management of 96–7
reflection 139–40
Rentokil 23
reskilling 75–6
rewards 100–1, 171–2, 211–12
resources 212–13
Roddick, Anita 159
roles in teams 90–3, 104–5
  evaluation of 137–8
  power of 148
  and processes 90–3, 104
  and professionals 145–6

and secretaries 67–8, 145–7
in UK managers 104
in various occupations 105
and work roles 145–8
rules 164–5

satisfaction
  and diversity 102
secretaries 62–71
  deskilling of 64–5
  development of 197–200
  and E-mail 66–7
  and IT 64–7
  job enrichment of 66
  and know-how 64–5
  and knowing beyond 67–8
  and knowing that 69–70
  and power 63
  and team roles 67–8, 145–7
  as wife and mother 62–4
sectors
  diversity in 10
Security Pacific 201
self
  confidence 100–1, 192
  defence 167–8, 171
  identity 29–30, 51, 100–1, 126
  promotion 172
She magazine 4, 128–30
Sheppard, Allen 30
Sinclair, Clive 161–2
Smith-Kline Beecham 159
social learning 140
social exchange
  and development 194–5
  and information technology 176–7,
      179–80, 184–5
stakeholders 23–4, 115
stereotypes 11, 145–8
structure
  organizational 52–3
styles
  learning 121–39
Sundridge Park Management Centre
      195
survival 25–6
Swiss Watches 23
systems
  organizations as 170–3, 191
  and professional knowledge 37–8